FOR I HEARD FROM
BEHIND THE VEIL

FOR I HEARD FROM
BEHIND THE VEIL

Insights & Messages Regarding Current Events in
Light of the Teachings of the Prophetic Kabbalah

R. Ariel B. Tzadok

For I Heard from Behind the Veil
Insights and Messages Regarding Current Events in
Light of the Teachings of the Prophetic Kabbalah

The KosherTorah School
for Biblical, Judaic & Spiritual Studies
www.koshertorah.com
arieltzadok@gmail.com

ISBN: 979-8-361-99887-6

Layout, graphic and cover design by: Dovid S. Brandes

PROUDLY PRINTED IN THE USA

Also by R. Ariel B. Tzadok:

WALKING IN THE FIRE

Classical Torah/Kabbalistic Meditations, Practices & Prayers.

PROTECTION FROM EVIL

Exposing & Neutralizing Harmful Spiritual Forces.

ALIENS, ANGELS, & DEMONS

Extraterrestrial Life in Judaism/Kabbalah & its Vital Relevance for Modern Times.

VISIONS OF THE END OF DAYS

A Kabbalistic View of the Book of Daniel With a Guide to Dream Interpretations

THE EVOLUTION OF GOD

Experiencing the Fractal Sefirot of the Kabbalah

SECRETS OF THE CYCLE OF TIME

A Prophetic Kabbalah Journey Through the Jewish Year

LET THERE BE... KNOWING!

Using the Prophetic Kabbalah & Ma'aseh Merkavah to Expand the Powers of the Mind/Soul

USING THE HOLY NAMES OF GOD

Developing Psychic Abilities Using the Secret Codes Within the Torah

THE GREATEST STORY NEVER TOLD

Torah: Not for Jews Only! The Bedrock of Universal Spirituality

THE KABBALAH OF RELATIONSHIPS

Between Men & Women You & Your Soul You & Your Body

THE SIMPLE PATH

Uncommon Common Sense from Psalm 119

Available on Amazon.com

Check out our courses in all areas of study

Available at **www.koshertorah.com**

YouTube: **KosherTorah School of Rabbi Ariel Bar Tzadok**

TABLE OF CONTENTS

SECTION FIVE
OPENING THE PSYCHIC MIND

SECTION SIX
THE WHEELS OF THE MERKAVA: SECRETS OF TORAH LIFE
ACCORDING TO THE MA'ASEH MERKAVAH

SECTION SEVEN
THE HOLY GORAL OF AHITOPHEL

Important Introduction

As I awoke one recent morning and performed my routine meditations, I could see the image of this book forming in my mind. I had no plans to arrange this text, indeed, I am presently in the middle of writing and arranging another book. But I could clearly hear that "still soft voice" that speaks within my heart say to me loud and clear, "Let my people know!"

And I knew right away, as if information was downloaded into my mind, what it is that I am supposed to do. And so, I have been guided to quickly arrange this text, and to reveal these lessons publicly, and to allow each of you, those who wish to see, a glimpse "behind the veil" as to what is really happening in our world at this time.

Some of this material is new, some of it is old. What is unique is that I am putting it here all together for you in a single volume.

I confess that I am not allowed to spell out everything as clearly as some would have me do. But be this as it may, I am providing herein all the pieces of the puzzle. The one who knows "how to connect the dots" will be able to properly arrange all the materials herein and see behind the veil, which is the purpose of rushing this book to press.

Among the topics I have included herein are:

- Secrets of what is coming, and who is really behind it.
- Practical guidance for expanding consciousness through psychic development.
- The secret of the Pre-Adamic races who still survive and are active among us.
- The secret of Inner Earth and identifying those who dwell there.
- The coming New World Order.

We all know that we are living in troubled times. Long ago, our Prophets and Sages have warned us that these times would come.

The majority of us do not have a clue as to what is really happening now all around us. We do not see the bigger picture. And now, more than ever, we need to gain a glimpse at the Big Picture if we are going to survive.

Many are now asking themselves: What is going to be happening in the immediate foreseeable future, and what must we do to prepare ourselves? Without some insight into the hidden realities surrounding us, we simply do not know what we can do, and what it is that we need to prepare.

Overwhelmed by the pressures of modern times, many are already in denial. They believe that everything the way it is now will continue to be this way, and that nothing great is going to change. One hundred years ago many then also believed like this. They did not survive. We all know what happened to them. We commemorate their loss to this day. Both history and common sense demands of us to learn from the mistakes of the past, not to repeat them!

No one knows for sure what is happening and what is going to happen. We have no prophet today to enlighten us. And even the wisest of Sages will not dare to predict certainties that may indeed not happen. We are left to our own devices to best cultivate understanding and wisdom so as to gain a sense of what it is that Heaven wants from each of us as individuals.

Heaven is our guide. And we do have what it takes to expand our senses of awareness to enable us to gain a sense of inner knowing (a psychic intuition) of what is it that Heaven will want of each of us individually.

For this purpose has this book, Behind the Veil, been rushed into publication. This book contains vital information that you the reader needs to know that will assist you in expanding your awareness about a great many things.

This is not a book about meditative practices, although a small number of such practices have been included herein. For those of you seeking meditative exercises, I already have available for you three of my previous books. These are: Walking In The Fire, Let There Be... Knowing, and Using the Holy Names of God. For those of you seeking the actual practices and exercises of the Prophetic Kabbalah, these other books are available for you now.

But Behind The Veil offers you that which these other books do not. Behind The Veil, like its name implies, is here to reveal to you insights about the true nature of our world in general, and to reveal why what is coming upon us needs to come, be it now or later, or in one form or another. This book is here now because the times require that it be so. And thus, here it is.

I have written about many of the topics herein over a period of years. Most of these writings, messages, and warnings I have never published. The time then was not yet right. This has now changed.

Psychic wisdom is not something to be intellectually understood. Psychic wisdom is something that is taken to heart. One embraces it because one recognizes within it a truth that seems to be speaking directly to you, aimed directly at your heart.

The messages herein are not academic lessons, but rather they are insights and warnings that you need to hear in your heart right now. Once the seed of these words are planted firmly in your heart, God will water them and make them grow. The Tree of Life must be revived inside of you.

Many fear our unstable future. Many believe that somehow magically Mashiah will appear out of nowhere and come to save the day. I am here to advise you that this will not be the case. Mashiah will indeed come when Heaven so ordains it to be. But the time of the End is not yet upon us. There is still much to come as the prophetic scenario unfolds. I have explained much about this in my book, Vision Of The End Of Days, which is a Kabbalistic commentary to the revelations in the Book of Daniel. For those of you interested in the prophetic scenario, I recommend to you this book.

For right now, you my reader must come to see the bigger picture of what is happening around us. I want for you to see, with your own eyes who are the real major players here and now. I want for you gain insight into our past, and into our present. For in doing so, you will gain insights into our future. And if not now, then when?

Before Divine Judgement visits this world, we must cultivate understanding and wisdom. We must be ready to detach from that which binds us to slavery and destruction. We must be willing to let go, and to let God! Behind The Veil is here to assist you in this most sacred endeavor.

May God bless you with an open heart to receive His Living Word, and open eyes to see the movements of His Living Hands. May God bless you with the fluidity of movement, to go where you need to go, and to move when you need to move.

Do not fear! God is already with you. It is now time for you to be with Him!

Learn now what it is that you need to know, and allow God to guide your heart and your actions to do what you need to do.

Take a peek behind the veil, and see with your own eyes what is really happening. And remember, do not fear! God is with you, always.

Shalom.

Ariel B. Tzadok
19 Heshvan 5783
12 November 2022

SECTION ONE

INSIGHTS INTO
WHAT IS HAPPENING NOW

Chapter 1

Experiment Earth - Endgame Insights in the War of Gog & Magog

Experiment Earth. We are in the midst of it. And the Endgame has commenced.

We understand so very little about the reality in which we all live. However, we have all been blessed in that the visionary language of the Kabbalah has revealed to us profound insights into the true nature of our world. Yet before we attempt a gaze at a bigger picture, let us first focus on the little picture, that which we think is real.

First, and foremost, we must understand that absolutely everything that we experience with our physical senses only reveals to us a small fraction of everything that there is. One cannot put together the pieces of an intricate puzzle if one has only a small fraction of all the pieces. This is why our world and everything that happens in it will never totally make sense to any of us. We do not, and we cannot see the whole picture.

Experiment Earth is described by the Kabbalah as being a process through which a state of imbalance is restored into balance, and that which has been damaged is repaired. This description is metaphorical. As to the nature of the actual reality underlying the metaphorical, we can only mentally speculate, or psychically experience. But, at present, due to the limited span of human consciousness, both cannot be merged into a singular whole.

In our infantile minds, limited as they are to three-dimensional reality, we believe that the most direct route between two points is a straight line. But the reality of our multiverse is that we live in far more than three dimensions. We are aware of only the three, and thus we expect reality in general to conform to the limited reality that we perceive. But this is not the case.

Experiment Earth is directed by those entities who exist in higher dimensions. They are what we are not, and they are where we are not. They can see what we cannot. They can do what we cannot. We, and everything on this Earth, exist for them like specimens in a laboratory, or like variables in a computer program. We are watched. We are moved. And when necessary, they intervene and inject change or alterations to direct or redirect how the experiment is to proceed. They can manipulate the fabric of our reality in a way similar to programming a computer.

We cannot understand the grandiosity of what is really going on. We cannot comprehend why the Experiment is taking the course that it does. Certainly, the experiment has not unfolded in a way that takes us from Point A to Point B in a straight line (as we understand such things in the third dimension).

Yet, the Experiment proceeds according to the plan set and established in five-dimensional reality, or perhaps even ten-dimensional reality. We have no words to describe such things. We do not even have thoughts that can conceive of such realities. Yet, such realities exist!

Whether we like it or not, or whether we chose to believe it or not, those who dwell in the higher dimensions control our destinies. And there is nothing that any of us can say or do that can influence the Experiment. It will unfold and reach its conclusions as it has been ordained.

Consider Experiment Earth to be a computer simulation. The Experiment has been planned and programmed since before that which we call "The Beginning." The Experiment Program operates according to plan, while we are the variables within the Experiment Program who are observed, and monitored.

With all this said and done, each of us individually must recognize that part of the Experiment is to observe which of the variables (human souls) will be able to rise to the top and begin the shift outside of limited three-dimensional reality and into the higher ones. Consider this similar to the separation of parts within a liquid when it is set to boil. Heat, friction, and subjectively experienced conflict, strife, and turmoil, always lead to the most-refined rising to the top, making it ready to be collected from there and removed from the rest of the boiling concoction.

The Kabbalah, using its typical method of highly abstract metaphors, describes our reality as the "sifting of sparks of Light that have fallen amidst the pieces of the shattered vessels of the Primordial Kings who reigned in Edom prior to there being a King in Israel." In no way are the Kabbalists, when alluding to this Biblical reference, referring to any kind of literal, or historical connection with the ancient (or modern) peoples of Edom or Israel. Such associations of historicity and Kabbalistic metaphor must be totally disconnected.

Kabbalah attempts to speak in the language of the fourth dimension. Therefore, its terminologies and ways of thinking, logic, and analysis are radically different from how these methods are understood and practiced here in three-dimensional reality.

What for us, here in 3-D is limited and confined, is for Kabbalistic thinking in 4-D unlimited and free. It is very difficult for the 3-D mind to conceive of anything in 4-D. This is why 4-D thought is not something achieved, but rather it is something received (and thus we have the meaning of Kabbalah, which means "to receive").

4-D thinking makes no sense in 3-D. When those who reach the limits of 3-D and take their first steps into 4-D, they are misunderstood by all those beneath them, and are treated with scorn, derision, and even fear. Such thinkers are called crazy, and insane. And why? Because those who experience the fourth dimension can see that all of the 3-D world, and everything happening within it, is nothing more than a controlled reality, similar to a laboratory experiment, similar to a computer simulation.

Those of you reading these words will either accept the truth of them, or reject them. Our opinions, in the long term, really do not matter. What does matter is not so much what we think, but rather what it is that we do. As living parts of Experiment Earth, we are each an "entrapped spark of light." The goal of the Experiment is for each spark to free itself from the shattered vessels that make up our world, and for each spark to allow itself to naturally flow back up, unhindered, and unimpeded.

Sometimes the ascent is easy. Other times it is very difficult. There may even be forces (entities? experimenters?) that are seeking to draw out the experiment, making it longer than necessary (at least in accordance to how we know and measure time here in 3-D). When these forces see sparks rising out of the 3-D and towards the 4-D, they intervene and seek to push the sparks back down again, to observe if whether their ascent is with intent, or by chance. They observe the sparks to see what they will do next.

And so it has been through the progression of the Experiment. And we, our souls, enter, exit, and reenter the Experiment Program over and over again. Each time we enter to learn new and different tasks. Each time, we "sift out more fallen sparks, and elevate them to their Source above" (whatever this really means). Yet, to everything finite in 3-D reality, there is its beginning, and then there is its end. In other words, the Experiment Program does have its own lifetime, and its own process for termination.

That which we know as our Experiment Earth will eventually wind down and conclude. This does not mean the destruction of Planet Earth, nor does it mean the end of 3D reality. What it means is that the Experiment being performed with our souls will run its course and conclude. When this occurs, all souls will have reached the level that they are going to reach. And then the separation occurs.

Those souls who ran the course of the Experiment successfully in accordance to the expectations of the Programmer will move on into greater and more elevated work positions. Whereas those who failed to make progress will again be recycled from scratch in yet another program, somewhere else in a different dimension, place, and time.

Those souls who failed this experiment will be divided up and separated out, each in accordance to that one's failings. Each group will then be placed in future Experiments that will be monitored by yet other Watchers, who in times to come may very well be the successful souls from this version of Experiment Earth.

Those who dwell securely in their little 3D worlds know nothing about how to understand the times, and what the times say about the progression of the Experiment, and of its imminent conclusion. But those who have elevated themselves to draw close to the border of 4D, they can sense and see that Experiment Earth is presently drawing to a close.

The final sifting between ascending souls and descending souls will soon occur. As this final procedure occurs, "all the sparks of holiness will be released from their entrapments, and will be elevated and rectified." Experiment Earth, this time around, will be complete. And after a break, the new Experiment will begin for other reasons and purposes.

At the time of this writing, here in 3D space and time, it is the time of celebrating the Biblical holiday of Succot. The meaning of this holiday is itself most sublime, and I have written about it in my book on Jewish holidays and festivals, Secrets of the Cycle of Time. There is one theme pervasive throughout the holiday, and that is the message of the End of Days, or as we will call it, the Endgame of the present Experiment Earth.

In the prophet's readings (Haftarot) for the first day of the holiday, and for the Sabbath within the holiday, reference is made to the great war that is to occur in the End of Days. Most read these Biblical accounts and view them as nice stories without any modern relevance. But this very limited 3D view of prophecy is about to be shaken. The Hand of the Experimenter is active, and there is movement within the Experiment. This is clearly sensed by those close to the 4D, whereas those who are entrenched in 3D are for the most part oblivious, and uncaring. And so the Experiment goes.

I offer these insights so that my words may be contemplated, and that if and when upheavals do occur in our world, that we should know that this is all part of the plan. We each are being tested, we each are being observed. Everything that happens is monitored. Everything that happens is recorded. Everything that happens will be weighed, measured, and fully analyzed by powers and forces not of this Earth, and not even of our 3D universe.

If one is able to remove oneself from the illusions of 3D reality, one may gain a glimpse of the 4D and see how what is being done there is directing what is happening here. The sparks of holiness do need to rise. So, the Experiment must run its course.

And this is all that I have been given to communicate at this time.

Chapter 2

The Coming Not-So-New World Order
Insights into the Modern Nephilim
& our Collective Future by Divine Design

A New World Order is coming.
There will be total control, total compliance, and total participation!
You will no longer be an individual, you will be part of the greater whole.
You will be a cog in the machine.
You will approve of it all, and you will like all of it.
Resistance is futile.

All your needs will be provided for you. You will be given everything that you are told that you need. There will no longer be choice. Even the word "choice" will be removed from the vocabulary, all the more so will such a thought be removed from the mind. You will do what you are told. You will think what you are told to think, and you will believe what you are told to believe. But none of this matters anyway, because there will no longer be allowed expression of thought or belief. You will be assimilated into the New World Order, and it will absorb every part of your being.

These are the dreams of the formers of the New World Order. This is what they want for you (but obviously, not for themselves). But there is just one little problem with this New World Order. There is nothing new about it at all. The "New" World Order is just the most recent attempt to establish total control. This has been attempted by so many, so many different times, that to enumerate a list of attempts would be rather lengthy.

Since the earliest periods of recorded history there have been attempts made by a small group of privileged elite to completely dominate over everyone else. Every time that they have tried to implement their plan, they met with dismal, destructive failure.

Lifetime after lifetime, reincarnation after reincarnation, the small group of privileged elite rise to the heights of political, economic, and social power all in the attempt to take control over the whole. With history as judge, this small powerful elite do not have a good track record. Every attempt that they have made worked a little bit, lasted a short time, and then came crashing down, bringing disaster upon themselves and to world that they tried so hard to control.

And here we are again, sitting back and watching as the ancient, small powerful elite try yet again to manifest their plan for global domination. Only this time they have at their disposal the technological terror of computerization that they have made. With such an ability to control, they reason, how can they go wrong this time? And so we witness their plans unfolding. They have been very busy since the end of the last World War, preparing for the next World War, and the New World Order that they are planning to unfold in its aftermath.

This power elite is a group of very old souls. They have been around since the early dawn of humanity. They came to our Earth when our present Adamic civilization was still young. They hatched their first plan in the aftermath of the Great Flood. They set up their representative Nimrod and taught him how to ensnare human souls, which is an area of expertise well known to this power elite.

Most of us are familiar with the Biblical story of the Tower of Babel. Unfortunately, the way that the story comes across in translation makes it appear like a non-historical legend, and fable. It is unfortunate that most who read the story, even in its original language (Hebrew) remain oblivious to the concealed and hidden messages buried in the Biblical text that reveal the secret truths of what really happened in Babel in ancient times.

The Tower of Babel was not just a big brick Ziggurat. As big as such a construction was, it could not contain within itself the entire growing world population. There was clearly a city being built alongside the tall Tower. Babel was the building of a new civilization, the first of many New World Orders to come.

A detailed understanding of this historical construction is irrelevant today. That subject is best left for the archeologists to explore. What is relevant is the purpose and reason behind the Tower and city. This psychic, psychological, spiritual reason very much concerns us today, because the underlying reality of human (and extraterrestrial) nature has not changed much over the many centuries.

Let us look at a brief review of what happened. The generation of the Tower had vivid memories of the global catastrophe of the Great Flood. They saw the remnants of a great, and destroyed civilization all around them. The water did not wash away all the remnants of the past. Some of those pre-flood secrets were smartly and safely protected from the flood's destruction. Maybe you have heard about what today are called, "Star Gates" buried in the deserts of Iraq? According to one Rabbinic opinion, based upon the Zohar, this may very well be real.

The ancient pre-flood world was certainly not primitive. Legend (which seems to be backed by numerous archaeological discoveries) states that the pre-flood world was a very developed, highly advanced, technological society. These same legends speak about a group of Extraterrestrials (referred to in the Bible, Gen. 6, and the "sons of God"), coming to Earth, interbreeding with human beings, and providing to the masses advanced technologies without them having to work to discover them naturally. All this was supposed to be wiped out by the Flood. But was it?

The ancients were no fools. Like Noah, their leaders knew very well natural disaster was coming. Their one mistake was that they thought that they could use their knowledge and science to avoid it.

They were wrong. There was a Higher Hand that was working against them to thwart their efforts.

The scientists of old are thought today to have been magicians simply because we misunderstand their technology. Tried as they did to avert the coming natural disaster, they discovered long before the end came that they would fail. Many of the ancient leaders, especially the Extraterrestrial corrupters and their children (the Nephilim), took refuge in many different places. Some returned to space. Some shifted form and settled in a parallel dimension. Some took refuge in Inner Earth.

All these legends are enlightening and entertaining. We would quickly dismiss them for being the stories that they are, if it were not for the fact that these same old ancient ones always pop up again and again throughout human history trying to rebuild that which they once had. Although these ancient ones come under a different guise each time, their purpose, their methods, and their intentions are clearly always the same. It is easy to recognize them if one knows what to look for.

The true Power Elite are not fully human, as we understand genetic humanity today. But they themselves are in control of all the institutions of science that experiment with these things, and which make these things public. If it were ever discovered that someone (or a small group of people) had unidentifiable DNA, no one would recognize it as extraterrestrial; no one would define it as Nephilim. There would simply be an anomaly, without any further interest or desire to explain it.

But do not fear that our present human civilization is inundated with the bloodline children of the Nephilim. Their numbers are few, by design. This is nothing new. Long ago they developed a technology of transformation to conceal their non-human origins. They have been using this technology for centuries, speeding up their plans in recent generations.

For centuries, there were stories of demonic abductions. Today we have relabeled the experience and refer to such bizarre events as alien abductions. For the most part, all these experiences have been conducted by those of the children of the Nephilim who centuries ago shifted into a parallel dimension, leaving them non-corporeal in this world. Their so-called breeding program was established to reconnect themselves with physical human bodies. Today, they have mastered the ability to fully incarnate as 100% physical human beings. This has been documented in the writings of the Kabbalistic Sages centuries ago.

Mind you, this has not gone by completely unnoticed in society at large. Some secular investigators today are aware of this, and have even written about it. These authors have no idea who in fact they are talking about, and consider this to be some sort of an "alien" agenda. But these entities are not at all aliens. They are from here, from Earth. They are given the name "hybrids." The generation of the Flood, and the generation of the Builders of Babel hve returned, and live among us. They are, by all means, totally concealed. No one will ever be able to identify their "spiritual" origins.

The only way that these "hybrid" beings can be detected is energetically. While they may be fully physically human, their energetic signatures (their auras) cannot hide the fact that their souls are definitely not fully human. They integrate into human society unnoticed. As such they serve as the behind-the-scenes influencers to pick and choose, groom, and elevate their chosen human candidates who, when ready, are placed in positions of power so as to (once again) implement their plan of global transformation and domination.

So, the world leaders and power brokers who today we see as "running the show," are in fact doing no such thing. Every world leader has a hidden master behind him, directing his/her thoughts, feelings, and actions. Just like God hardened Pharaoh's heart in ancient Egypt to manipulate him in order to unfold the Divine Plan, so too is it today. Behind today's power brokers are hidden beings, with a hidden agenda.

But fear not the "powers-that-be," (whoever they really are), for behind these hidden personages, are their angelic overseers. This body of angels serves God, and carries out "to the letter" the Divine Plan and Heavenly edicts. We know of these angels from the

Bible. Dan. 4:14 states, *"By the decree of the Watchers is the matter and by the word of the holy ones is the edict, in order that the living should know that the Most High rules over the kingdom of man, and to whom He wishes He gives it, and the lowest of men He sets upon it."*

And so, here we are today watching as our current events unfold leading the world into some most unsettling conditions. We see all around us social disintegration. There is no more any fear of God, or fear of wrongdoing. In many places anarchy is already ruling the streets. The global economy is shaking, and its present form may indeed collapse. Nations are fighting nations, as other nations are preparing for even greater wars. It looks like everything in our world is going from bad to worse. But is it?

The Watcher are doing their jobs. The children of the Nephilim are also doing their jobs. What we may think is happening randomly around the world is actually a grand well-thought-out plan for our world, and for all humanity. Make no mistake about it, God is behind this all!

It is God Who is giving the ultimate orders which are being carried out by many different levels of subordinates, many of whom do not have a clue as to whom it actually is that is giving them their "marching orders." And with all this being the case, we must remember the wise words of King Solomon, "there is nothing new under the sun." All that is happening now is what has always been happening in the past. And it is going to continue to be just like this.

In other writings of mine, I have referred to this Divine Plan for humanity as Experiment Earth, for indeed, all of human history, past, present, and even future, is all being guided and directed to serve the greater cause that only Heaven knows what that is. All we know is that the Divine Plan does end well for Earth. Eventually, an evolved, and spiritually mature humanity will inherit the Earth. We call this time period "the days of Mashiah." As for what this will really be like, we will have to wait and see.

For now, we should be paying attention to what is happening right here, and right now, for the Divine Plan is in full motion. And this Plan takes into account the future of the children of the

Nephilim, their fathers who are the angels that violated Heaven's law and came to Earth to sire them, the Watchers, whose job it is to oversee everything that is going on, and us. The Divine Plan sorts out the fate and destiny of us all. So, let us realize that everything that is happening now is for very good reason, and these reasons may indeed include concerns for other intelligent, indigenous races of beings here on Earth, other than us humans.

So now, let us return to discuss the coming "not-so-New World Order" and explore its purpose. This will help us recognize in advance its coming form, and where those who remain faithful to God are going to fit in (or not).

Jewish, Christian and Islam share a common core understanding that before the world is rectified with the coming of the Messiah, there will come before him another person who is going to be his dark-opposite. This dark-opposite messianic person is given many names. In Judaism, he is referred to as Armilus, the Christians call him the Anti-Christ, and Muslims refer to him as Al Masih ad-Dajjal. Whether or not this is an actual individual or whether the name can be applied to a system in general is something that we will see in time.

Whatever or whomever this is to be, one thing that we believe is certain is that this Armilus/Anti-Christ will be none other than the reincarnation of the Biblical Nimrod. In other words, the man who in the beginning tried so hard to enslave the world will now be allowed to succeed and to accomplish his plans.

The Armilus/Anti-Christ person is said to be human in form only, with a soul that emanates from one of the fallen angels from Genesis 6. As such, the Armilus/Anti-Christ will be a modern day child of the Nephilim, possibly even their leader.

The greatest problem that human beings face from the children of the Nephilim is that unlike human souls created in the Image of God, these souls do not share such Divine origins. As such they do not possess certain higher characteristics found in evolved human beings. This is why the children of the Nephilim have no sense of human morals, values, and good character. They embrace immorality as their norm, as we can plainly see today by the influence they exert over society through social media.

The children of the Nephilim have no regret, and no remorse for conducting their affairs with malicious deceptiveness. For a very long time they have infiltrated political, social, and economic movements and organizations around the world, corrupting everything that they touch.

Their methods are clearly identifiable. They chose to attack their opponents emotionally, and to conduct character assassinations. They seek to sow confusion and doubt in subtle yet disruptive ways. They tell the big lie over and over again, until most people believe that it is true.

And using these tools of deception and derision they have again captured the minds of the peoples, and enslave their bodies to their will. Only those with knowledge of higher things could have conducted such a campaign against humanity in such a successfully destructive way. Nimrod, Pharoah, and Nebuchadnezzar are proud of them.

So, why is God allowing all this to happen? The answer is simple! Because, by Divine decree, the Watchers are watching, and they are watching for who is going to succumb to the lies and deceptions, and who is going to make the efforts to free themselves from such controls!

God has commanded the Watchers to allow the scenario to develop under which every soul is going to be tested to see which one choses freedom, and which one chooses slavery. And once the choice has been made, it will determine which souls evolve forward into (what we call) the Messianic age, and which souls will devolve backward, and reincarnate elsewhere to again suffer through cycle after cycle of lower-lifeform lives in order to cultivate the proper mindset for reintegration into the cosmic/Divine design. This long and arduous process of rectification is the reality of that which we have come to call, Hell.

We live in a society that is actively engaged in a war against Heaven. The reality of this means that, for centuries, our modern so-called "science-based" society has made every effort to remove from human minds the ability to see beyond the limitations of confining physical reality. Everything that is included in the greater experience of psychic development is dismissed, rejected, and deceptively destroyed. This is how war is waged against Heaven, by disconnecting human souls from having any access to Heavenly realities.

A human soul that cannot personally see and experience higher realities is one that is enslaved within one's intellect, and lacks any true way of knowing the difference between right and wrong, truth and falsehood, light and darkness. Such souls continue to eat the forbidden fruit of the Tree of Knowledge, Good and Evil. Such souls are easy to control and manipulate. Such souls stay enslaved forever.

And so, here comes the New World Order, which is in and of itself, not anything new at all. The only newness about it is the technology that will be used to control all areas of an individual's finances, healthcare, livelihood, and personal choices.

It has always been the Dark Path to seek control over the minds, hearts, and deeds of people. Now with modern computer based technologies, and their virtual realities, total control can be enforced with the click of a mouse. Today we have credit scores, tomorrow we will have social scores, health scores, and who knows what other measures of control that will be shortly implemented.

Who will take a stand against the system? Who will move out of the system and leave behind all that it offers? Who has the faith in God to face life without all the modern conveniences that we have all become so addicted to? The number will be very few. Then again, the numbers of the righteous have always been very few. And so, the great separation will be!

God is allowing the New World Order to take the control that it will, and is allowing it to express the ruthlessness that it will. All of this is for the sake of individuals to choose which life they are willing to lead.

Will one continue to eat from the forbidden fruit of the Tree of Knowledge, Good and Evil? If one chooses to continue on this diet, then it will lead one to death. If, however, on the other hand, one chooses to embrace the Tree of Life, and to partake of its fruit, then one must return to the Garden in order to access it. For the Tree of Knowledge is planted in the heart of the human jungle where the rule of "dog-eat-dog" is the rule. The Tree of Life is planted in the Garden where the rule is "to lie down beside the still waters."

The New World Order is the final test of souls. The test is from Heaven, and each soul will pass through it. How each of us will be affected is up to the individual to choose. Know then that it is coming.

Know now what it is that you, the individual, is supposed to do.

Chapter 3

Aligning with the Divine Plan

There is an old Yiddish saying, *Mann Tracht, Un Gott Lacht*, "man plans and God laughs."

However fatalistic this may sound, it has been proven to be true many times over.

We walk a razor's edge between being masters of our own destinies, and being nothing more than pliable clay in the Divine Hands of our Maker.

Experience should teach us that there are those aspects of our lives that we seem to have under control, and then again there are other aspects of our lives that are totally out from under our control.

We are blessed that as human beings we have (or at least we should have) reasonable, intelligent minds. We can look out at any situation around us and decide for ourselves how to act and behave under the circumstances. Sometimes we chose to act wisely. Other times, intentionally or not, we chose poorly and thus act foolishly.

Consequences are the natural outcome of our choices. When we chose wisely what to do, things should work out well for us. On the other hand, when we chose poorly, things usually do not work out as good. And then again, sometimes as much as we do what is right, things do not turn out right, at least not in the way that we thought, and the way that we planned.

When we make foolish choices and bad things happen, we are not surprised. We act foolishly and nature takes its course. This is the definition of consequences. Some will even call it karma (destiny). But be this as it may, sometimes even when we make the right choices and the best of plans, even when we make every effort to ensure that our expected outcome materializes in the way that we wish, *Mann Tracht, Un Gott Lacht*, "man plans and God laughs."

Sometimes it seems as if Heaven and God Himself conspire against us and stand in the way of our accomplishments. This is sometimes true, even when one is seeking to perform the Will of Heaven, and to perform a commandment or other good deed (mitzvah). Yes, sometimes one can feel as if all that one does for God seems to not amount to much. So, what is one to do?

The first thing that one must do is to dispel any negative feelings that one may have towards God and His Divine Plan. Remember even the smartest and sharpest human mind is far too small to contemplate and understand the least of God's Divine Plan for the universe. There is just so much that we do not know. When one wishes to put together a puzzle one needs to have all the pieces. What kind of puzzle can one construct when one has less than 5% of the pieces?

We do not understand what God does or why. Plan as we do, we pray that our plans may be favorable in the Divine Eye, and that our plans are bestowed with Heavenly favor and blessings. Sometimes our prayers for blessings are answered as we wish them to be, and sometimes they are not. How prayers are answered is one of those things that, try as we will, we cannot manipulate or coerce a positive response.

The only way to successfully work within the Divine Plan is for one to follow the wise advice recorded in Pirkei Avot (2:4), in the name of Rabban Gamaliel the son of Rabbi Judah HaNasi. The Rabbi said, *"Do His will as though it were your will, so that He will do your will as though it were His. Set aside your will in the face of*

His will, so that he may set aside the will of others for the sake of your will."

In these simple words, the Rabbi has revealed to us the secret to successful living. The secret is not such much about what we do, but rather more about what we don't do!

We all make plans. We have to. In order for anyone to live any semblance of a structured life, plans and plan making is common sense. However, not all plans are equal; some are more thought out than others. Some plans include many different contingencies just in case something happens and the course of a plan is interrupted. One can always redirect from Plan A to Plan B, or even Plan C if and when necessary. However, unless one has made a Plan B and C and so on, if and when Plan A goes awry, one will have nothing to fall back upon. This is not a good plan.

Life is ever fluid. No one knows everything that can, and will, happen. Even science recognizes that there is a random element of chance in the otherwise rigid laws of nature. The random element may not be so random at all. It may indeed be the invisible Hand of Almighty God intervening in nature, to redirect whatever it is that He wishes into whatever direction that He may will. Try as we will to pin down every detail and to cover every contingency, *Mann Tracht, Un Gott Lacht,* "man plans and God laughs."

In all due respect, God is not really laughing. The course of human events, be it on the individual or collective level, is not a laughing matter. But God does not share our list of priorities. Here on Earth we prioritize what we consider to be important. In Heaven, God prioritizes what He believes to be important. And being that God is God and that His Wisdom and Knowledge encompasses all, we can rest assured that God's priorities are what's best, whether we like it or not.

The secret of a successful life is surrender to the Higher Knowledge and Will of Heaven.

Only God knows why God does what He does. God does not always reveal to us what He is doing, all the more so why He is doing it. Sometimes, in the past, this information was passed on to humanity through the revelations of the prophets. Today, prophetic communion has been terminated and we no longer receive direct revelation about immediate Divine Plans. We know that the day will come when prophecy will be restored. We are working hard teaching and practicing the prophetic techniques that one day will enable a new generation of prophets to arise. But this time has not yet come.

Step One in the practice of the prophetic techniques is called Bitul, nullification. How this is practiced has already been described to us by Rabban Gamliel. This type of surrender to Heaven is essential if we ever want to serve as ready vessels willing to be filled with Divine Light and Heavenly direction.

As much as we plan and do the things that common sense dictates for us to do, we must still nevertheless recognize that the Will of Heaven may or may not coincide with that which we have decided.

If our daily walk through life proves to take us in a direction other than that which we have planned, rather than fight the Hand of God, one should instead embrace it. The Hand of God is the Hand of our Heavenly Parent. Daddy/Abba will not steer His precious child down a wrong or dangerous path. We have to learn to accept this and to trust Avinu She'b'Shamayim (our Heavenly Father).

The Gemara (Macot 24a) teaches us that the entire Torah can be summed up in the prophetic words of the prophet Habakuk (2:4), *"the righteous lives in his faith."*

Surrender to the unknown is always a challenge for the human intellect. It is most unsettling for the human mind to have to admit that it cannot figure everything out, and that it cannot control everything that it wishes. It is our human intellect which is at war with faith. It is the intellect that tries to rationalize everything and to strip away the dimension of faith. But the intellect cannot accomplish this task. For faith belongs to the realm of the spirit, and spirit is above mind in the same way as Heaven is above Earth.

Faith, spirit, trusting the invisible, letting go of the rigid and embracing flexibility, these are matters that belong to the soul. The soul is that part of us which comes from Heaven, and remains attached there all the while that a part of it resides within our physical bodies. The voice of the soul cries out and says, *"trust God, surrender to the Divine Will; let go and let God!"* But alas, how many of us hear the voice of the soul, and all the more so comply with its inner message?

God knows the many paths that our future can manifest. Of all the multiple choices that lay before us, only one is the right and the best. And what is that one right and best path for one to walk? Don't ask me! I am not Heaven's messenger to tell anyone what their path is to be. However, within each and every one of us there resides our soul. When one cultivates hearing the voice of the soul, and accomplishes becoming sensitive to its inner message, then one will have acquired for oneself a Magid, a spirit guide.

Turning away from one's own true inner voice also turns one away from the Path of God. God knows all the paths that one can take. God thus speaks to one's inner soul. One's inner soul serves as one's spirt guide (Magid) who will always speak to one, not with audio words but rather with NVC (non-verbal communication).

The Magid communicates today through deeply-felt impressions that strongly influence us to sense and to know what is right and what is wrong, for the person, for the moment, for the situation and for the circumstances. But we must have faith to accept the inner voice, and to follow its direction, regardless of how unintellectual or how highly irrational it may seem. When one senses the conviction of truth within oneself, it becomes an obligation upon one to remain true to oneself, and by thus doing so, remaining faithful to God in Heaven.

So make whatever plans that you normally do. Detail them as best as you can. And once all your plans have been made, and you are ready to implement them, recite a short and simple prayer to God. *"May it be Your Will Master of the Universe that you bless the work of my hands, and may it manifest in accordance to Your Divine Will. I surrender my plans and myself to you. Blessed are You*

HaShem, the true Master of paths, and my faithful Guide along my personal way."

Being successful depends upon how we define the term success. When one surrenders oneself to Heaven and commits to being an open vessel for the fulfillment of the Divine Plan, then one's success is guaranteed.

As for any and all other types of plans, they are in God's Hand, much more than in our own. It is always best to bend the knee before our Creator, before we arise and set foot along the paths of our choosing.

Being by God's side is the best way to having God at one's own side. This is how one's path is blessed and made successful, even if that path experiences major ups and down along the way.

When one walks with God, one will be successful, regardless of what one considers the definition of success to be. In the end, and hopefully even along the way, one will come to the recognition best expressed by the wise Sage, Nahum Ish Gamzu, Gamzu l'Tova, "this too (whatever this may be), is for the best! Give thanks to God, for He is good, and His mercy endures forever, amen.

Chapter 4

The Cry of the Righteous & the Coming Judgment

God hears the cries of the righteous! As human behaviors sink to lower and lower depths of depravity and debauchery, the cry of the righteous grows in equal opposition.

God knows the suffering of the righteous. All the righteous want to do is to live righteously and to shine the light of freedom, and righteousness wherever it is that they go. The righteous know that behaving properly brings its own rewards. Therefore, they do what they do, because it is who and what they are as human beings.

The wicked who perpetuate depravity and debauchery have a different way to them. They despise righteousness for one simple reason. Righteousness dictates the equality of all human beings. Each individual has the rights and privileges of freedom. Each person cultivates one's own strength and one's own independence. The righteous only bend the knee to God in Heaven, and not to any opposing human authority. The wicked will have none of this!

The wicked will not extend the rights and privileges of freedom to any other. The wicked are essentially self-centered, selfish individuals who care only about themselves. In the eyes of the wicked, other exists only to be used and exploited. In the eyes of the wicked, others are meant to be controlled and completely dominated. In the eyes of the wicked, others are merely a resource to be selfishly used, and then discarded. The wicked thus embrace the very essence of depravity, and practice every form of debauchery simply because it pleases their selfish desires.

As the wicked grow more and more in their wickedness, the more and more they see the righteous as intolerable opposites, whose mere existence can no longer be tolerated. Thus the wicked use every power at their disposal to cause the righteous to stumble and fall. In so doing, the wicked prove themselves to be the stronger. For the wicked use guile and deception as their tools of choice to rob righteousness from the righteous.

The righteous in general pursue righteousness. Although some also pursue wisdom, not all do. Therefore, without wisdom, the righteous can fall victim to one of the many scams that the wicked perpetuate in order to entrap them, and to imprison their minds. Righteousness protects the bodies and souls of the righteous; wisdom protects their minds and hearts.

God knows the ways of the righteous and God sees all the behaviors of the wicked, both revealed and concealed. And God judges, in His own way, and in His own time.

Judgment will fall upon the heads of those who deserve it. This is unavoidable. However while it is unavoidable, it can nevertheless be delayed. When God gazes out and sees the struggle of the righteous with the wicked, God moves to act on behalf of the righteous. When, however, the righteous and the wicked mingle together, Judgment is delayed.

God will not punish the righteous alongside the wicked. And the wicked know this. For this reason they make every effort to ensure that the righteous are forced to live in their locations. When the righteous live among the wicked, Judgement is postponed. God watches and waits. If the Divine Eye sees the righteous being overcome by the wicked God judges the wicked accordingly.

If the righteous dwell amongst the wicked by choice, then together the two will face a single Judgement. When however the righteous are forced to dwell among the wicked, simply because they have no place else to go, then God's judgment is patiently withheld.

God hears the cries of the imprisoned righteous and God sees the arrogant depravity and debauchery of the wicked. By keeping the righteous enslaved, the wicked buy for themselves time. In this stolen time, the wicked continue to siphon off all the life-force energy from the righteous. The wicked steal all their money, rob their souls of their chastity, and seek every way to corrupt the righteous and to turn them into being wicked, just like themselves. In this way, the wicked conspire to stay in power and to hold back Divine Judgement.

Essentially, the wicked are holding the righteous as hostages. And God sees, and God knows!

As things get worse, the enslaved righteous cry out with greater intensity for their Master in Heaven to free them from the burdens of their slavery. Their cries arise on high, and God hears them. God extends His patience all the while that He works behind the scenes to free the righteous from the grasp of the wicked.

Once the righteous have been segregated and set apart Judgment then comes upon the wicked. This is the way that it has always been. When, however, the righteous choose to live with the wicked, and by doing so extend to them their shield of righteousness, God also watches and takes note. For such compromised righteous persons, God also hears their prayers for patience. But for the righteous who chose to live among the wicked, regardless of their merits, God will bring judgment on both righteous and wicked together. We have seen this happen many times throughout history.

Today we find ourselves living in a society that once tolerated and even encouraged righteousness in its midst. But these days are long gone. Society today prides itself upon praising the wicked and their wickedness, and at the same time condemning the righteous, and in many cases, actually persecuting them.

The righteous are slow to respond. The righteous have a hard time believing and accepting that the society that once welcomed and supported them, now no longer does either. The righteous have become complacent and watch the rise of evil. And instead of trying to rigorously fight it, they (for the most part) just sit back and watch, doing nothing to intervene. And God watches and God knows!

God knows the hearts and minds of every individual. God knows who cries out in anguished prayer reeling under the pain of encroaching evil, but who find themselves powerless to confront it. God knows His own.

There are many others who also offer their prayers to God. But these offer their prayers as if by rote, as if they are merely reading words from the page of a book. And God watches and God knows.

God hears the prayers of the sincerely righteous, those who mourn the encroaching evil. When the moment of Judgment comes, God will grant these righteous souls their due protection and salvation. If these souls are held hostage and imprisoned within the present evil society, God will break their shackles and set them free. But once free, these redeemed souls need to go very far away from the society that enslaved them. For that same evil society will seek to enslave them again, in their continuous effort to thwart the Plan and Hand of God.

God knows the heart of every soul, be that soul righteous or wicked. God knows which souls can evolve and move even closer to holiness, and He also knows those souls which can devolve, lose their humanity, and thus incur severe and harsh rectifications.

In the Eyes of Heaven, the Judgement of God does not come to punish, but rather to repair. God knows what souls can bear, and when their salvation is called for. God knows that to every depravity and debauchery there is an end. Though that end may be postponed for a short while, it is never postponed indefinitely. One way or another, at one time or another, both Judgment and Justice come!

Crying out to God in sincerity does not even require words of prayer. Sometimes a deep heart-felt sign is all that is needed. God knows who belongs to Him. The righteous are precious in the Eyes of Heaven. God will comfort the righteous and encourage them to be patient until the great sifting between the righteous and the wicked is complete. And we are drawing ever closer to the conclusion of this process as more and more individual souls are picking sides in a culture war that will inevitably conclude with the Judgement of Heaven upon wicked and evil persons.

As the battle around us wages, it is incumbent upon every soul to finally decide once and for all where one wishes to stand. Is one with God, fully 100%, or is one against God, however small or great. God knows His own and will judge all souls in accordance to the truth of their beings.

The separation between good souls and evil souls is ramping up. It is God who is guiding the course of human events so as to push every individual soul to make one's decision. In the end, before the Judgment, souls will either be 100% for God, or 100% against God. The present culture war will guarantee this. God is behind this all. It is the Way of the Divine to test all souls to see who is who, and what each is willing to do, or not to do.

Let the righteous know the Way of God and of His Judgment. Let them separate from this wicked society and the perpetrators of evil within it. As the righteous move out of the way, they enable the Judgment of God to manifest.

Then again, if the righteous do not move out of the way, then God takes note, and in its time will Judge both righteous and wicked together by the same standard. This is a fate that I pray the truly righteous will make every effort to avoid.

Cry out to God in the anguish of your soul. But at the same time, do not remain docile in the face of evil. One must act. One must move. One must make every effort to protect and to defend one's righteousness, or otherwise one stands every chance to lose it.

Repentance before God is a lot more than merely saying, "I'm sorry," especially if such an apology is insincere with the individual continuing one's wanton behavior. God despises the hypocrite. Repentance means change. Change must be on both the inside and the outside. Change must be sincere. One must elect to do the right things. Action talks clearly when words speak confusion.

Judgement is coming, maybe not today, and maybe not tomorrow, but it is coming. And when it arrives, it will sweep away all wicked and evil parties that stand in the way of Divine progress. As it was in ancient times when Moses redeemed Israel from Egypt, so too will it be today, without or without a Moses character to lead the way.

Let the wise heed this message and reaffirm one's bond with God. As for the rest, like the family of Lot, let them remain in denial until the fire and brimstone of Judgment consumes them all.

Whenever this will be, however long it takes, this day will definitely come. Be ready for it, for no one knows the time. It may be close or it may be far. So act now, choose righteousness and live it, distance yourself from evil and do good. And trust that the Master of the Universe (Ribbono Shel Olam) is watching and that He sees all and knows all.

Draw ever closer to God's side under the protective wings of the Divine Presence. This is the path of salvation and the answer to the prayers of the righteous. May God bless and keep His righteous ones. Amen, may it be the Will of Heaven.

Chapter 5

Blessings & Curses,
Nature's God = God's Nature

It is no secret that the prophetic curses listed in Leviticus 26-27 have, in one form or another, all come true, often many times over. Throughout the centuries, the children of Israel, whether they have been religious or irreligious, righteous or wicked, still suffered under repressive government/religious regimes that promoted against them pogroms and holocausts. There is obviously something very unbalanced here.

God does not send punishments upon humanity simply as a whim. Such a concept of God would be nothing less than attributing human attributes to Heaven. According to some, this concept of humanizing God is the very act of idolatry.

God does not punish humanity as some form of wrath, similar to that of a human king. Although Scripture may indeed speak in this language, the Sages are clear in emphasizing to us that this type of talk is only for human understanding, and it, in no way, reflects the true heavenly outlook upon the universe.

The key to understanding human suffering, curses, and the like, is rather very simple. These occurrences come about due to a lack of balance in the natural order and affairs between Heaven and Earth, and between we ourselves, and our fellow man.

Human suffering comes to us as a warning for us to realign ourselves. If we listen, then all turns out well and good. When, however, we fail to listen, or worse, refuse to listen, this is when push comes to shove, and the forces of natural realignment, inherent in the natural world, placed there by the Creator, push hard to realign.

This leads us to a concept, no, a reality, which many people have a real hard time understanding today. The reality is that God is Alive. God is a living, vibrant, and conscious Force.

As Creator, God permeates creation, and therefore, all of creation serves as the "hand" of God to bring about what we can call the Divine Purpose. Nature, therefore, is God's servant. Thus when natural law is violated, God is violated. And when natural law acts to realign itself, it is God acting through natural law that makes this happen.

Now hear this! God is the consciousness of existence. God is the soul of creation. Without a soul, we are dead. Without God's soul, the natural world around us (including what we call the supernatural) would also be dead.

God's "soul," God's presence thus imbues all things, in all places, at all times. Whatever therefore happens, be it for us a blessing or a curse, the "soul" of God is within it. Cultivating a recognition of this and learning how to experience it is one of our greatest human goals.

Prophecy makes one thing clear, that in spite of our feelings or beliefs to the opposite, God, and God alone is the source, the author of all things, both good and evil. Isaiah 45:6-7 states, *"In order that they know, from the shining of the sun, and from the west, that there is no one besides Me. I am YHWH and there is no other. Who forms light and **creates darkness**, Who makes peace and **creates evil**. I am YHWH, Who makes all these."*

Nature itself manifests and reveals the Will of God. In order for us to know God's Will, we must in turn, be in-tuned with creation, nature, the living, breathing manifestations of the Way and Will of God. Knowing God, and understanding "His" Way, is not as hard a task as one might assume. The path and the instruction are all around us. They have always been all around us, and they always will be.

If we only open our eyes to the natural Way, if only we would open our ears to hear the natural sounds, we would see the moving spirit of God in creation, we would hear nature's song, and learn to sing along with it.

God revealed commandments to humankind. Some of a sort, "He" commanded exclusively to Israel, others "He" ordained to be observed by all humanity. We do not need to get overly academic here by identifying and elaborating which commandments are which. Rather, we must know and understand a simple point. *All of God's Laws in the commandments given to humanity, are mere archetypal reflections that mirror the natural Laws ordained by God to govern the universe.*

One cannot have natural Law, without the concept of a natural "Law-giver." God is the Will and Way of creation. When we live in sync with this, this is how Divine blessings are received. When we live in contradiction to this, this is how Divine curses are received. It really has nothing to do with a "wrathful" God, and everything to do with energy alignments, balanced polarities, and achieving harmony between the dimensional planes, which we refer to as Heaven, Earth, and human consciousness.

Israel, as a nation, is also an archetype, and fulfills a unique role in human history. Israel was chosen by God to serve as a tool to serve the Divine Intent. Being Israel certainly does not make one any better than anyone else, not smarter, not richer, not more beautiful, and most certainly not necessarily any closer to God realization, or any closer to God's absolute truth for humanity.

Israel, as a nation was chosen as God's tool of work. The nature of a tool is to be used, often to be banged around, often used to perform hard tasks. God's tool Israel certainly fits this definition. And yet, throughout centuries of being used as God's tool, most rank and file everyday people of the children of Israel live obliviously to what it is that God is doing with both the nation, and with each individual (personally), therein.

Most religious people today are content living their very unnatural lives, while they continue to use their religion as a tool against God, to block out of sight, and out of mind, the very natural Way of God. Most religious people today hold up their religion to "God's Face" and proclaim their self-righteousness, thinking that this should solicit Divine favor, and thus earn them the right to Divine blessings. Yet, nature and reality show us, day after day, that regardless of how religious one is, bad things still happen to good people.

Religion might want to explain away the Will of God as being something mysterious, but is there really something mysterious going on? Rather than to dismiss the natural Way as something mysterious, one should instead explore the natural Way (the Living Torah) and come to recognize just how far away one is from the true Will, Way and Torah of YHWH, the creator.

To show us just this, the Creator shines darkness upon us, in order to help us recognize and appreciate light. Those who wish to walk in, and live in the light, had better learn to understand the true nature and purpose of darkness. *Darkness, like light, is a creation of God. Both serve "Him" as "His" tools. Both are agents of the Divine Will.*

While we may not like this reality, it is still a reality that we are unable to deny or prevent. God uses both good and evil, both light and darkness, as our teachers. It is up to us to learn the lessons in order for us to realign our souls with God's natural world. When indeed, we accomplish this, we will indeed have solicited Divine favor. This will clearly result in blessings. Balance and blessings go together like hand in glove.

When however the opposite occurs, then nature, the universe, and God all work in harmony to bring realignment, be it to the individual, to a community, to a nation, or to the whole world at large. This is the natural way of things.

Seeking God, learning to see God is the Way to walk the natural path of Living Torah. In the Torah, we are actually commanded to do this very thing. The Torah calls this bonding with God, in Hebrew, Devekut.

This commandment is nothing mysterious or nebulous. It has been written down and is readily available to be viewed by those who desire to know it. In his book, Peleh Yo'etz, (Dalet), Rabbi Eliezer Papo writes regarding Devekut:

"Devekut (bonding) with God is one of the 613 commandments. One is obligated, in accordance to one's ability; to make all efforts to properly observe this commandment, at all times. One must be bond with God continually, with great yearning, and with sparks of burning love. There is no greater attribute than this, for all things are included in it. The difficulty in achieving it (devekut) is in direct proportion to its level of importance."

The Ba'al Shem Tov, founder of the Hasidic movement, addresses how to cultivate this learning experience. (Sefer Ba'al Shem Tov, Noah 7)

"When a father wishes to teach his toddler son to walk, what does the father do? He stands his son up and places him before him. He stretches out his arms to the sides so the child does not fall. Thus, the child will walk between the two supporting arms of his father.

When the child reaches the father, the father then moves back a little bit so that the child will again move forward and come close to the father, each time the child does more. In this way, the child learns to walk correctly. For if the father would not back up, the child would have no place to move forward... This then is the way of the Holy One, blessed be He with His creation. When a person strongly desires to bond with God, God removes Himself a bit. If not for this, a person would never develop strength and continuity in their bonding. However now, as God backs up, the individual needs to strengthen himself in meditation more and more. Thus one grows in strength (and seals the bond)."

In accordance to the investment of effort, is the amount of the reward. If we truly wish to align with nature, and nature's Creator, then **we have a lot to learn, and equally a lot to unlearn.** Balance, alignment, proper polarities, all these things serve us in becoming bonded to God. Only a bond with God enables one to see, to understand, to know, and to this do, that which is right and proper.

Chapter 6

To Fight the Great Lie

Look over here – not over there!

This is how deceptions begin!

Entertainment always blinds education.

Addiction to comfort and ease is partner with death.

Tolerance towards the immoral and the unjust is how evil flourishes.

Taking away one's rights is the definition of what is wrong.

Feelings have their place – but they must never override the rule of calm thinking.

Responsible individuals always act responsibly.

Irresponsible people always act irresponsibly.

Actions define the person – be they righteous or evil.

A person of confused thoughts is weak.

It is easy to manipulate such a person through one's compromised emotions.

Such a one is a danger to others and to oneself.

Clarity of thought is simplicity – It says, I am responsible. I act responsibly.

One with a clear mind sees all with simplicity.

In simplicity the deceptive arguments of the wicked become clear.

One who uses deceptive arguments to cloud simplicity is an agent of evil.

Many today are simply vile, revolting creatures of evil.

They care nothing for God, country, morality, and dignity.

They are easy to recognize – they are the ones who use every means

to rob you of your rights, and to destroy your spirit of independence and self-reliance.

Creatures of evil seek to destroy every good value and moral behavior. They create every opportunity to take away the power of the righteous to resist their evil onslaughts.

To stand up when everyone is being told to lie down takes courage and resolve.

Unrighteous authority is no authority at all.

It is righteous and right to stand up against the unrighteous and wrong!

Embrace simplicity – to do not allow yourself to be distracted by unnecessary complexity.

Complexity, as opposed to simplicity, is what leads to deceptive arguments.

Deceptive arguments rob the mind of peace – and enslave the soul to confusion.

This is how the wicked attack and destroy the righteous.

Stay clear – Stand tall – Be responsible – Be strong.

Embrace what is right – fight what is wrong.

Do not fear misguided authority – fight it in every way possible.

Know that God is watching – and that God alone is the Judge of the souls of all mankind.

SECTION TWO

WARNINGS & ADMONITIONS

Getting Ready by Getting Right
with God, Ourselves, & with One Another

Chapter 1

The Curse of Strife
From Sefer Darkei Shalom – The Ways of Peace,
Chapter 5, Section 3, Pages 54-56 by Rabbi Mordechai Potash

In the book Even Shlomi, Chapter 11, letter Het, it is written that there are "five types of mixed multitude (Erev Rav) within Israel. These are:

1. Masters of argument and slander.
2. Masters of lust.
3. The (two-faced hypocrites (lit: those whose inside is not like their outside).
4. Those who hunt after honor so as to make themselves famous.
5. Those who hunt after money.

The Masters of Argument are the worst of all, they are called Amalek.

The Son of David shall not come until he (Amalek) is blotted out of the world. Any argument that is not for legitimate spiritual reasons (meaning, for the sake of Heaven) is because of the mixed multitude, who jump at any chance to give themselves power and take the glory, as it is written, "Let us make for ourselves a name" (Tikunei Zohar 46B).

In the book Hafetz Haim, Section "Guarding the Tongue," Subsection "Remembrance" Chapter 15, it is written in the name of the Rambam: *"The prophets have prophesied and the wise have spoken all together condemning the evils of arguments, and still could not condemn it enough."*

The Hafetz Haim has also written that, aside from arguing being a great sin in and of itself, it is also the cause of many more grievous sins, such as pure hatred, slander, libel, anger, insult, harmful speech, public embarrassment, vengeance, bearing a grudge, cursing, causing the loss of one's livelihood, and many a time the desecration of the Name of God, which is the greatest sin of all.

By this, one also comes to godlessness, and then one draws others to become involved with his arguing. By this comes mockery; they mock those of the opposing view in order to draw more people to support their side. Even if, at the beginning, all this evil was not the original intention; even so, by the end they will not escape all of the above-mentioned sins. This is certain to all who are experienced and know the way of the world.

In the Gemara Hulin 89A, it is written:

"Rabi Ila says, the world stands only upon he who is silent at the time of conflict."

The source of this lesson is the Zohar (1-25A). There it says, *"There are five sections to the Erev Rav (mixed multitude): They are the Nifilim, Giborin, Anakim, Rifa'im and Amalekites. Because of them, the final Hey (of the holy Name YHWH) has fallen from Her place."*

The Zoharic commentaries *Yedid Nefesh* and *HaSulam* both have interesting details regarding this passage, but this is not the place to elaborate upon those details here. One thing clear from all the commentaries is that the Erev Rav is to be identified, not as a blood-line, but rather as a spiritual connection.

The Erev Rav are identified as those who behave in certain ways. They most definitely include those secular Jews who with arrogance and with scorn reject the Torah. The Erev Rav also includes many religious Jews who observe the faith hypocritically by appearing religious on the outside, but who all the while express a personality and behavior which is the opposite of Torah righteousness.

The Yedid Nefesh, on page 188, writes of Amalek: *"They make themselves appear as good Jews, as Hasidim and as Rabbis."* Above we read other aspects of Amalekite action, i.e. causing strife. It is terrible misfortune that this spirit of ungodly conflict imbues any number of members within religious communities today.

As with Pinhas the son of Eliezer, the son of Aharon the Kohen, we must always stand up against those who would seek to weaken the Torah, even if those individuals are "leaders" (religious or secular) as was Zimri, the leader of the tribe of Shimon, who by his actions caused death to reign in Israel.

Yet, we must not sink to their level to fight them; we cannot defeat the Erev Rav by imitating their immorality. On the contrary, we can only defeat the Erev Rav among us by our own righteousness.

Chapter 2

The Waves of Opinions

Opinions are neither right nor wrong.

Opinions are not facts, they are the beliefs that one holds based upon whatever thought process that led one to draw the conclusions that one does.

One can agree with an opinion, and one can disagree with an opinion.

But one who declares another's opinion to be either right or wrong is only expressing one's own opinion.

There are facts. They are truths which can be proven true.

Some may approve of such truths, and others might disapprove of them.

The good thing about facts is that they can be shown to be true, beyond the imposition of opinion upon them.

For example, one may agree or disagree with something written in the Torah (or elsewhere).

One may like what the Torah says, or dislike it.

But one thing is certain, and very easy to prove, and this is that the Torah does (or does not) indeed say a specific thing. One can look it up and quote "chapter and verse."

What the Torah says is fact. What you think about what the Torah says is opinion.

Our Sages of blessed memory did not all agree with one another.

Our Sages of blessed memory interpreted the facts, and based upon their interpretations expressed their opinions on matters.

Some opinions of the Sages were well embraced and accepted. Others were not!

And so it is too this day!

Deot (opinions) are deot! Take them or leave them.

Halakha (Torah Law) is Halakha. One may choose to observe it, or not. But one may not randomly change the Halakha simply because one's opinion is against it.

All true children of Torah live by Halakha, and live for Halakha.

Halakha is how we bond with God. No Halakha, no bond. – Is this opinion or fact? You decide.

Debate opinions, yes! Argue over opinions, no! Emotional anger has no place in a Torah discourse.

The Torah and Talmud are compared to the ocean.

There are always mighty waves, highs and lows, calms and storms. This is the "way of the territory."

Don't fight the ocean – learn to navigate it.

Torah in your head can always be debated. Torah in your heart is beyond such debate.

Torah in your heart is knowing, being and doing. – Is this opinion or fact? You decide.

But before you decide, first embrace Torah in your heart, so that you can judge from a place of knowledge and experience.

And allow the waves to do what waves do!

Chapter 3

The Meaning of Life

Life means expansion. Life means taking on all new forms made from all new combinations. The universe was created to give expression to life. Thus, in order to live there must always be free expression that seeks to build, to grow, to compliment, and to expand, all the while expressing balance and harmony with all other forces and forms that are doing the same.

Any force that seeks to curtail the growth of expressions through which life manifests, without purpose or cause to better serve the growth of life, is considered a force opposite life. We call such a force death. The definition of the word death needs to be expanded beyond the mere separation of soul from body.

The force of death is the universal principle that acts opposite the force of life. Sometimes death serves life, sometimes it does not. Sometimes death acts on its own. When this occurs, death is to be opposed. When, however, death acts in the service of life by bringing to an end one form in order for a fresh new form to become manifest, then death acts as the force we call good. When death acts on its own accord to sow destruction not based on healthy rebuilding, this is the force that we call evil.

Life and death, good and evil are universal constants. They define the course of existence, in this and in all worlds, and in this and in every dimension. Sentient beings who are the higher expressions of life itself are all subject to these forces, and act within their context.

Fires that burn out of control can cause destruction to all things. Whereas a fire that burns under control, a controlled burn, can be very useful, and successful in removing worn-out old forms, to make way for the revival of life in better new forms.

Life always seeks to improve on its ability to express itself. Life manifests itself in sentient conscious beings, each one of whom is a unique expression of the general life-force of the universe. Sentient beings seek to grow, to become more aware of the greater universe, and how one's individuality fits into the greater picture of all existence. As sentience expands, so too does one's awareness of the common good and the needs of each individual. Greater sentience brings one closer to seeing and being aware of the greater purpose of existence, and the need for life's expansion.

Freedom leads to life. Subservience leads to death. Subservience is not destruction in order to rebuild. Subservience is a death that serves itself. Its purpose is to stifle the force of life and expansion, and to control the force of life, limiting it, or cutting it off altogether. As such, subservience is the primary force of evil.

We must understand that the greatest forces of the entire universe play out their roles in even the most miniscule places of life expression. Our Earth, and our lives here on this planet, reflect the greater cosmic ways of the greater universe. Whatever happens here is because what is happening here is also happening elsewhere. All the universe (and multiverse) reflects itself into all its individual parts. As such human daily struggles reflect a cosmic struggle happening everywhere within the universe.

Life and death, good and evil all exist, and are meant to exist, but their existences are meant to be properly balanced and harmonized. This expression of harmony, or the lack of it, displays itself in multiple, and possibly in an infinite number of forms. Some manifestations are more balanced than others. Some have found complete balance. Others have found complete chaos. Life grows and expands by experiencing all these things, and thus learns how best to grow, and how best to avoid the obstacles to growth. This is the process of maturation. This is the same as evolution. For evolution is never random, or haphazard. All evolution is purposeful, intentional, and guide by a Higher Hand.

All that happens here on Earth, in our everyday lives, is an expression of this natural evolutionary give-and-take between the universal forces of life and death, and good and evil. All life on Earth here and now is guided and directed by a Higher Hand in order for all life here on Earth to find and maintain its proper, natural state of balance, in its unique expression and form, in accordance to the greater principles of the universe.

Greater consciousness and lower consciousness are both ingredients in this evolutionary mixture that combine and recombine daily leading towards the fulfillment of the balance that is natural for our race, on this planet, at this time. Once this balance is achieved, those who have achieved it will be ready to move on into new forms to start the process of alignment and balance all over again at a higher level in the universe that corresponds to the higher level of consciousness achieved during previous efforts.

In order to experience the meaning of life, one must expand consciousness in order to experience this personally and directly. The meaning of life is to be found in the "here" and in the "now." One who gazes above and seeks to see what is above, will only see little to nothing. Life is not "out-there." Life is right here. One who lives life here and now, placing focus on the microcosm, will learn from it, with proper observation, the ways of the macrocosm.

The big picture will always be found in the little picture. Seek that which can be sought. See that which can be seen. And from it, the wonder of the whole can be experienced. Within the one is the whole, and the whole is just an expression of the one.

Do not seek to understand this, instead seek to experience it. Consciousness grows with experience far better than with mere academic understanding. Indeed, there is no true understanding without experience. Seek to understand experience and integrate the understood experience. This is how consciousness expands, and how evolution is expressed.

Human beings incarnate here on Earth to learn lessons about the true fluid nature of life. In order to accomplish this, human beings need to be free to express themselves in whatever manner that they see fit, that is not harmful to themselves, or to others. Freedom by definition means that one learns to become self-reliant so that one can be free to choose one's path through life, and not be held back by force of circumstances, or by the imposing will of others.

There is a natural order. Human beings are supposed to know this order, internally and intuitively. Because present human consciousness is so low, the vast majority of human beings are out-of-sync with nature, and thus they are out of sync with themselves. This loss of natural internal balance is the cause of all human chaos. This is where evil enters into the human experience with all its accompanying pain and suffering. If only human beings led balanced lives in harmony with nature, pain and suffering would be things outside the human experience.

Life here on Earth is our personal microcosm, from which we learn about, and experience the macrocosm. We are here on Earth, not to learn how to be a human animal, but on the contrary, we are here to learn how to be faithful children of both Heaven and Earth. This embraces the highest ideals of our humanity and transcends them as well.

Once the individual soul learns this, it can graduate out of life on Planet Earth, and take its rightful next step as a full-fledged citizen of the universe. The quest for life will then guide the soul to where it needs to be next, on whatever planet, in whatever dimension, in whatever form.

Most souls incarnate now on Earth are far away from reaching this most lofty of goals. There are many lessons yet that each souls needs to learn about living a life in proper harmony and balance with all forces that be. Balancing good and evil, and life and death is first an internal struggle within each individual, and this struggle manifests into all the matters experienced in human societies.

We come to Earth to learn how to get along with ourselves, each other, and our planet in general. When we master life here on

Earth, and separate out from it death, we can then continue to embrace life elsewhere in all its multiple, wonderful forms.

Beings of Higher Consciousness serve us as teachers while we reside here on Earth. Living as they do in higher dimensions; we do not experience their presence within the context of the sensorial senses of the physical body. This is not so much by design. In other words, it doesn't have to be this way. We do not see different dimensional realms as a matter of choice and education.

If, indeed, we chose differently, and we were educated differently, we would indeed be able to regularly commune with the Beings of Higher Consciousness that direct and instruct life. Indeed, in every generation there are those individuals who make the efforts to learn the necessary lessons thus enabling them communion with the Beings of Higher Consciousness.

Of course, there are other beings out there, who seek to stifle the growth of life. They seek to capture and corral weaker human souls, whom they recognize as embracing death, more so than life, and feed off of them, in the same way as human beings carnivorously feed off of animal flesh.

The Beings of Higher Consciousness see all this happening and use this interaction as tools for instruction, to educate human souls about the dangers that the forces of death and evil pose to them. Only after many cycles of reincarnation under the subjugation of these other forces, do human souls finally become aware of their need for change.

As this need for change dawns in human consciousness, we see born individual souls who crave for, and cry out for freedom. Finally, the individual soul recognizes those forces intent upon holding back its natural progression of growth and life. In oneself, and in society the now enlightened soul proclaims the message of freedom and seeks the alignment and balance of natural forces. In societal terms, this balance is called, Justice.

There has always been guidance provided to us by Beings of Higher Consciousness. They are the ones who have, throughout human history, served as the internal Voice within select individuals that directs and motivates the fluid expansion and expressions of life within them.

In all fields of human endeavors, the Voice of the Beings of Higher Consciousness directs and influences the development of human culture, directing it to more manifest the universal principles that favor life and growth. Through the fields of the arts, sciences, literature, and philosophy, internal Voices from Beings of Higher Consciousness speak within the minds and hearts of men, directing them to express their life-force in positive, altruistic ways.

Life is expressed through consciousness. The more consciousness, the more life. The more life, the fuller the expression of meaning and purpose is revealed throughout creation.

In some systems of metaphysical speculations, the expansion of life and consciousness is often symbolized as the awakening of the Mind of the Creator. All metaphysical speculations are just that, speculations. However, as we have just said, Voices of Higher Consciousness regularly speak within the confines of the human mind placing thoughts therein that are meant to lead to the manifestation of deeds. Maybe what for us finite human beings in this world are metaphysical speculations, may indeed be revelations about the reality of the universe coming to us from the inner Voice of Higher Consciousness.

After all, Earth is our schoolhouse. Maybe we come here to learn how to recognize and hear the Voices of Higher Consciousness, and how to distinguish between these voices of life and good, and those voices of death and evil. Life seeks to expand and grow in its own rightful and proper way. If life in this physical plane serves as a distraction from enabling consciousness to distinguish between good and evil and between right from wrong, then Schoolhouse Earth is the right place wherein one is meant to learn such discernment.

The Voice of Life speaks to us all the time. So too does the Voice of Death. Sometimes the message of Death is the right one, when Death comes to end the old in order to make way for the new. But sometimes the Voice of Death speaks for other reasons, to spread evil and to do that which is wrong. How is one to discern the difference?

This is one of the many lessons taught by the Voices of Higher Consciousness. The wise pay heed and learn. The fool has not yet learned wisdom, and continues, lifetime after lifetime to repeat the same mistakes, by not discerning the difference between good and evil. Such wayward juvenile souls will return to Earthbound life in multiples forms one after another until their lessons are learned. No soul leaves the Earth-plane until it has finished its learning, passed all its tests, and thus "graduates" from the need for Earthly existence.

Lesson of Higher Consciousness are not spelled out for the learner. Such lessons need to be internally recognized and discerned. Lessons of Higher Consciousness speak to the inner mind. The intent is for the inner Mind to speak with the outer Mind, and for the outer Mind to recognize the Voice of the inner Mind, and to pay attention.

This is why the accumulation of outside distractions serve to hinder the development of the connection between inner and outer Mind. When the outer Mind is drawn towards external attractions, the attraction towards internal matters is weakened; oft times it is even broken altogether and forgotten. Such disconnected, lost souls require a long and arduous process to break them of all the distractions that cling to them like a second skin. Schoolhouse Earth thus remains open and remains a very busy necessity.

The meaning of life is simple: growth, expression, and the freedom to materialize such expressions. When life manifests properly in peace, harmony, and balance with the universe, with one's place and within one's self, then one has become the proper piece within the cosmic body, serving its unique and rightful function. Getting to this place requires one to pass through the many cycles of death and rebirth as one grows in form.

Distraction along the way abound. These lead to evil, corruption, imbalance, and disharmony. Life seeks to root these out so that the whole can exist in cosmic health, balance, and harmony.

The meaning of life is simple. The Voice of Higher Consciousness reveals this to us at all times. Freedom. The Way of Life and the Way through Life equally come to us from the inner Voice. Freedom.

School is in session. The teachers are teaching their lessons. The good student pays attention and learns how to shine the Light of Life. May we each merit to be good students, and to faithfully learn our lessons.

Seek the freedom of life. Shun servitude, reject submission to those who seek to enslave you. This is what leads to needless death. Grow as we are meant to. See within the freedom of life, the Light therein.

Chapter 4

The Ways of our Heavenly & Earthly Parents

"And I said: Call Me 'my Father,' and do not turn away from following Me."

Jeremiah 3:19

"Train a child in the way that he should go, and even when he grows old, he will not turn away from it."

Proverbs 22:6

There is a wide gap of division between the Creator and His creation. This gap does not exist in space or in time. Rather this extensive gap exists in the realms of understanding, wisdom, and knowledge.

This gap should not surprise us, we experience a similar one every day here on Earth with the extensive gap that exists between the mind of a small child and that of a mature adult.

In the mind of a child, what it is thinking makes sense. The child cannot fathom the depths of adult thinking and does not understand why Mommy or Daddy does not allow them to do the things that they very much might want to do. But the alert and protective parents watch their children well. They provide for their beloved child all the freedom that they can safely have. They provide for their beloved child many opportunities for education and growth. And at the same time, they make sure that the child, who does not understand the harsh realities of this world, is properly protected from them.

Not for naught are we called the children of God. This status does not confer upon us any rank or privilege. Rather, it should reveal to us how it is that we are perceived in Divine Eyes. Just like mature and responsible human parents hover over, and protect their adolescent child, so too does God watch over us.

When our children misbehave and intentionally act bad, sometimes throwing fits or otherwise causing serous disruptions for no necessary reason, then the mature and responsible parent acts to discipline their child. Due to the nature of the severity of the wanton behavior, the mature and responsible parent will impose whatever punishment that might be appropriate. This can be something as simple as a time-out, or something as severe as a serous spanking.

Only very bad parents refuse to discipline their children, and to spank them however harshly, when needed. Punishment is not abuse! When bad parents refuse to punish their children when needed, the children grow up without fear of punishment. They thus feel free to misbehave in any way desirable, without fear of consequences or repercussions.

Bad human parents cause otherwise good children to make bad choices. When children are not raised properly with healthy discipline, and proper punishments, when necessary, these children become adults who are oblivious to boundaries and parameters. They quickly act in ways that are harmful to themselves, to others, and to the world at large. And they are oblivious to the harm that they cause, and consider their behaviors to be their freedoms.

When human parents do not act to raise their children in the right and proper way, human society as a whole becomes more and more imbalanced. As the society as a whole becomes more and more corrupt, our Heavenly Father takes note and is forced to intervene, as is necessary.

We are the children of God, and God does not defer His Divine duty as Heavenly parent. Our problem is that because our human parents never taught their children the right and proper truths about Heaven, these same human children, who are now human adults, are oblivious to the Hand of God disciplining them, first putting them into a time-out, and only when necessary and proper, instituting a full and harsh spanking.

As children of God, we are subject to the authority and direction of our Heavenly Father, and of our Mother Earth. This metaphor needs to be explained.

When we refer to our Heavenly Father, yes, we are referring to God, but one should never be so childish as to think that God is actually some type of Heavenly super-human-being wearing a long white robe, with a long white beard, wagging a finger in our faces, proclaiming, "thou shalt not!" Such an idea is childish at least, and idolatrous at most. Our Earthly Mother, in Torah, is always a reference to the Divine Presence, the Shekhina. This Presence is what defines and manages the laws and parameters of our physical space-time universe.

Our Heavenly Father is the energetic pattern that is the underlying construct of creation, and is thus its Creator (In Kabbalah, this is the Ten Sefirot of Zein Anpin of Atzilut). Our Earthly Mother is what embraces this pattern and uses physical matter to construct the multiple forms and structures of the multiverse (In Kabbalah, this is the Partzuf of Nok d'Z.A.).

The energetic realities of Father and Mother permeate everything around us and within us. Thus Daddy and Mommy dictate to us, their children, how we are to behave properly.

The disciplining Hand of Daddy and Mommy is never too far away. But we are uneducated children! More than one generation of parents have denied their Earthly children right and proper religious and spiritual guidance as they grew up. Thus today's adults are no better than wayward bad children. They are oblivious to the Presence of the Divine, and have come to arrogantly rebel against any suggestion of proper discipline.

People today have no understanding about the true nature of God, nor do they have any wisdom to intuit and sense the natural Way of creation. As such the peoples of today all seek to live lives whose very form contradict the Way as ordained by our Heavenly Father, and established for us by our Mother Earth (Z.A. and Nok).

Everyone goes about their lives thinking them to be so important, all the while that they live unnaturally and continually provoke both Heaven and Earth, causing God to respond with appropriate punishments.

And the wayward children will respond by denying and condemning any mention of punishment. The wayward children will continue to arrogantly carry on their lives and lifestyles with growing ignorance of the Natural Way. The wayward children will go so far as to redefine what is natural, and they will even boldly proclaim that there are no Heavenly parents at all. Just like their human parents never punished them, so too are their no Heavenly parents to punish them. And so the misbehaving children will go on their merry way, and boldly live the lives that they lead.

But we are the children of God, and God while patient and tolerant, still does not allow His wayward children to succumb completely to consequences of their dangerous and harmful paths. Proper and mature human parents will many times allow their children a semblance of freedom to behave in a borderline dangerous way so as to experience the consequences of not listening to parental warnings.

When human parents do not act in this way, and children grow up without fear of the consequences of their behaviors, then the society that these children build becomes one that is wicked and evil. And this is where we are today. And God, our Heavenly Father watches and sees all.

And here we are today! Weak parents have raised wayward children. These wayward children grew up and raised a generation of even more wayward children. And these children grow up in the arrogance of rebellion. The society that they create is one that itself is totally abusive to the individual.

The greatest abuse that society can impose on its members is slavery to its system. Manipulating the minds and thoughts of individuals through entertainment, education, and social media are the tools of the trade. And their tools have succeeded in creating a society of slaves. Today most individuals are like mindless sheep, they are no longer free-thinking private individuals. They have all become indentured servants to a system that makes every effort to prevent people from returning to their Heavenly Father and Earthly Mother with sincere and profound remorse and repentance.

And so Heavenly punishments progress from being a mere time-out into something more serious. It is the job of our Heavenly Father and our Earthly Mother to arouse our slumbering souls. It is their job to punish us for our bad behavior, especially when we refuse to admit just how bad our behaviors have become.

Up until now I have endeavored to describe the reality of our spiritual problem using the language of symbolism. As I conclude here, I will reiterate my points using the language of Kabbalah and psychology.

We human beings live in a multidimensional reality. However, our present addiction to rational thought has molded a society that acts as if it is allergic to psychic development. Our entire reality as experienced by the rational mind is but a poor reflection of the higher realities in which we live. But because we have been brainwashed over generations to ignore, and to ultimately deny the higher realities, we live day-by-day performing actions, and living a lifestyle that brings us into direct, constant conflict with it.

Day-by-day the masters of our society feed to the masses more and more of the forbidden fruit from the Tree of knowledge, Good and Evil; causing them day-by-day to become more and more distant from God, Eden, and the Tree of Life.

Blind and arrogant human beings are day-by-day living lives which they consider to be normal. But in the Eyes of Heaven, modern civilization and the lifestyles of those who prosper within it, are an offense to Heaven, and an insult to Earth.

Like rebellious children who refuse to behave properly, people today cling to their unnatural lifestyles, thinking that these ways will last forever. But this will not be the case. Heaven and Earth will both (together) make sure that humanity will be set back along its proper path, regardless of the cost that this will take in human life. Don't deny this! We have seen it happen many times in the past. Only an arrogant fool will boldly proclaim that it cannot and will not happen again.

The higher Source Pattern of Life is the world of Atzilut. An aspect of this exists within us. This is the Supernal Man, Zeir Anpin (Z.A.) of Atzilut. Z.A. is Adam above, as we human beings are Z.A. (Adam) below. Z.A. is also the Source of emanation from which comes forth the Universal Way for the universe. We embrace this Universal Way through the vessel in which we received it. The vessel is the Torah.

The Torah is both written, reflecting Z.A. of Atzilut here into Asiyah, and the Torah is Oral (which is now also written), reflecting Nok, the Divine Presence of Atzilut, as She is cloaked here in space-time within the order of natural Law, and as the active, conscious, and sentient soul of our planet Earth (ref. RaMBaM, Y.T. 3:9).

One who violates Torah Law also is violating natural Law. The truth of this is not subject to rational explanation, but it is still a vital psychic fact. Those whose diet consists of the forbidden fruit of the Tree of Knowledge are those who continually refuse to develop their innate and natural psychic abilities. These disconnected souls continue to live contrary to nature. All their lives are devoted to building and praising the technological terror that has been established to keep their human minds enslaved. The Tower of Babel has been rebuilt!

We are bad, wayward, and rebellious children. And Daddy (Z.A.) and Mommy (Nok) will not tolerate our wanton ways forever. Correction and punishment will arise from within us (from Z.A.) affecting our minds and our thoughts. Our inner, higher selves will create chaos in the rational mind until such time that the rational left-brain mind, gives way to embracing psychic intuitive right-brain knowing. This is why almost all individuals in modern society are disconnected from themselves.

When Mommy (Nok, the Shekhina) moves to act, this is when we will see the fall of our modern civilization, as we know it. This is beginning to happen now. The downward spiral of events will continue until those individuals who have chosen to be behaving children will be identified. They will be protected by Heaven as the world around them continues to enslave souls, and to fall apart at the same time.

Getting right with God is one's only salvation. But getting right with God is not a concept or an idea, it is a series of decisions that must guide one's thoughts, feelings, and actions.

One must embrace Torah and natural Law in its entirety. One must shift one's politics, and one's views of societal norms away from that which is unclean and unnatural as defined by Torah.

One must embrace that which the Torah reveals to us to be the Supernal Pattern. This embrace must be from the psychic intuitive side of our minds. We must not water it down and contaminate our inner knowing with intellectual rationalizations of any kind. Doing this is nothing new. Doing this is the commitment we already made to God back at Mt. Sinai, when we together declared, "We will do, and we will listen" (Ex. 24:7).

We act first based upon psychic intuitive knowing, and only afterwards do we seek to make rational sense of that which our souls already know to be true.

Thus it is incumbent upon us to return to God, and to behave as good children. We cannot understand or fathom the Divine Way, but we can (and we must) be obedient to it and to follow it. This commitment on our parts, in order for it to be real, must manifest in our embrace of proper and correct Torah-based politics, social issues, and social associations. This is not a political statement; this is a spiritual necessity. One cannot call upon God and His Torah all the while that one is cloaked in a filthy garment, and a contaminated mind.

We have been told a lie! We have been deceived. We have been told that "times have changed," and that we must adapt to the modern ways of thinking. These are the words and rationalizations of wayward, misbehaved children. Mature and responsible adults do not follow in the footsteps of their misbehaving children. On the contrary, it is the responsibility of the parents to discipline their children with whatever form of discipline that it takes to get them to stop misbehaving!

As individuals, we have our work cut out for us. As we have been taught (Psalm 34:15), *"Shun evil and do good."*

It is not enough to change one's thinking. This must be only the beginning. One must change one's ways. Only corrected behavior is considered true repentance (teshuva) before our Creator. We need to reattach Atzilut (Z.A.) with the lower worlds of Be'Y'A. If we fail to act upon this in the proper way and in the proper time, then Heaven (Z.A.) and Earth (Nok) will act for us. And our parent's punishment will not be a pleasant experience!

"The sum of the matter, when all is said and done: Fear God and observe His commandments! For this is the entirety of our humanity."
Kohelet (Ecclesiastes) 12:13

Chapter 5

Herev D'Hakham – The Sword of the Sage

Open your heart, arouse yourself from slumber, remember the forgotten and embrace the truth of things that you have always known. Let us proceed.

Before one can lift up the sword of the Torah, one must merit to raise up the sword of the Sage.

Before one can lift the sword of the Sage, one must know well what it is he seeks to accomplish and who it is he seeks to be.

Let us start at the very beginning, put aside now your troubled and burdened mind, and open your heart to receive these words therein.

A Sage is a Gibbor, a warrior, a mighty man of war. A Sage is not just one who has mastered the spoken or written words that communicate ideas to the mind. A Sage is also the one who has mastered the ways and means of the human heart. A Sage can only be called a Sage because as a warrior he has conquered both heart and mind and subdues them both to the power of spirit. This and only this defines a true Sage. In Hebrew a Sage is called a Hakham.

Hakham literally means "one who is wise." A Sage is thus one who has wisdom. Wisdom, according to the ways of the Kabbalah embraces heart, mind, and spirit. Thus, the true Sage is the individual of integration, the one who stands with all inner aspects united as one.

In order to calm the raging heart and to tame the wild mind, the Sage must first acquire many attributes that will mold his character and spirit. The Sage must embrace the attributes of strength, courage, and discipline. He must before all things first become a warrior.

Before one can become a Sage of Torah one must first embrace the spirit of the warrior. A true warrior is not one who is a person of arms, but rather a person of strength whose character demonstrates victory over life's adversities.

To be a warrior one must learn the ways of battle. All of us today are in a battle. Some battles are physical, some are emotional, some are psychological, and some are spiritual. Whatever the battle, we are all under siege, we are all at war. If we wish success in life, we must have victory over our personal adversities.

Herein lies the secret of life's success, those who are happy in life have learned to be master warriors, masters of their own fate in the right way, masters of facing and overcoming adversity.

While we can never master that which happens to us, for this is always in Hands higher than our own, we are nonetheless always able to choose how we respond to that which befalls us. This is what defines the true warrior.

The warrior can never dictate when and how an opponent will attack. Yet, the warrior, once attacked is master of the battle. The warrior rises to meet whatever challenge faces him and molds himself to the circumstances before him to successfully overcome them.

The warrior thus bends like the reed before the wind and moves in harmony with the forces of the Higher Hand and thus accomplishes the task at hand, whatever that be, as ordained beforehand from Above.

There are many ways to meet the struggles that we face every day in life. The true warrior knows how to be pliant and to face every foe in accordance to the nature of that foe, and to thus defeat the foe, on the foe's own ground. The rule is that the pliant can bend like a reed in the wind, while those stiff like the mighty oak tree crack and fall once enough pressure is exerted against them.

The strength of the warrior is also the sword of the Sage, for one who wishes to excel in Torah must be mighty like the warrior (Gibbor). Indeed, to become a Sage also requires of one to face great battles, this time in the realm of mind. The lessons of discipline learned when training to be a warrior of life serve well the Sage assisting him to acquire his goals.

Without the tenacity and discipline of the warrior, one will never be able to rise to the level of Sage. For a Sage is not measured by how much knowledge he has acquired in his head, but rather by how much wisdom he has acquire in his heart. This is why a Sage is called a Hakham, the one who has achieved wisdom.

Learn a lesson from the laws of nature and know then the ways of God's world.

The path of ascent is from our Earthly bonds to Heavenly freedom. The path of ascent follows the naturally ordained way. As it is in the world at large so is it within the world within the human. In order to ascend, we must first pass through and conquer the heart, only then can one properly ascend into the mind and control it.

One who cannot control his heart will be controlled by it. The one who cannot control his mind will be held in prison by it. And the one who cannot control either heart or mind will remain in slavery and servitude forever being subject to whims and desires without control or discipline.

In Egypt, God set the Children of Israel free, freedom of the body, the heart, the mind, and the soul. In freedom, the warrior Sage knows to distinguish between silence and sound, between stillness and motion, between the sacred and the profane and between the right from the wrong. In his heart, the warrior Sage knows all these things because as it is written, the words that were commanded this day are upon his heart.

The heart is the center of the body, both the body physical and the body supernal. All from above and all from below meet in the heart. In the heart all merge into one. In the heart all is known, in the heart all is understood, as it is written, the heart understands.

The heart unites what is known in the mind and what is felt in the emotions. The heart unites and balances both. When the mind above and the emotions below merge as one there is equanimity, balance, and harmony; this is the true power of the warrior Sage. His Torah is his sword, his Torah is his heart; his Torah is his word.

The word of the warrior Sage emanates from his heart and pierces the heart of his opponents like a sword pierces flesh. In this way is the Sage a mighty warrior, strong in body, strong in heart, strong in mind and strong in spirit.

With this might, the warrior Sage seeks not the joy felt from those who praise him and feels no sadness because of those who would scorn him; all is equal in his eyes. The warrior Sage stands in the middle, in the center, as this place is the beginning of all things. He sways neither to right nor left but stands motionless and moves only as the spirit from Above moves him; and even in this movement he never loses his stillness.

For although the body may move from here to there, the heart, mind and spirit always remain in the center. In this way the warrior Sage serves his Creator, firmly rooted in truth, and thus reflecting the Image from Above in which he was created, the Image that emanated from the center point.

Knowing the center, the warrior Sage can go to all sides and to all places and never gets lost. For how can one know where he is going unless he first knows where he is? And how can one know where he is unless he first knows from where he came? In order to reach the end, one must know the beginning; for beginning and end depend upon one another. One cannot embrace the one without first knowing the other.

The center is the beginning of all things. It is the home of the warrior Sage. Long did he fight, facing all of life's adversities seeking to discover and know this place. Long did he struggle along the arduous path of life to arrive at this place. Yet, once attained, the warrior achieves the title of Sage, for he has learned wisdom.

Once achieved the warrior Sage is never lodged from his rightful place. For this place of the center is the place of freedom, balance, redemption, and salvation. It is the place of Torah and only through embrace of Torah can one ever find this place. Yet, in order to find this place by guidance of the Torah, the Torah must be embraced, not with hand, not with mind, but with heart, the place where His Words must rest.

The warrior Sage is the wealthiest of men, although he may own next to nothing in this physical world. Who is wealthy? One who is happy with his portion. And what is the portion of the warrior Sage? The wisdom and balance of his heart, his peace of mind, his inner silence, his embrace of knowledge of the Torah of YHWH.

In this place of the center the warrior Sage sees clearly and knows that he who has enough will always be satisfied with what he has. And when is this true? When the desiring eye looks within to see what there is instead of looking outside to see what there is not.

The inner vision viewing from the center sees the balance of all things. Knowing the center and seeing all things in their rightful place, the warrior Sage knows contentment and is thus happy with his portion. And why? Because he seeks not the portion of another.

What then does the warrior Sage seek? He seeks only to do the right thing. Above all, he is a man of honor. This is defined by the Torah and adapts to the time and circumstances of the moment.

This is why the warrior Sage is like the pliable reed; he nullifies his own will before the Will Above and thus brings balance and harmony wherever he goes along his travels in life. He walks the path of Torah, not by rote, or by word, but in action, in heart and in truth.

This is why the path of Torah is called Halakha, which means, "the way to go." For although one may endeavor to walk the path this does not mean that one is actually on it.

For in order to walk the path, the true Halakha, one must embrace it in the heart, know its beginning, know its end, and thus know where along the path one stands. Not knowing where one stands in life is the true definition of being lost. In the Torah this is called Galut, exile.

We were redeemed from exile. We were set free. Yet in order to experience freedom one must be bold like the warrior, like Joshua and Caleb of old. These were the warrior Sages who went into the Land and spoke the message of freedom, the truth that emanated from the center of Being. Yet, their words were heard only by slaves, those who were still in exile, those who were still imprisoned to that which would sway the heart, cloud the mind, and rob the spirit.

Joshua and Caleb were warriors. Those to whom they spoke were not. Thus, the warriors choose life and live, whereas those who were not warriors by definition chose to remain slaves to their undisciplined selves.

As such they chose death and although alive in body, they were no more than the walking dead. For this reason, were they destined to die in the wilderness. For only the warrior can embrace life, and thus freedom. Only the warrior who battles adversity and defeats it becomes a Sage. Only the warrior Sage lives to inherit the Land and walk therein. This walk above all others is the true walking of the path, the true Halakha, the true and only Torah.

In this is the honor of the warrior Sage. Knowing the path and standing in the center, he moves in stillness. He moves without being moved. Knowing the Torah, firmly entrenched in the heart, he speaks in silence. His words are heard not from his mouth but from his deeds. The warrior Sage is truly the free man. His freedom emanates from his very nature and shines like the sun on a clear summer's day. His freedom, his warmth, his simplicity, and his truth attract many to his side. The warrior Sage thus gathers in the lost souls and shelters them under the Shadow of the Almighty.

This is the honor of the warrior Sage. He is simplicity, the simplicity of the beginning, of the center. Simplicity is the true nature of Torah; it restores the soul to those who have lost it. *Torat YHWH Temimah* (the Torah of YHWH is simplicity). *Nefesh Hakham Gibbor Temimah* (the soul of the warrior Sage is simplicity).

"And you who bond to YHWH are alive everyone to this day." (Dev 4:4). How is one to bond to YHWH and thus merit life? The warrior Sages of old have answered and said, by clinging to the Sage.

The Hakham Gibbor becomes a living Torah that walks among us. Life comes through Torah. Torah is simplicity. The true Sage teaches both these things: Torah and simplicity. And the Sage must be a warrior to truly be a Sage.

Only the warrior Sage properly wields the sword and thus slices through the ignorance and slumber to free the fallen captives.

Take these words to heart. Fret not the challenges of your mind. Your thoughts at this time are too clouded to perceive all their truths.

Stand before the sword of the Sage and allow it to pierce you and penetrate your heart. Allow the warrior Sage to use his sword to remove from you your shell that encases you, separating you from the light of Truth.

Allow your heart to blossom, open it to the rays of the summer sun. Be revived in spirit.

Seek out the warrior Sage and let him guide you to the true simplicity of Torah that restores the soul. Let the warrior Sage teach you the true ways of battle so that you too may find the center, and from there set out on your life's path and thus walk the Halakha, even as you were destined to by the Higher Hand.

As the warrior Sage Hillel, once said, "if not now, then when?"

Chapter 6

Driving & Distractions,
A Lesson & Warning

You are behind the wheel of your car. You are driving out of control. Your speed is over one hundred miles per hour. The road is winding and steep. If not for the Hand of God that has buffered you, you would have long ago spun out of control, burst into flames and died horribly.

Now, as you struggle to maintain control you notice up ahead a solid brick wall across the entire road. Hitting it means certain death and destruction. So, then, here is the big question. Knowing well the big and final wall is dead ahead of you and you are speeding directly towards it, what then is the right course of action. Bottom line, what should you do? Bottom line, what will you do?

You might think that in such a clear scenario like this one's knowledge of what is right to do and what indeed one actually does would be one and the same. Unfortunately, human nature does not always allow what we know to be best and true to be acted out and materialize into reality.

Even when we know what is best and right to do, there are all too many times when we fail to act to do the right thing. Sometimes we can get away it this. Other times, it is like hitting a brick wall at a high speed; there will be no escape, there will be only disaster.

83

Now, to answer the question posed above. The rational and logical step to avoid an inevitable disaster would be to step on the brakes and to best slow down and get better control over the vehicle. Yet, instead of doing just this, you the driver are too busy watching the newly available DVD monitor installed for back seat passengers.

Instead of paying attention to where you are going and what you should be doing, you allow yourself to become distracted. You become involved in all too many other interests that keep you so busy that you have no time to think about what it is you are supposed to be doing instead.

Knowing well how distracted you are, God has protected you in the past from certain disaster. However, this time it is different. This time it is the end of the road, the brick wall runs across its entire face. There is no way to avoid it or go around it. Stopping the vehicle is the only way to avoid disaster.

In your distractions, you have always allowed God to be your co-pilot and to steer you away from harm. However, although God has done this in the past, He has still placed you as driver of the vehicle. How to drive and what is to happen is still ultimately your choice and responsibility.

God is not only the builder of the road; it is He who has placed the brick wall there across it. God placed this wall there to get your attention, to alert you to your obligations to drive safely and responsibly. Yet, instead, you choose to hop into the back seat and watch a video. What then, to do you think, is going to be the ultimate outcome?

Life is all too full of distractions. We all too often do not pay attention to what we must. We seldom do what it is we need to do and in timely fashion. We as a society are all heading towards the big brick wall in a vehicle speeding out of control.

All too many of us are distracted by all of life's diversions. So many of us are all so caught up in the illusions of the matrix of life, that we cannot perceive the true essence of life, and what it is that God wants from us.

God is patient with us, this is true. Yet, to all things there are limits, even to Divine Patience. Looking around the world and seeing everywhere disasters and threats of calamities, one cannot rationally argue and claim that God's brick wall is not quickly approaching.

In light of historical calamities and present day disasters, no one should feel confident to argue that God will provide and save us in the end, regardless of what we do to serve as the vessels for our own salvation.

God has indeed showered us with blessings. These blessings include us having sharps minds and keen eyes. God has blessed us with these so that we can see what is coming and to recognize what it is we need to do about it.

One who denies the blessings of God allowing one's eye to be distracted and for one's mind to become dull, in essence blocks God's Hand from intervening and saving one from disaster. This has happened all too many times in history; the two destructions of Jerusalem and the Holocaust are but three cataclysmic examples of this.

We are quickly coming to a point of no return. The brick wall looms ever so closer and ever more ominous. We are still in the back seat, distracted, watching the movie matrix of life, instead of paying attention to the real thing. Will we wake up in time? Will we take control of the vehicles of our lives and act responsibly in order to avoid certain disaster? This question remains to be answered.

There is so little precious time left to us. If we do not use the blessings and gifts we have already received from God, then He will not intervene further to save us.

If we do not take control of the wheel, no one else will. If we do not begin to act responsibly, then events in our lives will continue to spin out of control.

If we do not turn away from the distractions, we allow ourselves to succumb to everyday, then reality will soon hit us full force like a brick wall bringing to an end all that separates us from the ultimate reality of our obligations to God and towards one another.

It does not have to end this way...

<u>Chapter 7</u>

Charity B.S.I – The Best Survival Investment

"A wise son will make a happy father,
and a foolish son will make his mother grieve.

The treasures of the wicked will not work for them,
and charity saves from death!

God will not allow the soul of the righteous to be famished,
and the desire of the wicked is cast away."

Proverbs 10:1-3

In hard times, the hardest thing to do is to remain charitable. When finances become limited, we often forget that it is not only ourselves who are having a hard time, but so is our family, our friends, and our neighbors. Regardless of how bad things may be for us, it will not take long to find those who are much more unfortunate than we.

The test of righteousness is never about what we believe,
it is always about what we do.

It is no coincidence that the Hebrew word for charity is basically the same word for righteousness. Tzedaka is charity and tzedaka is righteousness. The meaning of this is simple. In "God's Eye" it is righteous to supply charity. And I might add that the opposite is also true, to withhold or deny charity is considered in God's Eyes as tantamount to wicked, evil behavior.

Today, in hard times, the great excuse is, "I don't have enough to give," or "I don't even have enough for myself and my family." All these excuses may very well be true, nevertheless in the Eye of God, they are nothing more than mere empty words!

We all have problems. We all have shortages. Many of us do not know where the funds will come from today to pay the bills that are due tomorrow. Many indeed wake up in the morning not knowing where the monies will come from to put food on the table for that very day.

And we complain about paying our high private school tuitions, credit card bills, medical bills, car payments and house payments! Granted, all these are important and must be addressed. Still, at least we have these things. Many do not have even that much.

Now, charity is not now, nor has it ever been meant to be a redistribution of wealth. Charity is not to give from the rich to the poor so that the poor become rich and the rich become poor. This is not charity, this is not righteousness. Indeed, this is madness and foolishness. Indeed, when a government taxes one segment of the population to provide free entitlements for another, this may indeed be institutionalized theft, a violation of the Ten Commandments and many other laws.

Public welfare in not now nor has it ever been the answer to individual needs. Loving your neighbor is not a government job, it is the obligation of each and every one of us righteous human beings.

Public welfare is in the hands of the public, not the government. This is a clear Biblical message.

When one is in need, we are supposed to turn to one another. When I turn to you and in turn you turn to me, we support one another. When we do this, God smiles upon us. This is what Proverbs meant went it said that "a wise son makes a happy father," in this case, our Father in Heaven.

When one turns to another for support and instead of receiving a kind response receives nothing (not even a kind word), this is an offense against nature itself. It violates righteousness and it denies charity. One who acts like this, in this one case, will clearly act like this in many other instances. By acting in this way, the miser thinks that he supports himself, but instead he hurts himself and eventually undermines his own foundation. Again, this is what Proverbs referred to when it said, "a foolish son makes his mother grieve."

Those who do not give charity exhibit a serious character flaw which will come back to haunt them. Those who do not give do not receive. True, there are the mega-rich who revel in their financial success and look with scorn at the "little people" less fortunate than themselves. Somehow and in some way, there is justice in this universe and those who laud their wealth over others will in the end suffer because of it.

"The treasures of the wicked will not work for them." There will come a time when the wealthy will realize that they are in need of something that money cannot buy. On that day, God will look down upon them and judge. If indeed the faith of the rich has been in their money, then God will allow them to face their crises relying upon their money.

If however, the rich are righteous and thus charitable, at the moment of need God looks down upon them and showers them with His Grace, that which money cannot buy! This is what the Proverb means when it says that "charity saves from death."

God looks after His own. Now, it is true, that in order for us to be righteous before God, we cannot rely entirely upon the gracious giving of others. Each of us must work and do whatever it is that we can to provide for ourselves with the great bounty inherent in nature and there for us to partake.

This relationship is beautiful. We do what we can and God does what we cannot! And each of us serves as the hand of God when we fulfill our moral obligations to provide for others, with however much or little we have to give.

Everyone is obligated to provide charity. Ten percent of our earnings is the standard practice. Some may give more, but none should give less. When we give and provide, we will find that in turn we ourselves receive and are provided for. It is a cyclical relationship. It is inherent in nature. It is what God has created and has meant to be.

Therefore, when you begin each day, pause for a moment, and give thanks to God for all the good you have right now. Then commit yourself to set aside a portion of today's earnings to provide for others, thus making yourself to be the Hand of God. In one way or another, as you give, you will get! For just as you commit today to give to another, someone out there has in mind to give to you.

God puts into the thoughts of business people and regular people alike who to interact with. Your new client is sent to you by none other than God. Thank Him for the business and express your appreciation by serving as God's Hand and give a portion of what God has given you to someone else in need.

Whatever hard times do or do not come, charity is the way of the world. Charity is righteousness and charity is a life saver! Charity is a better investment than gold and silver. Charity can bestow upon you the Grace of God in your hour of need. No gold or silver, bullets or beans can ever provide that!

So, give! That's it! Donate! Provide! Help! Be there! And as you are there for others, God is there for you. Remember, "Charity saves from death." So, "Give thanks to God for He is good, for His mercy endures forever."

SECTION THREE

THE DANGERS OF
THE TRUE "DARK SIDE"

Chapter 1

The True Dark Lords: Modern Day Balaams & the Occult

The fictional evil character Darth Vader of Star Wars fame said it best: "You don't know the power of the Dark Side."

It is such a shame that many profound truths are often completely dismissed just because they are words from out of a movie. Yet, the Sages of Israel, (in the book, Pirkei Avot) long ago advised us that one who is truly wise learns from everyone, and I might add, from everything, including from pithy lines of dialogue found in famous movies.

Although we all know that the Star Wars character Darth Vader is fictional; nevertheless the evil that he characterized and more so the psychic powers he portrayed do actually have a source in fact here in the real world.

There really are "Dark Lords" amongst us. We do not refer to them by names found in movies. They go by other names, some known to us and some unknown to us. While they do not speak about the fictitious Dark Side of Force, they do speak about the actual and real Dark Side, which in Hebrew we call the Sitra Ahra, the Other Side.

The Biblical personage of Balaam (Number 22-24) was one such Dark Lord. He was no man of fiction or legend. There is archeological proof found in modern day Jordan attesting to his existence and to his ominous reputation mentioned in the Bible.

Yet, the Biblical sorcerer and wizard Balaam was only one of the many who came before him and after him. To this day many follow in his footsteps and master the arcane powers of the occult, thus knowing how to use these powers for purposes both benign and nefarious.

Yes, very real Dark Lords do live and walk among us today. Yet, unlike their Biblical counterparts the Dark Lords of today do not advertise and do not make their identities known.

More often than not they conceal themselves well with almost impenetrable disguises. Although, they are unseen to the eyes of the masses, they still nonetheless continue the arcane occultic practices and purposes that have been handed down for centuries. If there was ever a real underground secret society of conspirators, rest assured that it is the coven of the true Dark Lords of the Other (dark) Side.

In his day Balaam tried to use the powers of the Occult to curse the Children of Israel. Apparently, he found out only too late that the Powers guarding Israel were stronger than the forces he could conjure up.

Those Biblical days were miraculous times, when angels walked among men and even animals could be made to speak and be rational. While we think such times are long behind us, little do most realize that very similar type things continue happening to this very day, but not necessarily on the side of holiness.

There are stories reported in the media how upon being caught a murderer might say that he heard voices compelling him to kill. Modern psychologists summarily claim that such voices are coming out of the murderers head and are a form of mental illness. They categorically refuse to accept the notion that the voices may be coming into his head from an outside source. Who is to say that they are right?

Sometimes the information that these psychotic killers provide shows that they are either very well learned in occult practices or while ignorant of them, still very much subject to their nefarious influence.

Many a time psychotic killers are not born such, but rather created to become such over a long period of time due to being subjected to occultic influence and compulsion by someone or something that seeks the killer to do their bidding and to suffer the consequences for doing it.

Such stories abound and they all have a scent of occultic involvement to them. We live in a society today that is inundated with interest in the Occult. The most popular movies and television programs deal with topics of vampires, werewolves, and demons. Most people have no idea that such entities really do exist and they are certainly not as handsome, pretty or gallant as the Hollywood productions would portray them.

Even the occultic method of contacting spirits, entities and demons, the Ouija Board, is sold to children at toy stores alongside traditional children's games. Modern Ouija Boards even come in the color pink especially for young girls. While many might think this cute and benign, those with knowledge and experience with the Occult know just how dangerous such practices can be and see nothing cute about this at all. This is not somebody's idea of a joke, but rather somebody's way of getting innocent children involved with practices that realistically endanger their souls and their mental sanity.

Somebody or some group is "out there" promoting popular interest in the Occult. How curious it is that as we see a rise in the interest and practice of the Occult, we see an equal and opposite loss of interest in traditional religion and proper moral values.

It is with the loss of such traditional Biblical-based values that has opened the floodgates to an epidemic of drug abuse, alcoholism, sexual promiscuity and perversions, violent behaviors of all sorts and an unusual rise in the number of mental illnesses, emotional disturbances, and suicides.

The younger one is when they drift away from traditional morals, values, and religion, the easier, quicker, and deeper one often becomes ensnared in any of these harmful traps. Whether or not any of this is a carefully organized plot by any modern day occultic cabal, we cannot say. However to dismiss such a possibility is also equally wrong.

In Biblical times, when Balaam realized he could not contaminate the Children of Israel with his normal arcane way, he chose instead a devious conspiracy of sexual subversion and corruption. This organized plot, spoken of in detail in Numbers 22-24 caused massive damage to the Israelite nation.

We see similar damage being caused today throughout societies that also succumb to sexual subversion and perversions. Should we therefore not wonder, if not investigate if there is a nefarious agent behind our modern societies corruption just like there was in Biblical times?

Whenever there is widespread moral corruption in human society, rest assured that the enemies of humankind are not too far away. Granted there have always been social problems and forces that seek to corrupt moral values, but it is rare that such forces take over a society and destroy the whole thing from within. Yet, we see this very thing happening all around us today.

This growing perversion and subversion is not a normal course of events. Things on this scale do not just happen on their own, without direction or cause. Something is behind it and most of us do not want to know just who or what this is.

Just like the spirit of Moses lives on in all those who study his Torah, similarly the spirit of the evil Balaam lives on in all those who embrace the Occult. This is why, like Balaam before them, most modern Occultists are viciously anti-Semitic.

Just like Balaam hated Israel, Torah and the power of holiness that defeated his evil magic, so too do modern Occultists seek to break the back of Torah, Judaism, and the Jewish people.

What these agents of evil hate is God, His Word and anything associated with it, Jewish, Christian, or otherwise. This may explain why with the demise of traditional religious beliefs and values in many parts of the world we see an equal rise in anti-Semitism coming out from those same contaminated communities.

We cannot deny that the Occult is real and we should never deny the dark and sinister power that the followers of the Other (dark) Side possess. They are indeed real and they are indeed powerful, but those who cling to Torah and who live by the Biblical message have nothing to fear from them. For like the Children of Israel in Biblical times God has instructed us in ways and practices to keep ourselves safe from such nefarious influences.

Not for naught were Biblical commandments ordained by Heaven and later augmented by the Sages of Israel. Heaven revealed to us through prophetic revelation the true nature and mechanics of how the Occult operates. The commandments we received on Sinai were specifically designed to keep us safe from physic attacks and all from other forms of occultic penetration.

The Biblical story of Balak and Balaam proves this outright. For once certain members of the Children of Israel allowed their sexual desires to override the standing commandment of no sexual contact with foreign women, not only did sexual promiscuity begin to spread like a disease within the camp, but actual physical disease also followed immediately on its heels.

One lapse of judgment led to the deaths of numerous individuals, not all of whom might have been involved in the sexual promiscuity. If only the few had safeguarded themselves, all would have been safe. Yet, once the few opened the doors to psychic attack, then everyone fell into danger.

Yes, the "Dark Side of the Force" has its real-life counterpart in the Other Side and those who master its manipulations. What their agenda and goals are is not really relevant to us. They can have all their plans, conspiracies, and agendas. We can never stop them from trying to hatch their malevolent plots. All we can do is to stop them from succeeding. In order to accomplish this, we need sincere and honest, moral, and good human beings who are focused and strong in resolve and action.

Those who are merely religious on the outside while their discipline and morals are weak are part of the problem, instead of being part of the cure. Such religious hypocrites look good on the outside; they say and do all the right things, but their fundamentalism and superstitious natures betray their true identities. Such shallow people and their weak and emasculated shows of hollow religion attract the Other Side and often become it very first victims.

The Torah teaches us that the malevolent sexual plot concocted by Balaam was not squashed through our prayers and supplications and external displays of fundamentalist religion. Rather, the sexual plot was squashed through the acts of a single man who acted with zeal and manifested the proper deed for that proper moment, which by definition was itself a violation of the religion.

Unfortunate, but the moment required an especially violent response, and that is exactly what Phineas the grandson of the High Priest Aaron provided. He committed an act of zealous murder, a crime for which under other circumstances he would have faced the death penalty for committing.

Were it not that God intervened personally through prophecy to ordain a different fate for Phineas, indeed he would have been subject to the law and sentenced to death for his crime.

Phineas, a son of the High Priest knew very well what the law was and what penalty he could face. He was not a prophet; he had no mandate from God to act as he did; he had no promise from God that he would be pardoned for his actions. Yet, he acted as he did, with complete disregard for his own personal safety. He acted with resolve and determination to respond to such a serious breach that only a response of such a nature could address. His gamble paid off and came to serve as a role-model for righteous self-sacrifice throughout the ages.

Phineas and later the prophet Elijah came to serve as the role-models of righteous zeal against unrighteous foes. Although in both historical occasions acts of violence were used to neutralize the cancerous occultic influence of the times; still this is not a universal Torah message. Like Ecclesiastes 3 states, *"there is a time and a purpose for all things under Heaven,"* there is a time for peace and a time for war. While there is from time to time a need for violent responses to terrible provocations, just remember this, the forces of the Occult also know this.

In order to create havoc and destruction, the true lords of the Other (dark) Side use their psychic powers to confuse the minds of those under their influence, especially the religious fanatics, and get them to act like Zimri all the while believing themselves to be acting like Phineas. This is why we have so much insanity today in the religious communities. It has the suspicious scent of occultic influence upon weak minds.

Judging from the almost total lack of Occult knowledge and denial of its existence and powers in these segments of the religious community it is no wonder that we see so many of their members subject to occultic attack and succumbing to so many psychic illnesses.

True children of Israel and children of God's Word must learn the necessary spiritual sensitivities to become able to distinguish the "spiritual" times. We must never mistake the time for peace to be the time for war, nor must we ever mistake the time for war to be a time for peace.

Both confusions bring with them disaster. And it is this exact same type of confusion that the dark powers of the Other Side try to promote. We can learn how to clear our mental/psychic vision, but this can only come about once we clear our minds and inner vision from the illusions and delusions that presently block our vision. For this we have the fullness of Torah study, known as PaRDeS and not just the partial, censored forms of learning that are popular today.

The only defense against psychic attacks is for the properly prepared disciplined mind to be housed in a healthy strong physical body. Real Torah observance is centered on real health, both physical and spiritual.

One so balanced stands a chance against the ever-menace of the Other Side. Others who allow themselves to be weak in mind or weak in body are prime targets for the Other Side and will not escape psychic attack or the damages that they cause. Being religious only at the cultural or ethnic level is absolutely no defense.

The Other Side sees through religious hypocrisy and is attracted to it more than to anything else. Why not be a wolf in sheep's clothing? The Biblical Prince of Shimon, Zimri was such a man and he was seduced "by the Dark Side." As the Bible teaches, his wanton behavior cost him his life.

Like Balaam, Zimri was not the last of his kind. Religious hypocrites abound and their mere presence serves as a psychic danger to the entire nation. Many like Balaam and Zimri abound, but there are relatively few like Phineas today willing to confront them.

As long as we lack the appropriate number of people who embrace the spirit of a Phineas, ready to act according to the needs of the time and place we will have no one to confront the modern day Balaam and Zimri types. Thus the problems of the nation grow greater and not better, to the point where the very future of the nation is itself threatened. Religious hypocrites, fundamentalists and fanatics cannot help anything; they themselves are the problem and in no way can they contribute to the cure. Only those who are truly sincere, healthy inside and out can stand strong at the hour of the greatest testing.

Prophecy states that in the end of days before Mashiah comes that God would restore to us his prophet Elijah. Legend tells us of the unique identification between Elijah and Phineas. We need an Elijah today more than ever. Yet, until the real Elijah is revealed, we can all participate in his sacred mission. The prophet states that Elijah's mission is to restore the hearts of the fathers back to the sons, and the hearts of the sons back to the fathers. This is no minor task, but it is something that each of us can contribute to, if we know and understand what exactly it is that we are supposed to be doing.

Chapter 2

Balaam's Occult in the World Today

Let's be blunt from the start, there really is no such thing as hocus-pocus magic. Yet, never let this fact confuse one into believing that there are no such things as the Occult or real occultic powers. For just as magic is fantasy, the Occult and occultic powers are stone-hard facts!

Occultic powers are real, not because of magic, but rather because they work through manipulating natural forces, specifically those not very well known. Indeed, every master occultist is the first to acknowledge that belief in magic is nonsense. Yet, the master occultist also spends a lifetime studying many different natural law systems, especially what we today call psychology. Mastering knowledge of the human mind, the occultist uses this knowledge for psychic purposes.

What the occultist learns is how the human mind interacts with the external sensory world, and how the inner mind can be influenced by manipulating extra sensory perceptions.

The master occultist is an expert of knowing how the human mind is accessed through the unconscious. He knows how to manipulate thoughts and feelings. The master occultist also knows secrets about other technologies that manipulate sight and sound.

Through the manipulation of sight, sound and mind, the master occultist can make people sees things that are not there, hear things that make no sound, and believe and feel things that have no basis in reality. With control over the mind, the occultist can pretty much manipulate another to do almost anything.

Today many of the old secrets of the occultists have become common knowledge, although no association is made to their origins. What were once occultic secrets are now being taught in many schools and universities under all kinds of different, more scientific names.

Today, knowledge about how the human mind can be manipulated is found in most studies of psychology. Lessons from the arcane knowledge are even more prevalent in the studies of advertising and marketing, which use psychology as a tool for behavioral manipulation. Whereas psychology is geared towards learning about how and why people act, advertising and marketing is specifically geared towards manipulating people to act in specific ways, just like the occultists of old would do.

Today, we are not much different from the past. We are all still subject to psychic attack from master occultists who know the secrets of manipulating the human mind. The only difference is that today, the psychic attacks are far more sophisticated, using all forms of high-tech communication, and entertainment to not-so-subtly manipulate the way people think and behave.

Today, the mass media directly influences the way the masses think, to specifically direct the flow of their behavior. Whereas, in the past, the master occultist could influence only individuals, or small groups, today the masters in control can hypnotize and manipulate the entire world. Judging from what we see, it appears that this is exactly what they are doing.

The tools and techniques once reserved for the occult are now so common place that we see them all the time. We are so used to them, that we ignore their influence, and even go so far as to deny the manipulative power of their influence. Yet, anyone with a knowledge of basic science, and psychology, knows that we average human beings are susceptible to influence from movies, television programs and even commercials.

Billboards, advertisements of all kinds, novels and magazines show images and imagery that present certain people and ideas in ether a positive or negative light, and we observers, for the most part, go along with what we see. While our intellect might say to us one thing, the subtle influences of imagery speak to a deeper level within the psyche, and often override even the most logical, and skeptical of minds.

I believe that it is a fair and honest statement to say that all our political leaders are, knowingly or not, heavily involved with ancient occultic methods. While I do not believe that the majority of politicians are secretly involved with devil worship, or any other such nonsensical rituals, I do believe that governments, and their officials, use the public media to influence and control the minds of people, using the same techniques as did masters of the occult throughout the centuries.

Control in deed, when none is perceived, this is the motto of the master occultist, and it might also be said of the modern politician.

In order for one to recognize firsthand what it is that I am talking about, all one has to do is either read one of the many books, or watch one of the many television programs publicly available about how the human mind works, perceives things, and is then manipulated thereby. Books and programs on this subject are most revelatory, and although they will not show any historical connections to the occult, one can simply read older occult literature, and see the connections for oneself.

These phenomena of mind manipulations has been around since pre-Adamic times. Indeed, such occultic techniques of manipulation and seduction are first recorded in the Bible being used by the serpent in the Garden of Eden, who manipulated Eve, and then Adam into becoming stuck here on Earth in our present physical human forms.

The same techniques are used today, everywhere! It is no wonder then that many in religious circles believe that modern society is "ruled over" by the ancient primordial serpent. While this is a metaphor, the reality underlying the imagery is most real.

There clearly is a global conspiracy to control the minds of the masses through all the different tools of the electronic media. As to who is behind this conspiracy, all I can say is that "fruit does not fall far from the tree."

Today, people think and behave differently than they did just two generations ago. What was once considered to be right, proper, and stable moral values are today cast aside in place of a new set of values that are certainly very different from those that came before them, and not for the better. This is the result of mass manipulations through world outreach. Yet, this is nothing new under the sun. We have a Biblical example of this mass manipulation being attempted on a national scale.

It is recorded in Numbers 22, that Balak, king of Moab was terrified of a pending Israelite invasion. In order to covertly weaken his enemy, Balak reached out to the reknowned seer of his day, Balaam, to curse the children of Israel.

Balak knew that by using the occultic tool of the projection of negative thought and word, that somehow Balaam would be able to weaken Israel from within. Now, Balaam was no mythical figure. He was renown in his day and for many centuries afterwards. There presently exists modern archaeological evidence, found in Dier 'Alla, Jordan, that validates and confirms that Balaam was a historical person.

Balaam was renown in the ancient world as a master magician, but as I said above, there is no such thing as magic. Balaam wielded a real power, a power of knowing how to manipulate the collective unconscious of large groups of people.

The Biblical episodes are full of archetypal behaviors (altars of sacrifice) and the like, and culminates with the peculiar dialogue Balaam has with his taking donkey. We'll leave the interpretations of these things for other scholars. We need to focus here on what Balaam was trying to accomplish, and what indeed, he did accomplish.

After performing all his sacrificial tasks, which judging from the Biblical record were all failures, Balaam was, nevertheless, able to gaze into the collective unconscious (Akashic record) of the Israelite nation and discovered their one weakness, the soldiers would be susceptible to seduction by the Moabite women.

If the woman attacked the soldiers with sex, instead of with swords and bow, they would be able to neutralize Israelite hostility. Once the soldiers got a taste of the sweetness of Moab, they would have no intent, or desire, to attack them. Thus Moab would be able to launch an offensive military campaign against an enemy of weakened resolve. In such a state of weakened resolve, Israel would be been easily defeated.

Ancient records show that the daughters of Moab were instructed to initially arouse the Israelite soldiers, but to not submit to their sexual advances too quickly.

First, they were to flirt, then seduce. Yet, before allowing the Israelites any sexual conquests, the daughters of Moab were to involve the Israelite soldiers in their Moabite religious ceremonies, and worship of the Moabite gods.

Fired on by sexual passion, the Israelite soldiers would suddenly become very lenient in their tolerance to idol worship. Needless to say, this arouses the wrath of YHWH against the sons of Israel. This then was Balaam's plan from the start.

Balaam knew that YHWH would be aroused to anger against Israel, and that YHWH would unleash His wrath against the offending soldiers, thus weakening the might of the Israelite forces. Balaam's plan was to defeat the Israelite army, without having Moab to lift a sword. YHWH would be Balaam's tool against Israel, and both YHWH and Balaam knew that the rouse would work. And indeed, it did.

Balaam manipulated an entire nation. He blinded their eyes from seeing one thing by distracting them with another. This trick is used to this day in the public media, and by every magician who has even performed in public.

Balaam's deep knowledge of human psychology was for centuries called magic, and later the occult. Whatever name we call it, it is still a powerful tool of individual and collective manipulation that can either build or destroy, bless or curse.

The knowledge of ancient Balaam is still vibrant and relevant today, and is even more dangerous than it once was, because now these powers have fallen into the hands of those who seek to enslave all of humanity.

In ancient times, only those who stood firm against persuasion and manipulation were able to withstand the onslaught against their morals and ways of thinking. Today, in this regards, nothing is different. The only way to stand against a modern-day Balaam is to stand firm, with conviction and resolve, like a modern-day Pinhas. But, the topic of Pinhas will have to be covered in another essay.

Chapter 3

"Demonic" Attacks & Psychic Warfare

Do you believe in demons, and evil monsters? They really do exist! The only question is are they actual external autonomous life forms, or are they just figments of the imagination?

This difference is a very big one. But the difference is not whether one is real, while the other is fake. No, while actual external creatures could be very real, one should never think any less about the imagined creatures that inhabit our minds. They too are very real. Indeed, they may be more real, and pose to us a greater threat than any actual external, autonomous, evil life forms out there.

Learn this very important rule: a perceived threat is more dangerous than a real one. A perceived demon, or monster, is also more dangerous than a real one. The external world is not under our control, and in spite of any individual delusions of grandeur, the external world does not revolve around any one of us personally. Frankly, no one individual is so important that he or she solely merits attack from the world of demons.

This all changes when we discuss the psychological makeup of the individual. For each person is very much a world unto oneself. One's inner world very much does revolve around one's self. Therefore, all internal demons, bad feelings, and ill intent, all circle within one's mind, with one's self being the center. What this means is something frightening. Inside one's mind can be a place of beauty and light, or inside one's mind can be a pit of darkness, and hell. For the most part, one always chooses one's internal reality. One always chooses to give life to, or take life away from one's own internal psychological demons.

One's own mind is one's greatest weapon against evil, but at the same time, one's own mind can be one's greatest weakness. Strengthening of the mind, therefore, should be one's highest priority. One thing is certain, a wise and competent enemy knows how to best attack an opponent. The best attack is not one with physical weapons, or with superior numbers. The best attack is to attack the mind, and to allow the opponent's inner weaknesses, and fears destroy them from within.

This method of attack is as old as humanity itself. It is referenced in the Bible, and even recorded by the ancient Chinese military philosopher, Sun Tzu. Today, in official military circles, there is even an appropriate name attached to this, along with large investments of time, money, and effort made to seek its accomplishment. Today, we speak of psychological warfare, and even of psychic warfare. The first seeks to attack the conscious mind, and to manipulate it. The latter seeks to attack the unconscious, and to activate, and increase one's own internal demons.

This latter method is ancient, and is even seen used in the Bible, with the narrative about King Balak of Moab, and the wizard Balaam, who sought a way to attack, and thus weaken the Children of Israel. In the book of Numbers (22), King Balak of Moab is faced with a terrible threat from the perceived hostile Children of Israel at his border. Possibly considering his military options to be insufficient, Balak turns to another more sinister method of attack. If he cannot defeat Israel by force of arms, then he will seek to defeat them by force of mind. Balak turns to the master wizard of the day, Balaam, to use his Occult powers to curse the Children of Israel.

By some modern standards, believing that a curse could have any actual power to inflict harm sounds like a delusional hocus-pocus fantasy. Yet, in ancient times, and even in many cultures today, the power of the curse is considered to be an actual and powerful danger. For those who live in a mind-set full of psychic and cosmic energies, who believe in the supernatural, and in the existence of demons and evil monsters, the power to curse is actual, and real.

Those who believe themselves to be cursed can actually cause the effect that the one placing the curse desires. It does not matter whether or not the curse, in and of itself, has actual power. What matters is that such a power is believed to exist, and once the belief is accepted in the mind, it is the belief itself that creates the effect of the curse.

Indeed, it is these self-same belief patterns of the individual mind that create all sorts of demons, devils, monsters, boogie-men, and other assorted "things that go bump in the night." This does not mean that these things do not exist in reality. What it does mean is that, for most people, actual external reality is insignificant when compared to the self-created internal reality that each and every one of us creates inside our own minds.

King Balak hired the ancient wizard Balaam, seeking him to place such a curse on Israel. Once word got out that Balaam had cursed Israel, the superstitious people of the day, including many of the Children of Israel, would have become greatly despondent, and would fear to move against Moab, out of fear for further Occult consequences. This was indeed King Balak's plan. Balaam thought to play along with the charade, but at the same time, Balaam was a legitimate master of spiritual forces. In Torah literature, Balaam is considered to be an equal with none less that Moses, himself. While King Balak sought to deploy psychological warfare, the wizard Balaam sought to deploy pure, out-right psychic warfare.

Balaam is portrayed in Torah literature as a force to be reckoned with. Although Balaam is a servant to the gods and goddesses (see the Deir Alla Inscription), he can still (and does) receive messages from YHWH, the God of Israel. As the Biblical narrative goes, YHWH does not allow Balaam to curse Israel, but instead, on numerous occasions, Balaam is compelled to bless them.

So, in reality, what is the big deal? To bless, to curse? Being that this is all in the mind of the believer, who cares, and what difference does it make? It makes all the difference to the believer!

In Biblical times, everyone was a believer. In modern times, most people still believe, even if and when they consciously deny such beliefs. The Occult method to commit psychic attack is to seek to introduce thoughts into the unconscious mind, and to allow them to simmer there, to create, and exasperate one's own inner, worst fears. Today, the powers of the Occult are no less effective than they were in Biblical times. Being that we are all human beings, we are all susceptible to psychic attacks on the unconscious mind.

Psychic manipulations were once thought to be the realm of fantasy. Yet, modern research in psychology, and the science of brain functions show how the unconscious can, and is, influenced by subtle stimuli that, in many cases, goes unnoticed even by the conscious mind.

Psychic warfare is real, and is no longer a matter of hocus-pocus fantasy. We have modern psychological science to validate such things. Yet, such knowledge is not new, in ancient times, such sciences were also known. Then, however, they were called "arts," specifically, the "magical" arts. Today, we recognize how such "magic" worked, and we see nothing magical in it. Nevertheless, the underlying psychology, and its subtle ability to manipulate, is at present, active, and in use today, no different than it was in ancient times.

The power of denial does not make something go away. Something real is nevertheless real, regardless of whether it is an external reality, or an internal one. While the substance is different, the harmful negative psychological effects are no different.

There is real evil in this world. There are real devils, demons, and monsters. They are not going to come out at night to drink our blood, but rather because they are inside our minds, they are with us always, and can inflict painful suffering, and harm at any time that we let down our guards, and entertain the thought of their presence.

In ancient times, Balaam's plan actually worked. Balaam conceived of a plot to weaken Israel sexually. He foresaw that in this one arena, the sons of Israel would be significantly weak. The Moabite nation mobilized, and instead of sending out their soldiers to spill blood, they sent out their women to spill seed! And the women were greatly successful. They infiltrated the Israelite camp, even to the highest echelons. Israelite resolve against Moab would be destroyed. A woman's lips would do more to undo the Israelite military, than an army of soldiers with swords.

This ancient scenario has been repeated so many times throughout history that no history book could ever record all the incidences. How many today have not heard of the infamous WWI German female spy, Mata Hari? We even have more recent events with Anna Chapman, a beautiful Russian woman in the United States who was exposed as an espionage agent. It seems that best way to defeat a man is through a woman, and to this day, almost no man has learned any better.

One's own psychological weaknesses create internal demons, and monsters that can corrupt, and destroy the mind from within. Knowing how to exploit this is psychic warfare. One perpetrating this on another is a psychic attack. No external magic is necessary here, the only magic involved is the magic of the human imagination. And the human imagination is the greatest tool for both self-defense, and for self-destruction.

The only defense against such psychic attack is a strong mind. "The Force can have a strong influence on the weak-minded." We can take the "Force" out of Star Wars, and replace it with our faith in God, our personal discipline, and resolve to reinforce our weak minds. Mental disciple is part and parcel of true, authentic spiritual practices. This is why the Torah path places so much emphasis on education. Education helps to expose the falsehoods upon which are built all types of lies that enter the mind, and once there, begin to create our internal monsters.

Education, mind you, is not learning what to think, but rather learning how to think. This is the ability to analyze things critically, with penetrating wisdom. This can only be accomplished by the disciplined mind. One way to discipline the mind is by first disciplining the body. This is why immersion in the martial arts, physically and philosophically, is an excellent complement to the path of Torah and mitzvot.

The strong mind in the strong body is a temple that will not be defiled. In the place of inner strength no monster or demon can dominate. While our inner demons may not be chased away permanently, nevertheless, they can each be put under control, and kept in check. This is what transformational spirituality accomplishes, it creates psychological strength. This is why the forces of the Occult seek to destroy psychological independence. For the only defense against psychic attack is a mind capable of recognizing such attacks, and strong enough to stand against them with discipline, and calculated wisdom.

Religion today is being destroyed in what seems like a global psychic attack. As long as minds are weak, monsters will dominate, and evil will prevail. The change begins within each and every one of us. There is protection from evil in the power of the mind. I wrote the book on it to explain how to do it. Read my book, Protection from Evil, and learn more. But don't stop there. You must implement it, and put into practice what you learn.

SECTION FOUR

IMPORTANT SECRETS REVEALED FROM THE ANCIENT PAST TO THE MESSIANIC FUTURE

The Two Arks of the Covenant, Pre-Adamic Civilizations, Secrets of Inner Earth

<u>Chapter 1</u>

On Reality & Perspective

What is the definition of reality? What is real and what is not? We think that we know, but in reality, what do we know? How we define reality is very limited, and we can easily portray that there are realities that real, even when we think them unreal. Definitions are a matter of perspective, and so too is reality itself.

Reality and perspective, let us demonstrate. That is which is physical, and is evident before us, all of us most likely will agree is real. Granted there may be some debate over some details. But in general, the old rule applies, if I can see it, and touch it, then it is real. While this may not necessarily be true, we will return to discuss this later. Now, let us discuss reality and perception.

Let us discuss an idea, a belief, or a matter of faith. Let us not discuss religion as our example. This too we can discuss later. Let us use a clearer example.

We are all familiar with the character of Santa Claus, the fictional person associated with the Christian holiday of Christmas. Now, is Santa Claus real? How can I ask this? I just referred to him as a fictional character! But, here again, is it possible for a fictional character to be real? Like it or not, but yes, a fictional character can be real.

Santa Claus, for example, is real. This cannot be denied! Santa Claus is real? How can this be? The answer lies in our understanding the use of the term "real."

Rather than ask, is Santa Claus real? Better to ask Santa Claus is a real what? With this question in hand, we can proceed to define the type of reality that Santa Claus really is. Perspective, remember?

Santa Claus is not a real physical person, who wears a red suit, and who lives in the North Pole making toys for good children for Christmas. But Santa Claus is a real character, a fictional creation, whose reality is in the hearts and minds of (maybe) millions.

Santa Claus is very much alive; he may even be immortal. Hs reality in the hearts and minds of his devotees is as real to them, as the physical reality of other things is real to us. So, what is real? Only external physical things? No, we must include within the definition of reality those things which are inside our hearts and minds.

But we must also learn to distinguish the difference between inner and outer realities. For this confusion leads many to believe that which is inside one is as real as that which is outside one. Granted, both internal and external reality are real. But one should always be able to discern the difference between one type of reality and the other.

This becomes very important, even essential when it comes to the perceptions of reality offered to us by our many religions, How many are convinced that their inner faith is a reflection of outer truths. And woe to those who challenge our inner faith, for they become the object interpreted to be rejectors of the great truths of reality itself. And history has shown us what happens to those whom we define as different, and inferior.

There is an inner reality and there is an external reality. While we are in waking consciousness, external reality for us dominates all. Yet, when we daydream or sleep, inner reality takes over as the dominant form. This can be illustrated by the words of an ancient philosopher. He said that he once dreamed that he was a butterfly. The dream was for him so intense and so real that when he awoke, he contemplated whether indeed he was a man who dreamed himself to be butterfly, or perhaps he was really a butterfly dreaming now that he is a man! This is a profound contemplation, and who can definitely prove one way or another, which reality was indeed true.

The inner realities do not need to be experienced so visually. Inner realities include the gamut of our emotions and our thoughts. Any of us can daydream. Any of us can sit back, relax, and imagine being in our favorite places. Sometimes these daydreams can be felt to be so real, that we really feel that we are there. Sometimes, a hypnotic state can also induce similar states.

Many of us see the world and interact with it entirely based upon one's emotional perceptions. One many witness or experience a situation which is one thing and interpret the situation to be something entirely different than what it truly is. One then responds to the situation based upon one's perception of things, as opposed to the actuality of things. The need to address this type of inappropriate behavior keeps the offices of psychologists and psychiatrists very full.

It is well known that individuals suffering from schizophrenia and other related mental health issues see the world in their own unique way. These individuals see and experience things that others just do not. And their reality is for them no lie! It is as real to them, ass our reality is for us. These are the ones whose inner realities merge with and often override their external realities thus giving rise to their need for professional mental health intervention.

What we learn from all this is very simple. Reality is not so simple! Reality is not so real! We can augment to this some scientific facts.

We view physical objects as being real. I touch them, I see them, thus they are real. But just how real is anything physical. We all know from science that all physical things are constructed from tiny particles that we call Atoms. Atoms themselves are made up of smaller particles which are neutrons, protons, and electrons. As these sub-atomic particles form, and create atoms, and when atoms combine and create molecules, they are not packed together, touching one another. No! On a relative scale the distance between the center of an Atom (the nucleus) and its orbiting satellites, electrons, can be rightly compared to the distance between the Sun and the planets. And one Atom in a molecule is very distant from the next one. Essentially, what science has discovered is that physical objects, which appear very solid to us, are in reality, mostly empty space. That which we think is so solid, in reality really isn't.

What we have discovered is that our thoughts cannot define reality, and neither can our emotions. Even that which we are so convinced is physical reality, is in reality something very different. So, we return to the beginning to ask again, what is reality? What defines reality? Or maybe we should better ask, who gets to define realty? And also, we need to ask, does the reality of one override, and dominate the reality of another? Like I said above, it is all a matter of perspective.

Now that we have discussed the philosophical, let us go deeper into the experiences of parallel realities.

Thoughts are things. So are emotions. Each of us thinks and feels. Each of us perceives the world around us differently from one another. Although we might want to proclaim that there must be only one reality that is objectively true for everyone, we see with clarity that no one on Earth has access to it, despite the many claims to possession of the absolute truth. Ultimately, no one knows the whole truth; no one sees the real picture. Everything that we experience comes to us through the filters of our thoughts, our emotions, our prejudices, our perspectives, and our personal world outlook.

When one sees things in a certain way, then everything that one sees is twisted and turned until it is made to fit within the context of one's personal perceptions. This psychological function within the human mind leads each individual to become rigidly attached to one's perspective, and equally prejudiced against any perceptions of anyone else that does not conform to one's preconceived notions.

All these concepts of reality as defined by perception apply to the many experiences that we face daily in this world, or maybe better to say, in our perception of this world. For who knows what the real world is like? All that we know is what we experience, and what we experience is filtered through our personal perspectives. We can rightly ask, what is the reality of what is inside us and outside us beyond the filters and limits of our personal perspectives? This we cannot know!

For centuries those whom we call spiritual masters have taught us that we live in a multi-dimensional reality that expands out much farther than what our physical senses can perceive. We are taught that there are other worlds, not in the physical space that we know. We are taught that there are other dimensions parallel to ours right here on Earth, and that each of these dimensions is inhabited and is populated similarly to is our dimension. We are taught how one can expand consciousness, thus altering perspective, allowing one to experience these other dimensions and to interact with them.

Doubters and deniers will consider other dimensions to be fantastical. The limit of their experience is due to the limits of their perceptions. In other words, if one chooses to close one's eyes and not see something, then that something is both out of sight and out of mind. One cannot see, and will not see, that which they refuse to see. So, the lack of spiritual insight and vision on the part of most everyone is usually due to personal choice not to see as opposed to there being no greater reality at all to see.

To debate whether or not there are other worlds and dimensions is futile. How can one expect to prove such a thing? The only way to prove the existence of other realms is for one to actually experience them first hand. Without such personal experience all the debates and arguments prove nothing. So let me ask the question, how many of us have actually experienced other realities and other realms. Do not be so quick to jump to the conclusion and think that almost no one has had such experiences. For on the contrary, almost everyone has experienced an alternate reality. It is just that most to not recognize it when they see it.

So, if one directly experiences an alternate reality, and yet one does not recognize the experience, or worse denies that it ever happened, we are left to ask the question, did one experience anything at all? Perception is everything. Thus, even if you experience a thing, but you do not perceive it, then how one can know that one indeed did experience it? There is only one answer.

There must be some form of residual side-effect that upon observation seems to have no logical or rational source of origins. If something is there, and one cannot ascertain from where it came, one must conclude that it comes from a source not yet perceptible. One will either then search for the source and discover that which was previous unperceived, or one will not care enough to search and go about one's business as unobservant and ignorant as before.

Expanded consciousness only comes about through expanded perception; can't have one without the other.

Chapter 2

The Natural Order

There is an Order to the universe. We each call it by different names, but regardless of its title, the Order of the universe rules supreme. And no amount of human disregard will change the Way things are, and the Way that things operate!

The universe was created to operate efficiently. All natural events, from the largest cosmological ones to the smallest microscopic ones, all operate in accordance to the natural laws that define their creation. And everything operates together in peace. Harmony is maintained between all the divergent parts of creation.

And then along comes human beings. By matter of choice, we chose to ignore the natural order and to proclaim an order all our own. Human beings spread their unnatural order over the face of the Earth, thinking that they will naturally succeed simply because they themselves are the authors of their own form of natural order.

When human beings consider themselves to be above the natural Order and declare allegiance to an order of their own making, unnatural conflict naturally arises.

Human beings were themselves created to be part of the natural Order, and to function and to thrive therein. But when human beings act contrary to the natural Order, their behavior triggers natural responses designed to restore harmony.

Look around at our world today. We proudly and defiantly proclaim our liberty from both Creator and creation. We arrogantly define for ourselves what is right and good and defy any natural Order that dares to be different.

Both Creator and creation watch! How long will wayward humanity be tolerated? Human rebellion and the harm that it causes is tolerated for a time, double-time and half-time. But however long the times be, eventually they come to an end, and the process of adjustment begins.

Look around at our world today! Can you not see how far we human beings have drifted away from the natural Order? For if you can see this, don't you think, for your own sake, that you should start your personal return to the natural Way? For it is your personal choices and your personal actions that will decide your personal fate once the process of restoration moves into full speed.

Look around at our world today! If you like what you see. If you embrace the manmade unnatural order, and declare it your own, then you can contend with both Creator and creation when the move to restoration comes directly for you. Proclaim all you want how right you are. Both Creator and creation care nothing for your proclamations.

In the eyes of the Creator and creation unnatural human beings or unnatural anything else are viewed as nothing more than a virus in need of eradication. And the Creator has created in the natural Order the natural way to eradicate harmful viruses.

Those with eyes can see this now. Those who refuse to see will continue to do so. They will not see their own termination before it comes, regardless of how close it gets. To the very end, the arrogant cling to their arrogance until the natural Order is forced to intervene and to tear it away from them.

We are the cause of our own greatest harm. Both Creator and creation gives us time, double-time and half-time to set our affairs in order, and to return to the natural Way. It is the Will and Way of the universe for all of us to live together in natural harmony and peace. But when we break the peace, then the same broken pieces, that we ourselves have broken, come back and in like kind break us, in like fashion as we have broken them.

Look around at our world today! Contemplate the truth of the matter. Know the Creator. Know creation. Know the natural Order. Know these all, and realign yourselves with them, while there is still time to do so. And that time is quickly coming to its natural end.

If you choose otherwise, then know, as you are creators of your own choices, so too are you creators of your own fate. So be it. Nature has to restore harmony and balance. It must remove that which is causing great harm throughout the system.

What is soon to come upon us is only natural. For the natural Order rules all, both human beings, and all other non-human races. Order will be maintained. Harmony will be restored. Arrogant and rebellious human beings will be swept aside so that natural and normal human beings will again be able to thrive and prosper. It is they who will be welcomed into the greater universal community of natural and normal beings.

Look at the world around you. Pay attention. Learn. Decide. What more is there to say?

Chapter 3

Secret of the Two Arks of the Covenant

The Ark of the Covenant is gone, lost in time, concealed throughout the ages until the one who hid it comes again to reveal it.

There is an interesting legend told in ancient Merkava literature that when the Ark was secreted out of Jerusalem by the hands of the Levites, that they took it far away to a place that cannot be mentioned. There they were met by a group of angels called the Benei Elohim. These Angels took possession of the Ark from the Levites and were charged to hold it and guard it until such time when their Master in Heaven commanded them to return it to Earth. Those today who are seeking to find the lost Ark will search in vain, for it is nowhere to be found, anywhere on the face of planet Earth.

The Gemara (T.J. Shekalim 6:1, and quoted by Rashi, Deut 10:1) however does mention to us a little-known secret. There were actually two Arks made: one by Moshe and the later one by Betzalel. The earlier one held the Tablets of the Commandments until such time when Betzalel's Ark was completed. Then Betzalel's Ark took over as The Ark, and Moshe's Ark was dedicated to being the Ark of War.

It was Moshe's Ark that went out into battle before the Israelite army sending forth some type of "energy" that struck dead its foes before it. Whatever happened to this Ark, we have no record.

Perhaps this Ark is buried under the Temple Mount; perhaps it is in Ethiopia; or perhaps it is buried in a cave somewhere out in the Negev. Until it is found we will never know.

One thing is for certain, Moshe's Ark, as powerful as it was, still was not as powerful as Betzalel's Ark. Betzalel's Ark was unique, designed by the Hand of God, to reflect the image of the Heavenly Ark. We are taught that Betzalel was granted special wisdom, specifically the knowledge of the primordial creative forces in the universe. He apparently needed this knowledge to construct the Ark.

If the Ark was a mere box of wood and gold, however artistically intricate, he would not have needed such advanced technological information. Yet, such information was vital for the Ark's construction. What exactly Betzalel was taught and what technological secrets were used to build the Ark; we may never know until the Ark's return.

The only insight that we have is what we have already said; Betzalel was a master of the creative arts found in the Sefer Yetzirah and that he used what he knew to build what he did. Why and how and for what purpose is information lost to us along with the Ark.

The Ark of the Covenant was by no means a mere box of wood and gold. The Cherubim angels were much more than a mere pretty decoration. We are taught that when the Divine Presence filled the Ark, the Cherubim on top came alive. Their wings were in a state of movement, opening and closing. Turning statues of gold into living creatures is certainly a feat worthy of the Sefer Yetzirah, but Betzalel did not bring them to life, the Shekhina did. Betzalel merely provided the body; God provided the soul.

We should ask, were the bodies of the Cherubim magically animated or was there more to their construction that we know of. Was there some element of creation technology learned from the Sefer Yetzirah used here? We may never know but judging logically we can only conclude in positive confirmation.

We are taught that the Ark below was formed in the image of the Ark above. In essence, one Ark communicated with the other. Now, modern Sages are of the unsubstantiated opinion that all spiritual reality is absolutely non-corporeal. Being that none of these Sages have ever had any personal experience with any reality of these alternate dimensions, we cannot rely on their conjecture as having any validity.

This still does not mean that there is anything what we would call physical in Heaven. Still the Ark below was built in the image of the Ark above. Therefore, there is such an image and such a reality, which is far more than mere symbolisms. Let me compare it to what today we know as computerized virtual reality and holographic imagery.

If we were to don virtual reality suits and actually place ourselves in a computer game, are we actually physically there inside the computer program? Of course not. Yet, to the computer generated artificially intelligent characters in the computer game we are no different from them, with only one exception. Our program is not the same as theirs. We can come and go into and out of the virtual reality computer game any time we want. The characters inside the program cannot.

If those characters had any type of artificial intelligence, they might interpret our coming and going as something miraculous. Indeed, they might hypothesize that we take on forms just to be in their world and then disappear into formlessness, which they would consider to be our natural state. Yet, such formlessness is not our natural state, rather it is a state of transition that we pass through when we take off the virtual reality suit and come back into our real world; a world that the computer characters cannot possibly conceive.

Next time, you think of anything referred to in Torah as Above, remember this example. It will help you better understand the nature of our two worlds.

The Ark, therefore, was built in accordance to a pattern that would coincide with an already pre-existing Ark in what we call Heaven. No one can say for sure what its actual makeup might be.

Maybe someday we will know; then again, maybe not. All that we can learn is that there is an alternate reality and that it plays a very important role in what transpires here in our reality.

The Ark, as we know, was a communications device. It allowed a certain properly prepared individual (the High Priest) to make connection with Heaven and to communicate openly. However, the nature of this communication was far different from our modern technological means. The Ark was by no means a radio or telephone. The nature of the Earth to Heaven communication required many things.

First, the properly prepared individual, the High Priest had to be of a specific refined character. He was prohibited certain behaviors and required to perform others. These were no mere moral commands. Each of the laws of the High Priest was specifically designed to alter him down to the genetic level. Psychologically and even biologically the High Priest was prepared from the youngest age to take on his responsibilities as being the only one on Earth who could place the long distance call to Heaven. Just what type of transformations the High Priest went through cannot be publicly elaborated.

The High Priest would approach the Ark in a very precise way. He certainly did not approach it alone. He was required to wear the mysterious Urim and Tumim along with the Hoshen Mishpat, the Breastplate of Judgment. Inside the Hoshen was a secret pocket. Inside the pocket was the Urim placed. No one knows for sure exactly what the Urim were. We are taught that it had the holy Names of God written upon it. But this description is more of a non-description. It really does not tell us anything about the actual construction of the Urim or the Tumim, all the more so the nature of their operations and function. These are as lost in history as is the Ark.

In order to receive communication, the High Priest had to approach the Ark wearing the Urim, Tumim and Hoshen. He was then to contemplate his question. Apparently, no verbal communication was necessary. The communication between the High Priest and the Ark was apparently telepathic. He thought his question and somehow the Ark understood and transmitted the message. Receiving the response is when things got very interesting.

As the High Priest was meditating, or should we more accurately say, telepathically communicating with the Ark, strange things began to happen. The stones on the Hoshen would begin to light up, specific letters on specific stones would begin to glow and a strange high pitch whine would come forth.

Anyone watching, such as untrained Kohanim or the King would not be able to decipher anything from these lights and sounds. Yet, there were trained Kohanim whose job it was to record everything that was happening. They transcribed which lights lit up and in what order. They apparently had some insight into the meanings of the whining sounds and somehow recorded them too. After it was all over, it was time to decipher Heaven's response to the telepathic communiqué from the High Priest.

One thing was certain, the lights that lit up and the letters that glowed never spelled out any intelligible and rational sentence or words. The message was, from our rational point of view always a garbled mixture of letters and sounds. Here now is the key to their decipherment.

Like Betzalel before them, the Priests were also trained in the usage of the Sefer Yetzirah. Through the sounds they could intuit the proper order of the letters. They knew how to form them into rational words and sentences. The communication apparatus worked just fine; however, without the proper interpreters, the message from Heaven would never be decipherable.

The Ark therefore only worked in conjunction with the Urim, Tumim and Hoshen. One was incomplete without the other. This was the power of Betzalel's Ark over Moshe's. Moshe's Ark had the power, but Betzalel's Ark was the telephone to Heaven.

It is no wonder then as we entered into the historical period of exile that the Ark, along with the Urim, Tumim and Hoshen were concealed. Our direct communication with Heaven was disconnected. This also explains why prophecy came to an end soon afterwards. All prophecy channeled to the Earth through the Ark. Once the Ark was taken off the Earth, the means to make contact was broken. Granted, other lower forms of contact were still possible, but these are with the Angels, and never with the Master directly.

Over the centuries even the lower forms of communication with the Angels has been lost in time to all but the chosen few. Like the Priests of old, those today who know the secrets of angelic communication guard well both their secrets and their identities. What they know is not for prying eyes or for curious fools. When the time comes and the period of exiles grinds to its end, the lines of communication will again be opened; first with the Angels, and eventually again directly to Heaven.

We should not concern ourselves about the mysteries to be revealed in the future. We have enough to consider and contemplate today. There are still many secrets within the Torah, within its words and letters that we can extract and use today.

Long ago, our Sages revealed that the entire Torah is one holistic whole communiqué from God. In other words, we say that the entire Torah is one long Name of God. Its original form is not broken up into words and sentences. Therefore, when we come to study the Torah, we are not limited to that framework of reading.

We have numerous ways of reading Torah in non-linear ways. We have special formulas for combining different combinations of letters into different forms. These then form what is commonly referred to as Holy Names. Holy, these combinations are, this is true. Yet, they are not really Names as we would use the term. These letter combinations are more like formulas. They are used for many things, one being the focus of the mind for the purpose of expanding consciousness. Specific sound combinations reverberated (chanted) in a special resonance have an effect upon brain chemistry allowing the scope of consciousness to expand to perceive greater realities. Indeed, the Kohen Gadol made use of one of these formulas as he approached the Ark to commune with God. What formula he used; we may never know.

When we say that the entire Torah is one long Name of God, we should rather say that the Torah is one long code. Unraveling the code and discovering its true potentials is what we call the study of the secrets of the Torah.

In my opinion, it is a shame that this study is relegated exclusively into the hands of the non-scientifically trained religious. Their lack of scientific knowledge disables them from exploring certain avenues of exploration that can really tap into Torah's inner powers. Of course, secular scientists would have the same problem. Without the calibration acquired from living a Torah life-style, they would never achieve the necessary consciousness to know where and how to begin their research.

Let us not underestimate the power concealed in our Torah. Let me remind you that the proper term to refer to the origins of Torah is extraterrestrial. Do not be frightened of this word. Science and spirituality are two halves of the same whole. We must embrace them both to get the whole picture. We are the ones in the computer simulation. We must remember this, take off our blinders in order to wake up and see the true reality.

Like most other Torah faithful, I would love to see the restoration of prophecy and the return of the Ark to Jerusalem. However, I know what it will take to accomplish these monumental tasks. We need to approach Torah in the proper ways and extract its codes for the expansion of human consciousness.

If we all got together and send out loud and strong messages to Heaven, sooner than later they would have no choice but to answer and restore communications. Indeed, I do believe that Heaven is waiting for our call. Who has the proper number to dial?

Chapter 4

The Eden Episode
Decoded in the Extraterrestrial Torah

The entire universe is one great complex integrated machine. Our entire reality is merely a simulation program presently operating within the great machine of the universe. This insight has come to me (and to many) by contemplating the concealed messages hidden mathematically within the Torah.

The Torah does not conceal its origins. The Torah boldly proclaims that every word of it, from beginning to end, was transmitted as a whole to Moses from Heaven. In light of our present understandings about cosmology and the nature of Outer Space, has anyone paused to ask an obvious question? If Torah does indeed come from Heaven, then just where is, and what is this Heaven of which we speak?

In light of our present understandings of science, we do not have an answer to this question. True, the Torah Sages and mystic have answers, but these do not concern us at the moment.

When we say that Torah is from Heaven, then there is one thing that we are forced to admit about the Torah. If the Torah is from Heaven, then it is not of his Earth. As such, by logical deduction, we must confess that the Torah is extraterrestrial. It comes from "out there," wherever that "out there" realistically is!

We have an extraterrestrial Torah. This is a foundational statement of faith of Judaism, and for that matter, an equal statement of faith for our sister religions, Christianity, and Islam. When we say that the Torah came from Heaven, and clearly Heaven is not of this Earth, then we have an extraterrestrial Torah. And this takes Torah and all religious matters derived from it outside of the realm of religion, and returns them to their rightful place within the realms of nature, and the exploration of cosmological reality.

Torah is one grand mathematical document. No one on Earth has yet fathomed the depths of its secrets. God gave the Torah to Israel (and thus religion to the world). What God dictated to Moses underneath the exacting text, which must always be precise, is mathematical codes, of which we have only barely scratched the surface of discovery.

We know to look for numerical sequential relationships between equidistant letters. We know to translate letters into numbers, and to then look for numerical equivalents between words of equal numerical value. This process of exploration reveals to us discoveries of association that beforehand were unseen.

Torah traditions (the Kabbalah) have documented a good number of numerical values and their correlative significance. We know that the Name YHWH equals 26, and thus any equivalent value of 26, or any multiple thereof, will somehow be related to the Name YHWH, and contain within the number a concealed message about its specific significance.

The sheer number of mathematical possibilities already discovered in the Torah using the best of modern computer programs has clearly shown the validity of these once concealed Torah Codes. Nothing more than science itself now proves that the Torah is of extraterrestrial origins. What more awaits our discovery is only a matter of time.

The secrets concealed within the Torah do not require of one to use the latest computer analytical software. Anyone with a basic knowledge of simple mathematics can with ease gaze into the

Torah, and instead of reading it like a book, look at the Torah as one big mathematical, numerical puzzle.

One can start anywhere within the text and begins looking for numerical values between words. One can count equidistant spaces between letters for a specified number and see correlations between the letters.

In order to give you a small taste of this procedure, I am going to reveal to you some this coded material and the significance of these findings. I confess that we will only be scratching the bare surface. As for what lies underneath, as yet undiscovered; who knows?

Let us start in the very beginning with the opening words and verses of Genesis. The first verse in Genesis contains seven words and twenty-eight letters. Seven becomes a very important number in Torah, amongst other things becoming a standard measure of time. Twenty-eight is the numerical value of the word Ko'ah, which means "power." Right from the beginning, hinted to in the numbers, the Torah makes a statement about the "power of seven." As for what this power is, we do not find an over hint to this in the verse. So, we will have to look for a hint in another way.

One of these other ways in equidistant numerical spacing. We can begin with the first letter of the Torah, Bet, and count seven letters. The eighth letter begins the next sequence of seven letters. We repeat this to create seven groups of seven. The first letter of each group consists of our group of seven. These seven letters (Bet, Resh, Alef, Wav, Wav, Tav, Hey) are numerically equal to 620. And 620 is a very significant number in the Torah tradition (Kabbalah).

בְּרֵאשִית בּ

רָא אֱלֹהִים

אֵת הַשָמַיִם

וְאֵת הָאָרֶץ

וְהָאָרֶץ הָיְ

תָה תֹהוּ וָבֹ

וְהֹ

בְּ׳רְ׳אַ׳וְוְ׳תְ׳ה

ג׳ 620 ג׳ כֶתֶר

620 is the number of the commandments that were revealed at Mt. Sinai, the 613 commandments for the Children of Israel, and the 7 general categories of laws for all

humanity.

620 is also the numerical value of the word Keter (crown). This is the name of the first of the Ten Sefirot spoken of in the Kabbalah. Keter represents the Divine Will.

Right from the beginning, hinted to in the numbers of the first letters in the Torah, there is a coded reference to both the commandments of God and the Will of God. Common sense dictates to us to understand how the first message of the Torah is that the commandments of the Torah are the Will of God, and that they are the revelation of the Primary Sefirah.

The numbers speak for themselves. And this is only the beginning.

Genesis 1:1-2 contains twenty-one words. Twenty-one is the numerical value of the holy Name of God revealed to Moses at the burning bush, AHYH (Ehyeh). The Kabbalists associate this Name of God with the Sefirah Keter. It seems most fitting, and no surprise to see a hint to it here. But what significance can we ascribe to it? For this we need to look at Verse 2 to ask some often overlooked questions.

Genesis 1:2 says, *"And the Earth was tohu (voided) and bohu (chaotic), and darkness was on the face of the deep, and the spirit of God was hovering over the face of the water."*

Now, Genesis 1:1, a very famous verse, says, *"In the beginning God created the Heavens and the Earth."* So, in Verse 1 the Heavens and the Earth are created, but as we see, there are some missing details, for already in Verse 2 there exists a void, chaos, darkness, the deep, and water. There are five things here already in existence on Earth whose creations are not mentioned previously in Verse 1. So, when were they created? The written Torah does not say.

Torah commentators explain, often at great length, what things were like in the beginning, and the Oral Torah does fill in many of the blanks left in the written Torah. But one way or another, we see in Verse 2 that there is a state of void and chaos over an already existing darkness, deep and waters.

This description is summed up in the twenty-one words of these two verses. The twenty-one of Ehyeh is present. Ehyeh means "I will be." In the beginning, the state of the Earth, prior to the creation of Light, is in the potential state of "I will be." This again hints back to the relationship with Keter and its correlation to the Will of God. The primordial Earth is in the state that it is as ordained by the Will of God. This state is not static but flexible, subject to change, as we see with the introduction of Light, in the next verse.

"And God said, "Let there be light," and there was light. And God saw the light that it was good, and God separated between the light and between the darkness. And God called the light day, and the darkness He called night, and it was evening and it was morning, one day." Genesis 1:3-5

Twelve is also an important number throughout the Torah. We see it constantly repeated as the number of months, astrological signs, and of course, the number of the Tribes of Israel. If we look at the first twelve words beginning with Verse 3 that speaks about the creation of Light, we find something interesting that help us identify what exactly this Light is.

In the original Hebrew, this translation, *"And God said, "Let there be light," and there was light. And God saw the light that it was good"* has

וַיֹּאמֶר אֱלֹהִים יְהִי אוֹר וַיְהִי אוֹר:
וַיַּרְא אֱלֹהִים אֶת הָאוֹר כִּי טוֹב
ר״ת ויאיאיאיואיכ׳ט
ג׳ 67, ג׳ בינה

twelve words. Adding up the numerical value of the initial twelve letters of the twelve words (Reshei Tevot), we derive the numerical value of 67. This number is significant in that it is the numerical value of the word, Binah (understanding). Binah is the Name of the third Sefirah. Binah is the Source of the worlds of the Heavens (Yetzirah) and the Earth (Asiyah). Binah is the realm of the Supernal Mind, the Source of the Supernal Man (Zeir Anpin).

Binah is the "home" of the supernal higher Self souls which are called Neshamot. Binah is called the World to Come. Not only is it an afterlife for this life in this world, but it is also the final domain of all souls that have evolved through the lower domains of Yetzirah and Asiyah.

Even the standard commentator Rashi (note 4) mentions how this Light is not a physical light as we would understand it, but rather it is a special Light "put away" for the righteous in the Future to Come (the same as the World to Come). Many have asked what is the nature of this mysterious primal created Light. And now, by simply looking to the Reshei Tevot of the twelve words, we have our answer. Right from the beginning, we have concealed within the numerical value of letters, a subtle hint as to the nature of the Primal Light.

And remember this important fact! Knowledge of the Sefirot, and their Names and functions did not exist (in its present forms) in the days of Moses. While Moses knew the Hebrew word, Binah, he would not have associated it with the many concepts that we do today. Yes, Moses did not do this, but we today can do it, and we do!

From the beginning, the code is there. But the keys to unlock the code only came many centuries later. The Reshei Tevot always were numerically equal to 67, Binah, but it took many, many centuries for us to spiritually evolve in order for us to be able to understand (Binah), what exactly the hidden clue is there to suggest. While we had to wait centuries to unlock this code, the code was nevertheless there waiting to be unlocked. How many more codes, and more hints are waiting for us to discover the ways and means of their unlocking?

If we take the totality of the verses discussing the creation of the Primal Light (verses 3-5), we have a total of 31 words. Thirty-one is the numerical value of the Divine Name El, short for Elohim (the Creator), and the suffix found on the end of many angelic names (Mikha'el, Gavri'el). Light is also related to the Elim.

The Benei Elim (children of the Elim) are mentioned in Psalm 29:1. RaMBaM (in Y. T. 2:8) mentions the Benei Elohim (children of the Elohim) as the one of the ten species of angels. Is the presence of this species of angel hinted to here concealed with the telling of the creation of Light? These angels are the conduit for shining the

Primal Light in the Heavens (as we humans are here on Earth to perform the same task).

The Benei Elohim are clearly involved with human affairs, as is suggested by Job 1:6. And we see from Job that there is one specific angel who is amongst them who is called the Satan. Is he one of the Benei Elohim? We will address the subject of the Satan shortly. But first, let us finish with these initial verses in Genesis 1.

All in all Genesis 1:1-5 contains within it 52 words. Twenty-one words (Ehyeh) discuss the beginning phase of creation; thirty-one words (El) discuss the creation of Light. 52 is again one of those significant numbers that is well-known in the Kabbalah.

We have already learned that 26 is the numerical value of the Name of God YHWH. Also, any multiple of 26 equally relates to the holiness of the Name. The first 52 words of Genesis speak about creation in general, and then about the creation of Light, and nowhere in these verses is the Name of YHWH mentioned! But although its mention is not outright, its presence is there, however concealed.

Two times twenty-six (2 x 26) is 52. Concealed within the number of words is not just one reference to YHWH, but to two. Being that two topics are covered and that two other Names are concealed in the numbers (Ehyeh and El), it is no wonder then, that the Name YHWH would be present twice. Also, in later Kabbalah one of the expanded spellings of the Name YHWH (Havaya of Ben) has the value of 52. This is the Name of YHWH as it associates with the Asiyatic dimension, which is after all, the Earth spoken of here in the Genesis creation story.

Now, let us return to the topic of the Satan, whom we introduced above. Although there is no overt reference to such an angelic character in Genesis, the Serpent referenced in Genesis 3:1 has always been associated with him. Let us turn to the verse and see if we can discover any clues to his presence.

Genesis 3:1 says, *"Now the Nahash (serpent) was cunning, more than all the beasts of the field that the YHWH Elohim had made."*

We all know the Garden of Eden story. The serpent tempted Eve to eat of the forbidden fruit; she gave it to her husband; God got mad, and kicked the two of them out of Eden. A simple perusal of the surface telling of this story leaves the reader with incredible confusion! Here are some points to consider.

The verse clearly states that YHWH Elohim created the Nahash (serpent). Did God not know that the Nahash (serpent) was capable of doing his "dirty" deed when He created him? Why did YHWH Elohim create a Nahash (serpent) capable of doing what he did. Wouldn't it have been better to have created a lesser cunning creature?

When God created Eve, did He not realize that there was a flaw within her that would make her susceptible to the temptation of the Nahash (serpent)? Why did He create her in this way? He must have known the future, and could have taken the steps right away in her creation to have avoided it.

We can ask the same question with regards to the creation of Adam. When God created Adam, did He not foresee all that could and would happen with Eve and the Nahash? Why did God create things the way that He did knowing that these results would ensue?

If one would wish to claim that God gives man free-will to choose, and that in His All-Knowingness God knew that everything was to happen exactly the way that it did, then why go to all the trouble to set up the scenario, knowing full well the way it was going to end up?

Are we going to say that All-Knowing God didn't see what was coming? Did All-Knowing God not know that the Nahash was cunning, that Eve was naïve, and that Adam was weak? God created everyone the way that they were. God knows everything! He knew what He had created. He knew what could and what would happen. And God let everything unfold and happen just like we read in the Genesis narrative.

Make no mistake! God was behind it all. God created the players (Adam, Eve, and Nahash); God created the scenario (all three together in Eden); and All-Knowing God foresaw everything that was to happen. And He let it happen just the way it did!

We are left to question just how much free-will was really involved in all this!

From a surface reading of the text, either All-Knowing God was not all knowing and He was easily fooled by the Nahash (serpent) that He Himself had made, or God, the All-Knowing let it all happen like it did. I am certain that the latter is the truth. God created the scenario and the players to interact exactly as they did.

Knowing that the so-called "fall" in Eden was an "inside job," let us explore some aspects of the verse quoted above (Gen. 3:1) to glean some insights.

וְהַנָּחָשׁ הָיָה עָרוּם מִכֹּל וַיַּת הַשָּׂדֶה אֲשֶׁר עָשָׂה יְ"הֹ אֱלֹהִים
רי"ת ו'ה'ע'מ'ח'ה'א'ע'י'א   ג' 216 ג' אריה, ג רי"ו   [3 x 72]

In the original Hebrew, the portion of Genesis 3:1 quoted above has ten words in it. Let us look at the ten Reshei Tevot (initial letters) of those words. The Reshei Tevot (initial letters) of this verse gives us the numerical value of 216. This is a most important number in the Kabbalah, and its presence here in this verse is most revelatory.

216 is the numerical value of the Hebrew word Aryeh, which means "lion." This, in and of itself, has a significance related to the spirit of prophecy, but I will not address this issue here because it will take us away from more important insights.

216 is 3 x 72, and 72 is a most important number. 72 is the numerical value of Hesed, which is God's mercy. 216, in and of itself, is the numerical value of Gevurah, God's severity. 72 (Hesed) and 3x 72 (216, Gevurah) show how God's "right" and "left" Hands work together in harmony.

Nowhere is this more apparent than with what is considered to be the holiest Name of God, the 72 Triad Name. This is the awe-inspiring Name that is used by practitioners of the Prophetic Kabbalah for psychic ascents, and according to legend, the Name that has the Power to do almost anything.

And here with regards to the Nahash (serpent), which was not only made by Elohim, like the rest of creation, but was also made by YHWH, as was Adam. The Nahash was entrusted with a profoundly important role in creation. God created the Nahash to be a very cunning creature. This was no mistake, no accident, and not the choice of the Nahash. God made Him the way that He was (and is).

YHWH Elohim made the Nahash from the power of the 72 triad Name of God. And in this Name is both the Power of Divine Mercy (Hesed) and Divine Severity (Gevurah). God is thus in charge of all things in the reality which He has created. Centuries later, God revealed this exact teaching to the prophet Isaiah (45:6b-7), when He declared, *"I am YHWH and there is no other; who forms light and creates darkness, Who makes peace and creates evil; I, YHWH, make all these."*

God created the Nahash, knowing full well what it was capable of, and what it was going to do. And God let it happen! As for the why of this story, this would take us into some of the deeper teachings and secrets of the Kabbalah. This is not the time nor place to discuss such details, but there is one such detail that is most relevant here, and this will provide for us a revelation into the true identity and mission of the Nahash.

The numerical value of the word Nahash is 358. There is another very significant word that shares this numerical value. This word is Mashiah (messiah). This association has not gone unnoticed over the centuries, and it has led to many questions and many revelations. Some opine that it will take the Mashiah (358) to fully rectify the damage caused by the Nahash (358). This is a good understanding. However, there is more.

The Nahash, as we see is associated with Gevurah (216), which is the "left" Hand of God. Many Kabbalists opine that we are presently living in an epoch (Shemitah) of time dominated by the Sefirah Gevurah. This is why our present cycle of human evolution and civilization is marked by violence, bloodshed, and other forces of darkness and evil. This is the "evil" that God has created. In this epoch, evil is used by God as much as is good to accomplish the Divine plan.

In this Gevurah epoch of time (Shemitah), Hesed and Gevurah, God's "right" and "left" Hands work together. This is the meaning of Isaiah 45:7 (quoted above). So, the Nahash, while working evil, is nevertheless performing the Will of Heaven. God ordained it to be this way. This is our inevitable conclusion after a thorough study of the Eden narrative.

Mashiah (358) is to come to bring the peace, to offset and rebalance the evil brough by the Nahash (358). When this is actualized, God's purpose in this cycle of creation will be complete. Even the Nahash and all that is within him will be restored to balance.

The Kabbalists use this source in the Torah to boldly say that when Mashiah comes all is to be rectified. The "all" will include everything that is evil, including all souls, even those of the archetypally evil, Kayin, Esau, and the Nahash himself.

One of the teachings of the Kabbalists on this subject is as follows. Through the centuries, the Satan accuser, who worked through the Nahash has been identified to be an angel by the name of Samael. This name is spelled with four Hebrew letters, Samekh, Mem, Alef, and Lamed. When the Mashiah comes, the Kabbalists say that Samael will be no more. And what is God going to do to him? God is going to remove the Mem from his name Samael, and leave it to be Sa'el (Samekh, Alef, Lamed). What the uninitiated do not know is that the name Sa'el (Samekh, Alef, Lamed) is one of the 72 triads of the Great Name. That which made Samael to be Samael will be no more. He will be transformed from something evil into something good. And thus evil, and accusations will cease forever.

All of this is hinted to with the numerical values of words, and Reshei Tevot. How many more secrets lie hidden in the Torah text unseen to our eyes simply because we do not yet know how to see.

The entire order, plan, and directions for the universe was preordained long before these things came into physical manifestation. As such all of creation operates in accordance to a master plan. The universe is thus like one great complex machine. There are many parts, but each part fits into its own right place, and not anywhere else.

Adam, Eve, Eden, Nahash and Mashiah are all integral parts of the machine's operations. We can see what we can see about the great Divine plan, and then only speculate about the rest that we cannot see. And what we cannot see is far, far, greater than what we can ever see. God has made it so in this Shemitah of Gevurah.

We have looked at the Keter, at Binah, and even at the 72 Triads. We can see that there is far more to Torah than meets the eye. Ancient ex-slaves wandering in a desert could not have crafted such a Torah as this one, encoded with all so many secrets, the likes of which, we have only touched the service. This indicates, if not proves that the Torah is not of ancient human origins. It is clearly a work that is from out of this world.

We need to reevaluate our relationship with Torah, at all its levels, and learn to recognize how it is our path to our future, even as it has been our doorway into the distant past.

Chapter 5

Lessons About the Pre-Adamic Civilizations

Is Tomorrow's Twilight Yesterday?

What if? Let's take a walk down a very pessimistic road into the future.

The modern global situation does not look especially positive. We all know what many of the problems are. What if?

What if we prove to be unsuccessful in addressing those issues that are tearing our world apart? Let's say that sometime in the next decade or two, global conflicts spiral out of control. Let's say the worst case scenario does indeed manifest. Global thermonuclear war.

In the devastating destruction of this apocalypse, 90% of the world population dies. At our present global population of 7 billion, the loss of 90% of the human population would still leave us with 700 million to rebuild what was destroyed.

Now, let's add insult to injury. Let's say that the global nuclear war triggers massive climate change. What type doesn't matter. What does matter is that compounded with the devastating nuclear fallout, Mother Nature's wrath wreaks havoc on the remaining human beings. Of the 700 million remaining after the nuclear war, another 90% of the survivors are soon dead.

After a period of a few years, only 70 million human beings are left alive. Essentially, in a few short years humanity has experienced an extinction event that has wiped out 99% of the human species.

But this is clearly NOT THE END.

70 million human beings are still a significant number. They can rebuild and rebuild they will! Yet, the Earth that they knew, and loved has been drastically altered. They will not be able to simply repair all that was broken, forget the past, and move forward. No, these survivors will be pioneers. It will be incumbent upon them to build a whole new society from scratch.

Everything will have to be newly defined. Granted, the first generation of survivors will try to keep alive the best of the old world, but after a few generations, the new population will have no direct memory of the past world. By their time, even the oldest of the original survivors will have passed on. The only thing that will be left will be the legends, and the ruins of the past. What the new generations will do with the legends of the past remains to be seen.

But let's change gears to speak about THE OTHER SURVIVORS.

It is well known that certain governments have been planning for Doomsday for decades. It is alleged that the US, Europeans, and Chinese each have massive underground support bunkers that can hold tens of thousands of survivors. These highly classified underground bunkers are more like entire underground cities. They are set up to be completely independent, and self-sufficient. They are capable of keeping alive their population of tens of thousands, and even have room for growth.

More than just surviving, these underground cities are equipped with the latest of technology. They have research labs, factories and more. While civilization might be wiped off the surface of the planet, civilization will not only survive, but it will also continue to thrive, and grow in its new underground environments.

And so, DECADES, and even CENTURIES can pass. Those surviving on the surface would have no idea about the existence of those in the underground cities. Those in the underground cities will be focused on their own needs, and growth. Reclaiming the surface might not be a viable option for them, for numerous reasons. As their technology expands and grows, so too does their population. If they cannot return to the surface of the Earth, then they just might focus technological development on space travel to find for themselves another Earth.

The underground cities were originally set up to be the continuation of human advancement. They will indeed serve this purpose. Yet, in a century or more, even these cities will need to expand. And so, to the stars humanity goes. Over the years, the scientists have developed successful faster than light space travel. They have discovered not only one new Earth, but many. The underground cities of the Americans, Europeans and Chinese have long ago put their differences aside, pooled their resources, and have been working together for decades. They each discover different new worlds, and they each embark to the stars to colonize each their own planet.

As the decades go by, more and more planets are discovered, and colonized. Within three hundred years since the Earth apocalypse, the underground survivors are now thriving on new Earths. Their populations swell into the millions. Their cultures, and civilization have adapted, and evolved so much that they too have only a faint recollection about life on the old mother planet, Earth. Their only knowledge of the old world comes from the lessons in ancient history, taught in their schools. In the future, they will learn about old Earth, in the same way that today we learn about ancient Greece, or Rome.

Let's skip ahead centuries. It is now the year 3022 A.D., one thousand years from today.

Humanity has been among the stars for centuries. Hundreds of planets have been colonized. An actual United Federation of Planets has been established and has served as the Galactic government for centuries. Let's keep things simple for now, and not bring into the scenario the other non-human extraterrestrial races that we will encounter among the stars. Everything in the universe looks pretty nice, with a bright and promising future.

There is however, one small problem. Mother Earth! What shall we do with our mother planet?

Over the centuries, the underground cities have been updated, and maintained. Earth has never been completely abandoned. Regular movement from the underground cities to the stars has gone on for centuries. Granted, not many stay in the underground cities anymore. They serve more as outposts than as anything else. One specific function the underground cities perform is to monitor life on the surface. They watch, and observe the surface survivors, and how they have managed to overcome all the adversities of environment, and culture building.

Surface humanity is primitive again. Technology is long gone. Even the legends of the old world have been shrouded with myth, and superstition. Yet, in spite of some unique evolutionary changes that the surface survivors have developed, they are, after all, still human beings. They really should be reintegrated back into the greater family of humanity.

With the advanced technology of 3022 A.D., cleaning up whatever damage remains on the surface of old Earth is an easy thing. Yet, to just swarm in, and to begin the cleanup would shock the surface people to their core. They never knew about the underground survivors of the old apocalypse. After so many centuries they do not even remember the old apocalypse, all the more so has all memory of the old world been long forgotten.

For the surface survivors, all that they know is that they are all alone in the universe. To expose to them the ancient truth so bluntly, and overtly would be a shock that they could not endure. Therefore, the advanced humans on the new Earths will devise a plan how to introduce new elements, and new ideas into the primitive Earth cultures, to prepare them for the eventual reunion of the human race.

Volunteers are selected. They will disguise themselves as surface dwellers of the old Earth and go live among them. These undercover volunteers will become teachers, and guides, philosophers, and scientists, to slowly reintroduce the old, lost ways to the people. This will be a long and hard road.

Culture building can and does take centuries. Nevertheless, in coordination with the underground city outposts, and in league with the United Federation of Planets, the volunteers who come to live with the surface dwellers of old Earth slowly but surely begin to steer the new surface civilization towards the values they will need to eventually be ready to meet their long lost brothers, to reintegrate with them, and to bring old mother Earth into modern times, as a full-fledged member of the UFP.

It is, after all, the least our space brothers can do. It is essentially, their obligation to reclaim, and remake the Earth.

By the year 4022 A.D., the plan to direct the surface survivors has been moving along excellently. Their civilization has advanced. Technology has been introduced, and they are slowly but surely beginning to unlock the secrets of the universe and are themselves beginning to look towards space. Yet, no one has told them about the ancient past. No one has told them about the underground bases monitoring their progress, or their brothers in space who are directing the entire endeavor. All things will be revealed in its time when everybody will be properly prepared to receive the truth. The revelation of these things is not deemed to be immediately important. These revelations can wait for yet a future date.

Now, here is the BIG QUESTION.

Is this what is going to happen in the year 4022 A.D., in two thousand years from now.

OR!

Did this already happen in 14,022 B.C., sixteen thousand years ago?

We can easily change the names of the US, Europe, and China to Atlantis, Lemuria, and Mu. Is this scenario a description of our ancient past, and not necessarily our distant future?

What if this were true?

What if all the great minds to have dawned on Earth, guiding, and directing human civilization have all been in touch, in one way or another, with our own space brothers, who today we would no longer recognize as being human like ourselves. While we might not recognize them, they have never stopped recognizing, and caring for us.

What if this were true?

If this is indeed true, then the ancient alien theory would have to be adjusted. For the ancient aliens, would not be aliens at all. They would, in actuality, be us! Maybe that is exactly who they are today? If this is indeed true, then it will explain so very much.

Now, here is an interesting fact. According to the legends of the Sitrei Torah (secrets of the Torah), this is indeed true. The ancient legends portray this scenario about an ancient, and long forgotten apocalyptic war that wiped out almost all of an ancient, technologically highly advanced humanity. The survivors went underground, and to the stars. Those who remained on the surface fell back into a primitive state. The secrets of the Torah were safeguarded to protect our ancient history, and to ensure the survival of our forgotten truths.

When the time comes, the ancient secrets will be exposed, and the truth will be known. When that day comes, we will be reunited with our long lost brothers and sisters and learn from the many wonders that they have discovered over the many centuries that they have been away from us.

What if this is true? Think about it.

"The domestic animals of the past epoch (Shemitah), they are the human beings of this epoch (Shemitah). Abel was their shepherd, and (thus) returned to shepherd sheep, as it is written. Moses [too] was a shepherd.

The days of those people of that epoch (Shemitah), which is the epoch (Shemitah) of Abraham (mercy), it is said about them, "like the days of a tree are the days of my people." They were very long. They ate of the fruit of the tree.

However the people of this epoch (Shemitah), which is the epoch (Shemitah) of Pahad (fear), they are the sheep of that other epoch

(Shemitah). Sheep eat only the fruit of the ground, therefore, they were commanded not to eat of the fruit of the tree. Therefore, they do not have length of days.

The children of Amram of that epoch (Shemitah) were like angels, and Moses was of that epoch (Shemitah). Therefore, Moses ascended to Heaven because he was an angel."

Yalkut Reuveni (Vol. 3, Arakhim), Shemitah 1
(Jerusalem, Vagshal edition, 1998, page 468)

Secrets of our Ancient Past
Have Mashiah and the Resurrection of the Dead Already Happened??

The wisdom of Heaven is always profound, but sometimes it is also shocking. Wise King Solomon said that "there is nothing new under the sun." Little do most of us realize just how profound and how in-depth a statement this is.

Nothing new under the sun tells us that what happens in life seems to happen in cycles, with one cycle being not so different from the next. We look at the Solomon's statement apply it to nature and understand it without difficulty. As King Solomon wrote, generations come, and generations go. The sun rises and the sun sets. Life goes on, through good times and bad.

But today we live in different times. Today we have modern technology, computers, space travel, nuclear energy, and nuclear warheads. We have conquered the entire surface of the planet. And certainly, life today is quite different from how it was just one hundred years ago. Can we still say that there is nothing new under the sun? Isn't what we have developed today in modern society new? Isn't how we live today different from any time in the past, ever?

Well, is it? Are we really different from our past, from a very distant past forgotten long ago? Is King Solomon correct? Was there a distant past not too dissimilar from our present? Is it possible that there really isn't anything new under the sun, including all the technologies of today?

149

There are many strange realities all around us whose origins are shrouded in mystery. There are many anomalies that challenge our present concepts of the age of humanity, and outright challenge our understandings of human history, and development.

Most who come and read the Biblical creation stories in early Genesis, often misunderstand the texts to be literal renditions of a historical account. Biblical scholars know differently. A literal rendition of Biblical chronology makes us think that the Earth, and all the universe is merely a few thousand years ago. Reality slaps us in the face with uncountable pieces of evidence that proves the opposite. The actual age of the universe does not prove the Bible wrong. All it proves is that our literal understandings of the Bible are wrong.

The Bible comes to us from a Source far beyond our human understanding. We should not be surprised that what it contains is also beyond human understanding. When we come and read the Bible, we extract from it much understanding, this of course is true. Yet, what we understand cannot compare to that which we do not.

The Bible tells us the stories about Adam, Noah, the Flood, about Abraham, Isaac and Jacob, the Exile in Egypt, and the Exodus under Moses. We read about the building of Solomon's Temple, its destruction, and even more exile. We read prophecies about the coming of the Messiah, the resurrection of the dead, and the renewal of the world. What if, like King Solomon said, that there is nothing new under the sun, and that all of this has already happened, from the beginning unto the end. What if the Messiah has already come, along with the resurrection of the dead, and the renewal of the world? What if this has already happened in the long distant past, to a long forgotten human civilization.

Yes, what if?

The anomalies are all around us. Yet, we always seek to ignore them or to dismiss them. We are not ready to acknowledge the reality of a long-lost ancient highly advanced human technological civilization, which in many ways, may indeed have been superior to our own.

And we turn to our religions, and ask, if there was such an ancient civilization wouldn't our religious literature reveal it to us? Those uneducated in religious literature will proclaim that there is nothing in religion to verify these claims. But those who are educated in religious literature know very well that the opposite is true.

So, without no further delay, let me introduce to you a piece of religious literature that will make statements, the likes of which are shocking to say the least. Let me introduce you to a small Kabbalistic text, titled, **U'me'Sheleg Albin** (Like Snow I Will Be Whitened), authored by R. Sa'id Ibn Albin, student of R. Eli.

In the brief translations I make here, you will find fantastic claims on behalf of the author. Yet, these claims are not his own. Like a true Kabbalist, he received his lessons from his master, who in turn received it from his, and on and on back through the generations. It has always been well known amongst the Kabbalistic Sages that our present human civilization is not the first to have developed here on Earth. What is shocking is that what we believe to be unique to ourselves, and our history, is not unique at all.

Here are the relevant selections from the text. At the end of this essay, I will include images of the full text for those who wish to engage the original source.

"Know this: that the previous Shemitah (Cosmic Sabbatical) was of Abraham [the Sefirat Hesed]. And in this Shemitah there was [a previous] Adam HaRishon (the first man), a Noah, a generation of the flood, and the a generation of separation (those who built the Tower of Babel), [a previous] Abraham, Isaac, Jacob and Israel, and [a previous] Israel [who] were enslaved in Egypt, who went forth from there and received the Torah by the hands of Moses, [they previously] built a Holy Temple, which was destroyed, and [a previous] Israel [was] exiled, and [a previous] Mashiah came, and there was [for them] the resurrection of the dead. Afterwards the world was destroyed." [All this already happened in the previous Shemitah, before our own].

"And then came the Shemitah of Isaac [the Sefirat Gevurah, our present epoch]. This is the secret of the verse, "the world is built upon mercy," meaning that the previous world (epoch) was the Shemitah of Abraham. In that epoch the name of Moses was Mahesh. And now he came into this Shemitah of Isaac. And know that the Israel that was in that Shemitah became angels. And the angels became sefirot, and the sefirot [became] Havayot [permutations of YHWH]. And with the Havayot was the [new] world created. This is the secret of "and he gazed and behold three men were surrounding him." Abraham recognized that in the first Shemitah they were men, who now had become angels."

"And know my brother, that the nations (goyim) that were in the first Shemitah, they are [now the] Israel of this Shemitah."

The entire history of Israel, including the coming of Mashiah and the resurrection of the dead have already happened, in full, to those human beings who lived before us. As shocking as this revelation may be to some, it is a validation to others, others including myself. I wrote about the Pre-Adamic civilizations in my book, **Aliens, Angels and Demons**. In my **Disclosure Essays**, available in the **Second Edition**, I discussed many secrets with regards to this. I encourage the interested reader to acquire my book, and to reference the sources therein.

It is truly profound that we see that there is a higher plan to human life and evolution. All things happen for a purpose. We can also understand now why what we think are aliens and extraterrestrials have such an interest in humanity. They are not alien! They are us! And this Earth was their old home. We are their younger siblings. This is how come members of this group called in Genesis, the Benei Elohim, could come down to Earth, be attracted to human women, and have children with them.

There are many secrets hidden from most of us. What is revealed here is only a drop in the bucket. As the past Shemitah went through the cycle through the prism of the Sefirah Hesed, we are now going through the same cycle through the prism of the Sefirah Gevurah. Once we finish our cycle, human civilization will again be rebooted from scratch. Whether this will occur through natural disasters, or by overt human hands, we will have to wait and see.

In the previous Shemitah, their civilization ended with an intergalactic nuclear holocaust. Mars was not always the way it is now. It was once richly inhabited. And there was once a whole planet once between Mars and Jupiter. We don't know how it was destroyed, but we see the evidence of it. The evidence of a prehistoric nuclear war here on Earth is numerous. But this war was not fought by aliens, it was fought by us, our ancestors.

And so, the secrets go. Yes, there is much for us yet to discover. And those who merit to access the secrets of Torah, gain access to those of our ancestors that now serve as Divine messengers, angels. We can access them and also many others, those who reside inside this Hollow Earth. But this is a lesson for another time.

Contemplate these truths and you will understand the wisdom of King Solomon. Contemplate some more and you will understand what the future holds for us, both the distant future, and the immanent immediate. In our literature, we have lessons that reveal much about the Shemitot that are coming. Let it now suffice for us to learn what is already before us.

Pre-Adamic Civilizations in the Teachings of the Sages
Secret of the Kabbalistic Shemitot

"For six years you shall plow your fields, but the seventh year shall be holy to YHWH, in that year you shall do no work." Lev. 25:3-4

One of the most controversial teachings among Kabbalists is the doctrine of the Shemita(ot), the cosmic Sabbatical epochs of pre-Adamic times.

According to many of the great Rabbis, Adam was not the first human to have walked the earth. These Rabbis teach that there were full pre-Adamic human civilizations that had arisen, and were eventually destroyed.

Among the earlier generations of Kabbalists, prior to the Ari'zal (R. Yitzhak Luria of Safed, d. 1572), the doctrine of the Shemita was written about by all Kabbalists, including the Ari'zal's Kabbalistic teacher, Rabbi David Ibn Zimra. These Kabbalists taught that not only is the source for doctrine of the Shemita to be found in the Oral tradition, but they also went directly into the simple and plain words of the Torah text to show that the history of time is not fully told in the Bible.

In the very beginning it is written, *"In the beginning God created the Heavens and the Earth"* (Gen. 1:1). Immediately, the following verse states, *"And the Earth was without form and empty"* (Gen. 1:2). The Kabbalists have noticed that the prophet Isaiah has written (45:18) that *"the Earth was not created empty,"* revealing an apparent contradiction between Genesis, and Isaiah. Yet, as it is known to every faithful believer of Torah, there can be no contradictions between what Genesis says, and what Isaiah says.

Something, however, is definitely missing. For when God created the Earth it was not empty upon its creation, as per Isaiah. How then did the Earth become empty, as related in Gen.1:2? This leads us to the inevitable conclusion that something is missing; not that part of the text is missing, but rather something has been intentionally left out of the narrative. This is glaringly obvious to any student of the Bible.

I have even spoken to one ex-Christian minister, (now an Orthodox Jew) who, upon learning about this anomaly, had mentioned that he had heard of this before from reading Christian Biblical commentaries. Therefore, it seems that we have a mystery, the secret solution of which, of course, is known to the Rabbis and Kabbalists.

In the Midrash (Gen. R. 3:7), a question is posed as to what was God occupied with, prior to His creation of our world? The Midrash relates that God was busy building and destroying other worlds.

It is written in Leviticus that, *"for six years you shall plow your fields, but the seventh year shall be holy to YHWH, in that year you shall do no work."* It is also taught by our Sages in the Talmud (San.

98A), *"six thousand years shall the world last, then for one thousand years shall it remain desolate."* Our Sages have learned from the secret meaning of the verse in Leviticus that the days of our world, meaning our civilization, will be measured in the same way, as is the Biblical Sabbatical year. Six years shall we labor, and in the seventh shall we rest. So, our civilization will grow for six thousand years, and then for a thousand years shall it *"remain desolate"* which means to be left alone to rest. After this time, it is said that God renews his creation.

The Bible proceeds to speak about the Jubilee year. We are instructed to count seven times seven years, and then to proclaim a Jubilee, a year of complete release. The Kabbalists have revealed that just as our civilization will last for the Sabbatical period of six thousand years, and one thousand years of desolation, so will there be seven cycles similar to this, corresponding to a cosmic cycle of Sabbaticals, and Jubilee. Therefore, according to this calculation, human civilization will rise and fall seven times, each for a period of six thousand years, with a rest period of a thousand years between.

Now arises the question, which Sabbatical are we in today? Many Kabbalists look back to the verse in Genesis and notice the discrepancy. They answer the problem of the emptiness of the land (Gen. 1:2), when this was not the way it was created (Is. 45:18), by saying that we are not in the first Shemita. The earth was indeed created full. It only became empty as a result of the previous civilization. They are the ones who left the land *"empty and desolate."* According to many of the Kabbalists, therefore, we are in the second Shemita.

Rabbi Yisrael Lifshitz, author of the authoritative commentary to the Mishna, Tiferet Yisrael, addresses the topic of pre-Adamic life in the introduction to the eleventh chapter of Tractate Sanhedrin. Drawing upon what was the scientific discoveries of his day, and the Darwinian conflict between creationism and evolution, Lifshitz points out that the Torah does acknowledge the existence of dinosaurs. These were the creations of the prior Shemita, he says.

Not only this, but Rabbi Lifshitz goes further to say that Adam was not really the first human being, but that there were countless people before him, which he calls pre-Adamites. This controversial view of Rabbi Lifshitz has placed his commentary, and other written works, on the taboo list in certain Jewish circles, who considered his revelations not in accordance with the spirit of Judaism. Needless to say, nothing could be further from the truth.

The Talmud, in Hagigah 13B, speaks of there being 974 pre-Adamic generations. One of the early Kabbalistic classics, the **Ma'arekhet Elokut**, states specifically that these generations refer to the pre-Adamic Shemita cycles. There are a great number of both earlier, and later generation Rabbis, Hasidic masters and Kabbalists who have spoken quite openly about the doctrine of the Shemita. With regards to the Shemitot, Rabbi Shmuel Lifshitz opens his discussion of the matter in his **Anafim Shatul Mayim** commentary to **Sefer HaIkarim** by saying, *"[I] open my mouth like a talebearer to reveal hidden secrets."*

Not everyone, however, accepted the doctrine of the Shemitot. Rabbi Haim Vital in his Sha'ar Ma'amrei Rashbi (44A) says outright that the doctrine of the Shemitot is Kabbalistically incorrect. Many later Kabbalists (such as R. Yehuda Fatiyah), follow Rabbi Haim's position on this. Nonetheless, many more do not.

In his Beit Lekhem Yehuda (2,66A), Rabbi Yehuda Fatiyah wrote questioning certain aspects of the doctrine of the Shemita. Yet, even Rabbi Fatiyah, in Minhat Yehuda (pg. 222), expounds on a section of the Zohar that speaks of the pre-Adamic parents of Adam. He even states that Adam's parents copulated on the "spiritual plane," that his mother conceived, and gave birth to Adam's body, which was completely non-physical. Where Adam's parents came from, Rabbi Fatiyah does not say. However, he makes it quite clear that they are individual beings, and not simply a symbolic, metaphorical reference to God.

Rabbi Aryeh Kaplan has written on this topic of the Shemitot and pointed out correctly that Kabbalistic learning does not follow the same line of reasoning, and authority as does Halakhic learning. Whereas in Halakha there is need of an authoritative conclusion to decide proper practice, this is not the case with Kabbalah. Therefore, although Rabbi Hayim Vital himself did not accept the teachings of the Kabbalistic Shemitot, this in no way makes his words the final authority, even more so seeing that almost every other master Kabbalist, before him, and after him, disagreed with him on this matter.

Interesting to note is the **Sha'at Ratzon** commentary on the **Tikunei Zohar** (36). The author, R. Shlomo Kohen, is one of the great later generation Kabbalists of the Rabbi Haim Vital/Rashash school. He is also the author of the authoritative commentary to Rabbi Vital's Etz Haim, Yafeh Sha'ah.

In his commentary to the Tikunei Zohar (36), Rabbi Kohen comments on the clear reference made there to the Shemitot, and then mentions Rabbi Vital's objections to this view. Rabbi Kohen then elucidates a brilliant compromise how the view of the ancients, and the view of Rabbi Vital can be synthesized.

Thus, no present day student of Kabbalah should be so quick to dismiss the doctrine of the Shemitot out of hand based on the comments of Rabbi Haim Vital. For as we see, they are open to various interpretations. Indeed, even the Gaon of Vilna in his commentary to the Tikunei Zohar (36) clearly states that the text is speaking about the pre-Adamic Shemitot.

No one in the Torah faithful, Kabbalistic community today would even consider the idea that R. Hayim Vital would hold onto a position on a topic that would outright contradict the Zohar. The entire system of Lurianic Kabbalah, pioneered by none other than R. Vital himself, would thus be compromised. The solution offered by R. Kohen thus becomes an important, and necessary reconciliation.

Those who are not Orthodox Jews may not recognize the following names, yet it is important to document them. This is only a partial list of those Rabbis and Kabbalists, from the earlier and later generations, which held that the doctrine of the Shemita is correct and true:

1. Sefer HaTemunah,

2. Sefer HaKana,

3. RaMBaN,

4. Rabbeynu Bahya,

5. Rabbi Yitzhak D'Min Acco,

6. Recanati on the Torah,

7. Tziyuni on the Torah,

8. Ma'arekhet Elokut,

9. Shatul Mayim on Sefer HaIkarim,

10. Sefer Livnat HaSapir of Rabbi David ben Yehuda HaHasid (Sefardi),

11. Sefer Shoshan Sodot,

12. Radbaz, Rabbi David Zimra (the Kabbalistic teacher of the Ari'zal),

13. Tekhelet Mordechai,

14. Rabbi Lifshitz's Tiferet Yisrael

15. Rabbi Tzvi Hirsch Eichenstein of Zidatchov *in his Ateret Tzvi commentary on the Zohar HaRakia,*

16. Rabbi Eliyahu, the Gaon of Vilna

17. Tikunei Zohar 36

This is only a partial list. Many Orthodox Jewish readers will recognize that these names are giants in the world of Jewish learning, and that they are the pillars upon which our Torah traditions rest. To say that all these giants of Torah are incorrect, because of the words of one rabbi kabbalist, regardless of that rabbi kabbalists stature, is to both dishonor these Rabbis, and the Torah itself. The legitimacy of the pre-Adamic worlds is firmly established in authoritative Torah literature.

Rabbi Tzvi Hirsch Eichenstein, in his commentary Ateret Tzvi (126B) on the book Zohar HaRakia, states that although the Ari'zal himself was silent on this matter, he definitely ascribed to the doctrine of the Shemita and that *"God forbid anyone would disagree with the holy Sages of Israel."*

As controversial as the idea of pre-Adamic civilization may be to some, we can rest assured that it is a known, and warmly embraced authoritative teaching of our Torah tradition

The Parallel Worlds of the Shemitot

Energy fields are real. Science has proven this.

The Ten Sefirot are energy fields. Science may also know the reality of these, although they be called by other names.

Each Sefirah and sub-Sefirah energy field generates its own construct reality.

In other words, each Sefirah and sub-Sefirah generates its own universe.

Each Sefirah and sub-Sefirah resides next to one another in accordance to the Secret of the Sefirot of the Igulim.

Each Sefirotic energy universe lies in space-time right next to its neighbor. These are the parallel worlds.

Each world developed differently based upon its Sefirotic energy signature.

Thus we have multiple parallel Earths, each with its own history that unfolded due to its individual dominant Sefirotic influence.

Each Sefirotic influence is called that world's Shemitah (cosmic sabbatical).

Each dimensional world begins with a different Sefirotic energy signature and follows its course of development and evolution based its source.

In this way, God sees all His multiple worlds simultaneously.

God sees all His Sefirot and sub-Sefirot as the whole pattern of His Tree of Life. In God's Eyes all the multiple worlds are one.

Here in our world, at this time, we are experiencing the Epoch of the Shemitah of Gevurah.

This Gevurah energy signature acts upon the human beings of this dimension, and serves as the source of what we call the Yetzer HaRa.

We all see the results of human beings who succumb to the influence of the Yetzer HaRa.

But this is not the case in all the worlds.

In the dimensional world next to ours, the Shemitah of Tiferet is in influence.

In that dimensional world, the one right next to ours, there never was, and thus there is not now, a Yetzer HaRa.

The source influence of that universe is very different from ours, and it has always been this way.

In the world parallel to ours, without a Yetzer HaRa to influence its development, the entire domain evolved radically different from our own.

In the world parallel to ours, without a Yetzer HaRa, life evolved without negativity, people never harmed one another, and nature never harmed anyone either.

In comparison to our world of Gevurah, the world of Tiferet is like paradise.

The world of Tiferet is not a future thing. It is a "now" thing for those who know how to open a vortex and to travel from one world to its parallel neighbor.

Someone from here going there would instantly leave behind the Gevurah influence and succumb to the Tiferet influence.

This would lead to the immediate cessation of Yetzer HaRa, and thus evil and the desire for wrongful things would be eliminated upon arrival.

The secret of the vortex locations is well guarded by those in the know.

Those who use their Yetzer HaRa to penetrate this secret and to go where they do not belong always discover that they are not welcome there. The powers that be in that place block entry to those who do not belong.

But there are others that can be granted entry, and from time to time are granted entry. Usually once granted entry, they are not granted permission to exit to any other Gevurah-based place.

In times of crises and trouble, those on the other side of the vortex reach out to those on this side who deserve not to be here, and invite them to come to the parallel world.

As the force of Gevurah increases here as the course of events unfolds as prophesied, more and more ready souls will be contacted and invited upon a journey.

As for who is who, these things are not known in the Gevurah universe. But those in the Tiferet universe do know, and they will act when the time is right.

As for us, our job is to lessen the influence of the Gevurah Yetzer HaRa energy field upon our thoughts, upon our hearts, and upon our actions.

The reason for this revelation is simply to let everyone know, that everyone has a change to improve oneself.

Everyone can go beyond Gevurah and into the Tiferet. For Tiferet is the home of the Torah, and is ruled by the Holy One, blessed be He.

Fear not the coming darkness. Resist it and detach from it.

Let your wisdom and understanding be your guide.

Chapter 6

Secrets of the Inner Earth
& the True Location of Eden

There is a great mystery concealed in the Torah story about Avraham's burial of his wife Sarah.

This mystery is not just another boring mystical mumbo-jumbo philosophical religious lesson that makes us want to yawn. No, this mystery is about a geological and geographical reality, spoken about for centuries in Torah literature and echoed in the literature of numerous cultures from around the world.

What I am speaking about is the Garden of Eden being a real physical place and the secret of its actual location.

So, where is the Garden you may ask? And who is living there now? In order to answer these questions, let us delve into Torah, to the time of Sarah's death and to the place of her burial, the "double" Cave of Makhpelah in Hevron.

The Torah story is well known. Sarah, Avraham's beloved wife, mother of Yitzhak passes away at the ripe old age of 127. Avraham, wealthy as he is, still does not own any property in his newly adopted homeland then called Canaan (modern day Israel).

In those days, there were no cemeteries. The dead were usually placed in caves which were sealed and protected as family tombs. Avraham sought to purchase such a cave for a family inheritance, where in later he would be buried alongside his sons and grandsons. Indeed, this we know is what happened and the Cave of the Patriarchs in Hevron is still a venerated place to this very day.

Now, of all the caves in the area, why did Avraham choose this specific one, which we know as Makhpelah? While the written Torah text does not delve into the issue (written Torah seldom delves into any issues), the Oral Tradition dating back to those days brings to us tremendous details, without which much of the written Torah will never be understood. The Oral Torah relates a story retold in many Torah commentaries. It goes something like this.

According to the Midrashic legend, which may or may not be historical, Avraham was out tending sheep one day when one of them ran off. He followed it through the hills and into a cave. Upon entering the cave Avraham was overwhelmed by the sweet fragrances coming out from deep within the cave. He enters deeper and to his surprise he founds that there is a second cave inside the first one and inside this second cave lay buried a man and a woman whose bodies had not decomposed at all. Amazed at this sight, Avraham prays to God for answers, what is this place and who is buried here. The male body then sits up and speaks, saying to Avraham that he his Adam and that this cave is the entrance way to Garden of Eden. This cave was the cave of Makhpelah and this episode was why Avraham specifically wanted it to for his own tomb, for himself, and his loved ones to follow. So goes the story.

Now, let us put legend aside and ask the necessary questions. If there is any legitimacy to Makhpelah being an entrance way to Eden, how it this physically possible? Gardens are placed where trees grow and flora flourishes. But these require the light of the sun in order for them to grow. We all know that caves are holes in the Earth, some rather deep, some going for miles and miles, and yet what they all share is that they are deep underground without any exposure to sunlight. One cannot have a Garden growing in a cave. How then is the cave of Makhpelah the entrance way to the Garden of Eden? Where on Earth is the Garden, or maybe better to ask where off the surface of the Earth is the Garden.

Torah Sages have forever acknowledged that the Garden of Eden is a physical location somewhere here on Earth. Since the earliest times, Makhpelah Cave has been associated with the Garden and is acknowledged to be the entrance way. Again, if there is more than legend to any of this, then we must ask: where is the Garden? To answer this we must delve into one of the greatest secrets guarded by the Sages of Torah. There is no better way to reveal it other than by being direct and outright.

There is an Inner Earth and the Garden of Eden is at the center of the Earth thousands of miles down, directly underneath the Cave of Makhpelah. The astounding proclamation is stated every so clearly in the Zohar and in other ancient sources.

The existence of Inner Earth should come as a surprise to no one. Such knowledge has long been known in ancient cultures for thousands of years, even expanding across the oceans. Even the ancient Native American Hopis know of these places. Even in the realm of science there have been some famous names who embraced what has become known as the Hollow Earth theory. Such scientists include amongst others Sir Edmund Haley, famous for the comet named after his discovery Haley's comet.

The existence of Inner or Hollow Earth is much more than a mere theological statement made by the Torah Sages. There have been numerous encounters between surface dwelling human beings and the numerous other types of life that inhabit the inner realms. Not all such encounters have been benign.

Our Sages have outlined that Inner Earth is actually divided up in seven sections which in Hebrew are called the Sheva Artzot. These are enumerated in detail in the Zohar (Hashmetut 1, 254a); Hesed L'Avraham 2,4 and Emek HaMelekh, Sha'ar 21. The Garden of Eden is said to be only one of the many locations in Inner Earth.

The Zohar teaches that it was here that Adam materialized on Earth; it was from the center-most domain (Eden) in Inner Earth that he was cast out; it was in other domains in Inner Earth that he lived and that Kayin and Abel were born.

It is stated that Adam left numerous other progenies throughout Inner Earth over the centuries of his life.

The Zohar says that many who escaped the destruction of the Tower of Babel did so by relocating to Inner Earth.

Inner Earth has long been said to be the domain of the fallen angels and the Nephilim mentioned in Genesis 6.

Inner Earth is said to also be the domain of many animals which we have long considered to be mythological, such as the unicorn, the phoenix, the minotaur, centaur, and dragon (ref. Hesed L'Avraham 2:4).

Inner Earth inhabitants are said to come in many different shapes and sizes, from what we would call giants, to the likes of what would call hobbits; indeed, there is even said to be a species of two headed human beings. All these things are proclaimed by our Sages to be physically real.

The Zohar states that the Garden of Eden is a real physical place existing in Inner Earth. In the "Garden" there are said to be numerous "palaces." This indicates that the Garden is no mere botanical location. It seems to imply that the Garden might not be a botanical domain at all, but rather a built-up domain similar to a modern city.

One of the "palaces" in the Garden is said to be the Palace of Mashiah. The Zohar teaches that Mashiah resides here and from here receives "powers and abilities far beyond those of mortal men." It is from here in the Garden that Mashiah sets out to Outer Earth to there fight the wars of YHWH and to conquer the surface for Him.

As is clear from Zechariah 14, Mashiah comes from out of the sky with an army of angels. Yet, if Mashiah is coming from Inner Earth, from where come the angels with whom he meets and takes their lead? Do they also ascend with him from inner Earth? If so, what then is their means of their transport?

Questions abound. Answers are plenty throughout the many works of our Torah Sages. One point that our Sages make is certain. WE ARE NOT ALONE ON OUR EARTH.

There are many races of indigenous intelligent sentient entities living in Inner Earth. Many of these species know about us and many of them have interacted with us for a very long time. Some of these races are benign or even benevolent. Others on the other hand are nothing but trouble.

One of these troublesome races is referred to as the Nishaya, after the name of their domain. They are one of the "Shedim" (demons) races spoken of by our Sages throughout the centuries.

The Zohar and other literature describe their appearance as being frail, short, with a greyish skin-tone, no noses, just slits to breath. Allegedly they have no females of their species and thus seek our human females with which to procreate.

Many might recognize the similarities between the Nishaya and the modern-day extraterrestrials called Greys, and so-called alien abductions, which are identical to age-old demonic abduction scenarios. While these experiences are definitely real, still, they are not the alien encounters that people think they are. There is far too much more to discuss about this than can be related here. Maybe it is best for people not to know.

The Garden of Eden is thus accepted by our Sages as a physical domain deep inside Inner Earth. Yet, just as the Garden is located there so are there other domains, even the physical location of Gehinnom (Hell).

These are not places of myth, or the repose of the souls in the afterlife. They are accepted as being physical inhabited domains, whose inhabitants very much interact with us on a regular basis. They know all about us. It is we who live in ignorance of them.

If there really is some sort of conspiracy of silence "out there" being perpetrated by the governments of our world, then it is knowledge of Inner Earth that "they" are trying to keep secret. Maybe, they have very good reason.

Chapter 7

The Seven Lands of Inner Earth
Teachings from the Zohar (1, 253b-254a)

Introduction

This is one of the few source materials that we have in written Kabbalistic record that documents the ideas and beliefs about Inner Earth (the Hollow Earth) and those that dwell there.

This short piece, while mentioning Gehinnom (Hell), the descendants of Cain, and those of the Generation of the Tower of Babel, is silent about the presence of Shedim (demons), as well as other known Inner Earth locations such as the Bird's Nest, which is the dwelling place of the Mashiah. The Garden of Eden is mentioned herein as being in Inner Earth (and thus the Bird's Nest is in it), but its exact location is not described.

There is much discussed about what today is called the Hollow Earth. Much of this modern information is shrouded in public disinformation. But knowledge of Inner Earth has been embraced by peoples and cultures around the world for millennia. Even many in the secular world have embraced this idea, some claiming it to be scientific.

Whether any of these places are physical inside the Earth is this dimension, or in another cannot be defined by what we have before us. We conclude with the obvious fact: these are the words of the author of the Zohar. Let them speak for themselves.

<u>Zohar (1, 253b-254a)</u>

The order of the world is [that there are] seven connected spheres. These are the seven lands that are spherical like a ball, one on top of another.

And the seven lands from below to above are called: (1) ERETZ; (2) ADAMA; (3) ARKA; (4) GEY; (5) NISHIYA; (6) TZIYA; and (7) TEVEL.

Above them all is our land which is called TEVEL. It is the most complete of them all because it is closest to the Kingdom of Heaven. It is the first to receive [Divine] influence. And [King] David said about this land, "And He will judge Tevel with righteousness" (Psalm 9:9), meaning that the Holy One, blessed be He will judge this world, which is called Tevel in accordance to the laws of the Kingdom called righteousness.

When Adam was kicked out of the Garden of Eden, he was cast into the place called ERETZ, the seventh place, the lowest of all the seven lands. This is a dark place that has no light at all. Neither is there any reflected light. There are no created beings there, no stars or constellations. For this land corresponds to the Heaven called Vilon, that also has no reflected light.

When Adam entered here, he was terrified for he had been kicked out of a place of light, and suddenly cast into a place of darkness and the shadow of death. His mind and thoughts were confused, and thus he knew that this was the edict of the King to punish him. For [there was] the revolving sword of fire that guarded the path [back to] the Tree of Life. And this fire burned in every corner of that land. There is no [greater] suffering in the world than to see once fire and then to immediately see darkness, a thing, and its opposite.

After the passing of the Sabbath, when Adam contemplated repentance, the Holy One, blessed be He raised him up [from there], and [brought him] to the place called ADAMA, which is one land higher than the lowest place called ERETZ, as it is written, "And YHWH ELOHIM cast him from the Garden of Eden to work the ADAMA [the land]" (Gen. 3:23). In this place there is a light that shines, and some things like the light of stars and constellations.

*There, in ADAMA there resides the children of men, [who are]
great (Eela'in) and powerful (Guvrin). [These are the ones sired by
Adam during the 130 year period that he was intimate with female
spirits. [As mighty as they are] they are most often depressed, they
have no experience of joy, at all.*

*These spirits fly about and come to this world. [Here] they turn to
the side of evil, and afterwards return home [and yet they do] offer
prayers [to God], for they become ashamed of what they did there.
They [also] plant seeds [in their domain], which they grind [into
flour to make something like, but not identical to bread] of which
they eat, but wheat is not to be found amongst them, or any of the
other seven types of produce [found in the Land of Israel]. In this
place were Cain and Abel born.*

*When Cain sinned [by killing his brother Abel], the Holy One,
blessed by He punished him by sending him back to that place called
ERETZ, as it is written, "You have banished me this day from the
ADAMA" (Gen. 4:14), meaning [that he was banished from] that land
called ADAMA. "And I will wander in ERETZ" (ibid.) for it is to there
that I have been banished, and "All who find me will kill me" (ibid.)
meaning the revolving sword of fire.*

*And [Cain] was terrified and he contemplated repentance, and
immediately the Holy One blessed be He raised him up from there
and brought him to ARKA, and [Cain] lived there and sired his
children [there]. In ARKA there is light from the Sun. Here, they plant
seeds and grow trees, but still there is not there any wheat, nor any
of the other seven types of produce [known to be in Israel].*

*And those that live there [in ARKA] are the descendants of Cain.
There are those that have two heads, and also those who are
powerfully (Guvrin) great (Eela'in). There are [also those] who are
small and young, but they do not possess complete knowledge like
the other people there. Sometimes they merit to turn to the side of
good, and other times to the side of evil. They are born and die like
all other human beings.*

*Now, Adam was in the place called ADAMA until the birth of Seth.
From then on, he ascended four levels and came to this world, which
is called TEVEL. When he surfaced here, he came out from the place*

[that the] Holy Temple [would stand in the future]. And [this place] TEVEL is the highest of all the levels, and it is [also] called by the names ERETZ and ADAMA. This is how it is called.

Adam skipped over three [of the seven lands], which are GEY, NISHIYA, and TZIYA. GEY is the fourth level from below to above. This place is wide and large, like the width and depth of Gehinnom.

In GEY, NISHIYA and TZIYA [there resides the descendants] of those who built the Tower [of Babel]. They had many children there because they angered the Supernal, Holy King. For this reason, they are close to the ignited fires [of Gehinnom].

Therein are very worthy human beings who possess great wealth with metals, gold, and precious stones. And if one from here, from TEVEL, enters GEY, they will give him a portion of their wealth.

Sometimes one leaves [GEY] and enters NISHIYA, and forgetfulness reigns there. One returns to GEY but does not know from where one has come.

GEY is in the middle between above and below. [GEY] is GEY ben Hinom [Gehinnom]. And a strip [of land] exits there and enters TEVEL. This is called Gey Ben Hinnom (the valley of Hinnom), or Gehinnom. And here is the opening to Gehinnom (Hell). And the people who reside there, because of this [being Gehinnom] are all wise in the ways of magic, and the dark arts (Harashin vHokhman). And here they also sow seeds and plant trees. But there is no wheat there, nor any of the other seven species.

In NISHIYA there are people who are short in stature, and they have no noses, only two slots through which they breathe. And whatever they do, it is immediately forgotten. This is why it is called NISHIYA. They sow seeds and plant trees, but there is no wheat there, nor any of the other seven species.

TZIYA, like its name indicates, is a place that is completely dry. The people there are very pleasant looking. Being that [this place] is dry, they will often ascend to TEVEL for water. The people there are have more faith that other peoples. They have lovely homes and great wealth. Due to their dry condition, they can only sow in small amounts. They try to plant trees but are mostly unsuccessful. Their desire is to bond with people from here.

Of all these people there are none that eat bread, other than those who dwell [here] in TEVEL. For TEVEL is the upper-most of them all, as it is written, "And He will judge Tevel with righteousness" (Psalm 9:9).

TEVEL has within it all that these other lands do. And all the names of these seven lands can also be found right here in TEVEL, for [TEVEL] is the seventh, and it includes within it examples of all the others. And in all these places dwell people different from one another, as it is written, "how numerous are Your works, YHWH" (Psalm 104:24).

Chapter 8

The Secret of the Zoharic Trinity

יְהֵא רַעֲוָא מִן קֳדָם **עַתִּיקָא קַדִּישָׁא** דְּכָל־קַדִּישִׁין. טְמִירָא דְּכָל־טְמִירִין סְתִימָא דְּכָלָּא דְּיִתְמְשַׁךְ טַלָּא עִלָּאָה מִנֵּהּ לְמַלְיָא רֵישֵׁהּ דִּ**זְעֵיר אַנְפִּין** וּלְהַטִּיל לַ**חֲקַל תַּפּוּחִין קַדִּישִׁין** בִּנְהִירוּ דְּאַנְפִּין בְּרַעֲוָא וּבְחֶדְוָתָא דְכֹלָּא.

It is time to reveal some of the as yet unrevealed secrets of the Zoharic Kabbalah.

There really is a Trinity in the Kabbalah of the Zohar. Of course, it has nothing to do with the Trinity espoused in other religions. The two are opposites, like day and night. The wise will understand the inference.

The Trinity of the Zoharic Kabbalah is most profound. It consists of Arikh Anpin (who we can also call Atika Kadisha), Zeir Anpin (Z.A.) and the Hakal Tapuhin Kadishin (NOK).

These Aramaic terms are translated as follows: Arikh Anpin – the Long Face, Atika Kadisha - the Ancient Holy One. These two are the same, and then again, they are not the same. Only the more advanced Kabbalists need to know the difference. For our purposes here, the two are the same. Zeir Anpin (Z.A.) – the Small Face, often called the Face of Supernal Israel. Hakal Tapuhin Kadishin – the Field of Holy Apples.

So here we have the Long Face, Short Face, and the Field of Holy Apples; this is the Trinty of the Zoharic Kabbalah. But what does all this mean? Words alone, by themselves, regardless of language, need to be interpreted correctly so as to safeguard them from the many misinterpretations that are applied to them by outsiders (hitzonim), those who have not received the secrets of the Kabbalistic system from a bona fide authentic Rabbi of the Kabbalah.

Those who look upon these words and the concepts associated with them, consider this Trinity to be referring to the "Godhead," and that the three Names are references to individual Sefirot within the "Godhead." This understanding is one of those misinterpretations that needs to be addressed.

First and foremost, there is no such thing as a "God-Head." God has no body or form. God has no head, nor body. We cannot speak of a God-head, or of a God-body.

The terms of the Kabbalah do indeed speak about Sefirot, but these too need to be understood correctly, to protect the knowledge of them from the outsiders.

Arikh Anpin (Atika Kadisha) are Keter. Zeir Anpin (Z.A.) is Tiferet. Hakal Tapuhin Kadishin (NOK) is Malkhut. These three represent the top, middle and bottom of the Center Column of the Sefirotic Tree of Life. But again, we have here more words and more symbols. What do they all mean? Without this application in practice, one cannot be consider an authentic Kabbalist.

Arikh is the Long Face of God in Keter. A Face? Zeir Anpin (Z.A.) is the Short Face of God in Tiferet. Another Face? Who is it then who gazes upon these Faces? Hakal Tapuhin Kadishin is the Holy Apple Field in Malkhut. It is called Feminine. Yet, it is not a Face that is gazed upon. Why are the two, Arikh and Zeir, Faces, and the Hakal Tapuhin Kadishin not a Face?

We must remember this; a Face is something that is seen from the outside. In other words, there must be an "other" to look upon the Face, for it is only the "other" that sees it.

We said correctly that God has no form, nor semblance of form. God has no head, no face, nor body. And yet, the Kabbalah is replete with such graphic images. Why? The answer to this takes us into the heart of the secrets of the Kabbalah.

We proclaim daily in our faith: God is one and His Name is one. This is indeed true. There are no parts to God, no Faces, long or short. God is a singularity in the most sublime way of integrated unity that encompasses all things. But this reality of God is something far beyond the comprehension of human intelligence.

We human beings, in our present state of human consciousness, can only know, understand, and experience a limited amount of finite knowledge about the Infinite Source that we seek to contemplate. Thus, when we gaze upon God, whether in meditative experience, or through intellectual contemplations and speculations, we recognize that there is that which we can know, and that which we cannot.

That which we can know, we call Zeir Anpin (Z.A.), the short, or limited Face of God. This alone is what is accessible to human meditative experience, and intellectual contemplation. That which we cannot know, we call Arikh Anpin, the long, or unlimited Face of God that is beyond human meditative experience, and intellectual contemplation.

Reference to this is found in the Torah itself (Exodus 33:20), when Moses asked to see God's Face, and God respond by saying, *"No human being can see my Face, and live."* This is because the human mind is limited in perception. Any experience beyond these limitations would require that the human soul leave the human body, and no longer to restricted by human consciousness. Of course, this means the death of the individual, and the soul's ascent into a higher dimension of consciousness and perception. Essentially, Moses was shown Zeir Anpin (all twelve subjective Partzufim therein). But even Moses could not be granted access to the higher Faces.

And aside from this, what else is there? There is us, our collective souls, which the Zohar refers to as the Hakal Tapuhin Kadishin. This is also called Keneset Yisrael, Collective Israel. This corresponds to the Sefirat Malkhut. In the later Kabbalah of the Ari'zal, this reference to the Sefirat Malkhut is called NOK, the feminine mate of Z.A. Two Sefirotic Faces are applied here to NOK, given the symbolic Names of the two wives of the Biblical Ya'aqob, Leah and Rahel.

God does not have any Faces. God does not wear any masks. But how God views God, and how humanity views God are two very-different things. Human consciousness and intellect create all kinds of imagery and symbols in order to give some semblance of form and identity to that which we humans experience. The human experience of higher dimensions is very unique and specialized for the human species. Others species do not share our limitations, and therefore do not share the need for our images and symbols of demarcation.

The secret of the Trinity of the Kabbalah is not that it is objectively real. There most certainly is no trinity within God. Indeed, such a thought according to Torah Law is both blasphemous and idolatrous.

This is why Torah so strongly condemns the mistaken ideas about a trinity within God that are found in other religions. They fundamentally deny the Absolute Unity of God. And more than this, these other religions, and those who misinterpret the Kabbalah, point to the true Trinity within the Kabbalah and (wrongly) proclaim that this validates their mistaken beliefs. This is only one of many reasons why authentic Kabbalists do not share the sacred teachings with students who are not ready or worthy to receive them.

Now that we have identified the true Trinity of the Kabbalah, we need to explain it, and understand it correctly so that outsiders (hitzonim) will not have foundation for their continuing mistakes. Let us turn to the words of the Zohar (3, 73a) itself for elaboration.

דְּתָנֵינָן תְּלַת דַּרְגִין אִינוּן מִתְקַשְּׁרָן דָּא בְּדָא, קוּדְשָׁא בְּרִיךְ הוּא, אוֹרַיְיתָא, וְיִשְׂרָאֵל.
וְכָל חַד, דַּרְגָּא עַל דַּרְגָּא, סָתִים וְגַלְיָא. קוּדְשָׁא בְּרִיךְ הוּא דַּרְגָּא עַל דַּרְגָּא, סָתִים
וְגַלְיָא. אוֹרַיְיתָא הָכִי נָמֵי סָתִים וְגַלְיָא. יִשְׂרָאֵל הָכִי נָמֵי דַּרְגָּא עַל דַּרְגָּא, הָדָא הוּא
דִּכְתִיב, ‏(תהלים קמ״ז:י״ט) מַגִּיד דְּבָרָיו לְיַעֲקֹב חֻקָּיו וּמִשְׁפָּטָיו לְיִשְׂרָאֵל. תְּרֵי דַּרְגִין אִינוּן,
יַעֲקֹב וְיִשְׂרָאֵל, חַד גַּלְיָא, וְחַד סָתִים.

"We have taught that there are three degrees that are bound to one another. The Holy One, blessed be He, Torah, and Israel. Each one, degree by degree, are concealed and revealed. The Holy One, blessed be He, degree by degree is concealed and revealed. Torah also is concealed and revealed. Israel, also degree by degree. This is what is written (Psalm 147:19), "He tells His Word to Ya'aqob, His rules and laws to Yisrael." These are two degrees, Ya'aqob and Yisrael one revealed, and one concealed." (Zohar v3, 73a).

The sacred Trinity of the Kabbalah, reflected in the unity of Arikh, Z.A. and NOK has its source in the unity of God, Torah, and Israel. God, Torah, and Israel is the true identity of the Trinty of the Kabbalah, hidden and concealed under the symbolisms of the symbolic Faces of God. Let us elaborate.

בְּגִין דְּאוֹרַיְיתָא כֻּלָּא שְׁמָא דְקוּדְשָׁא בְּרִיךְ הוּא

The Zohar (v3, 73a) teaches that *"the entire Torah is the Name of God."* As YHWH and His Name are one, thus YHWH and His Torah are one. The Torah is thus Zeir Anpin, the Small or revealed Face of God. Yes! That's right! The Torah is Divine. This is why we call it, The Word of God.

It is well known that in the synagogue prayer service called the Repetition of the Amidah, when the Name of God (Adonai) is recited in a blessing, *Barukh Atah Adonai*, the congregation responds, *Barukh Hu u'Barukh Shmo* (Blessed be He, and blessed be His Name). The Kabbalists have noted that God and His Name, of course are one, but within that unique singularity, there is still the concealed (God) and the revealed (His Name). Thus, we learn that the Essence of God is concealed, whereas the Name of God is that which is revealed.

To represent this reality, the Zohar established the concepts of Arikh Anpin, the Long Face of God, representing the concealed aspect, and Zeir Anpin, the Short Face of God, representing the revealed aspect, which as we have seen above is the Name of God, and is the Torah itself.

And now we come to the Hakal Tapuhin Kadishin, which we learn from the Zohar corresponds to the nation of Yisrael, or Keneset Yisrael. As with both, God and His Torah (His Name), Yisrael has both concealed and revealed degrees.

When discussing the nation of Israel, the term Keneset Yisrael, the Collective of Israel is used. Hakal Tapuhin Kadishin and Keneset Yisrael are two terms referring to the same reality. In Sefirotic terms, we are discussing here the Sefirat Malkhut. In other literature, this is most often referred to as the Shekhina, the Divine Presence.

Just as God and His Torah is one, so too is the Shekhina one with the Whole. The Divine Presence is not an independent entity or part of God separate from the rest of God. Such a thought is blasphemous and idolatrous. We uphold the foundation of our faith, God is one. God has no parts, remember, no form, nor semblance of form. Thus, if the Shekhina is the manifestation of God in the Sefirah Malkhut, what exactly does this mean?

In order to answer this and understand the answer properly, we again need to understand more Kabbalistic terms and concepts.

According to the Zoharic and later Lurianic Kabbalah, the Sefirat Malkhut (in all the worlds) is the receptacle, the vessel, and the body in which the Ten Sefirot of that domain congeal, unite, and manifest. Thus, the form and structure of every dimensional plane is its Malkhut. Our physical world is called the dimension (Olam) of Asiyah. The Ten Sefirot of Asiyah give rise to all the forms and realms of material existence, those seen and known to us, and those that are not. These include all forms of physical matter, dark matter, known energy and dark energy.

Throughout all these dimensional planes, the Divine Presence is there, functioning and operating as the Mover and Shaker of all things. The word Shekhina, is derived from the root *Shokhen* which means to dwell. The Divine Presence resides in the natural world. This is how God is manifest here in the physical dimensions of Asiyah.

In order for the Divine to manifest Itself in this dimensional plane of Asiyah, it takes a spark of Itself and encases it in a vessel of sorts through which it can operate, and function. This vessel, referred to here, is the collective higher soul of all humanity. This is "Supernal Man." According to the Kabbalah of the Ari'zal, this is what the Bible refers to as Adam in Eden (ref. Sha'ar HaPesukim).

This "Supernal Man" is Zeir Anpin (Z.A.). His "Mate" is NOK. NOK is Malkhut, the Shekhina. NOK is also that spark of the Divine which is the source of the Collective Soul of Israel, Keneset Yisrael. This is the concealed degree of Israel, as referenced in the Zohar v3, 73a. This explains the unique Singularity of the Sefirot of the Center Column of the Tree of Life. Arikh is Keter at the top. Z.A. is Tiferet in the center. NOK (Keneset Yisrael) is Malkhut at the bottom.

There is Israel revealed and Israel concealed. Israel revealed is the Twelve Tribes, descending from the Biblical patriarch Ya'aqob. Today we only know of those Israelites whom we call Jews. There are many other lost tribes, lost to us, but known to God. In Messianic times, these will be identified and reunited with the Jewish people to again become a united Israelite (and not Jewish alone) nation.

Israel concealed is another story all together. Israel concealed is the gathering of enlightened souls, those who embrace the higher consciousness earned by the patriarch Ya'aqob when he defeated God's angel in mortal combat. This famous Biblical story (recorded in Genesis 32) relates the powerful episode of how the mere mortal Ya'aqob rose above the natural influences of this spacetime dimension.

Ya'aqob grasped the higher dimensional plane, represented by the angel, and made it subservient to himself. Ya'aqob thus became Israel, and his insight into God rose from the level of Adonai, Elohim, Shadai (in Malkhut and Yesod) to the level of YHWH (in

Tiferet). Tiferet is the source of Torah. Thus, because Ya'aqob of Yesod became Yisrael of Tiferet, he and his descendants merited the Torah which also emanates from Tiferet. Thus, Yisrael and Torah are one, married together as husband and wife, as is often the metaphor used by the Sages to describe this sacred relationship.

Now we can understand the meaning of the Zohar when it says that Israel, like God and Torah has both a concealed and a revealed degree. The concealed degree of Israel is Keneset Yisrael. The concealed degree of Israel is the collective of human souls that activate and manifest the Divine Presence of Keneset Yisrael through their developed consciousness and holy behavior.

This is the secret of the unity of the Nation of Israel, the Torah which it received, and God who gave it to them. This is the singularity of Keter, Tiferet, and Malkhut. Like the Zohar said, *"There are three degrees that are bound to one another. The Holy One, blessed be He, Torah, and Israel."*

Revealed goes with revealed. Concealed goes with concealed. This should be obvious. The revealed Jews bond with the revealed Torah through what is revealed to us about God. They form the religion of Judaism as it is known and practiced today by the religious faithful.

Concealed Israel bond with the concealed Torah (the secrets therein, the true Kabbalah) through a higher, more concealed revelation of God that is accessible only to those who have made meditative ascent and interact with higher beings, just like Ya'aqob.

Keter at the top of the Sefirot represents God. Tiferet in the middle represents Torah. Malkhut at the bottom represents enlightened humanity (Israel). Thus, when Israel is faithful to the Torah at the revealed level then there are blessings at the revealed level. And when higher Israel is faithful to the higher (secrets of the) Torah then there are blessings in the concealed (secret) level.

Now for one last secret. As is well known from the teachings of the Ari'zal we do possess knowledge of the upper Sefirotic Face beyond Zeir Anpin. In matter of fact, our knowledge of these domains is quite extensive (the Olamot of AK, and the Akudim, Nikudim and Berudim, ref. Kitvei HaAri'zal). And still, no one has seen, or can see, the Face of God. And how can this be? The answer is very simple, although some might find it shocking.

Remember, all that we human beings can know about God in this present incarnation we sum up and call Zeir Anpin, the Small Face. So, whatever it is that we are discussing must be understood to be within Z.A.

All of Kabbalah, all the worlds spoken of, all the Sefirot and Partzufim (Faces) all exist with "Man" (Adam). For terrestrial man point by point is a microcosm of the macrocosmic Supernal Man. Be it Adam Kadmon (Primordial Man), Adam Elyon (Supernal Man – Zeir Anpin) or Adam Tahtone (Terrestrial Man – us), like the Holy One, blessed be He, Torah, and Israel; all are one.

All are revealed and concealed. And those who know the secrets guards them well. Even what I have revealed here in this essay only reveals the barest minimum of what still lies concealed, hidden away from unworthy prying eyes. Again, the wise will see and understand, and they too will remain silent.

For it is only in the Silence that the Still Soft Voice can be heard.

No more secrets for now.

Chapter 9

Why there will be No Animal Sacrifices in the Third Temple

Blood sacrifices were an integral part of Divine worship in ancient times. Indeed, much of Torah is dedicated to outlining the type of sacrifices that were to be offered in the Tabernacle, and later Temple, on a daily basis, as well as for all the holidays.

But why did God ordain that there be animal sacrifice? Was the reason because the life-force energies in the animals was necessary to offer upon an altar so as to somehow realign energetic imbalances? Did the blood of the sacrifice really erase the spiritual blemishes of sin? All we can say for sure is that this is what ancient peoples sincerely believed. And still some believe this to this day.

Lots of animals were ritually slaughtered all because human beings believed that when they violated the Divine Law that same Divine Law demanded that animals be sacrificed as an atonement. Indeed, we know what Torah Law says; God ordained the sacrifices. There is no denying this. However, we can ask why? Why did God ordain these practices? Was it for the sake of Heaven, or for the sake of humanity?

While the Temple stood no one dared question the validity of this practice or dared to challenge Divine ordinance. However, as the centuries since the destruction of the Temple have passed, important views, such as Maimonides (Guide 3:32), questioned why we needed to slaughter animals to atone for our sins. Indeed, it is asked was this not a primitive custom best gone and lost in time? Maimonides opines this view in detail.

In order for us to understand the Torah in general, we need to understand the ideas and concepts upon which its present form has been established. Long ago our Sages have taught us that the Torah was expressed and put into its present form based upon the understandings of the Children of Israel 3500 years ago. While the Torah itself is eternal, and is never to be changed, or exchanged, nevertheless the form of Torah that we received from Sinai was subjective and subject to the language and culture of its historical period.

The Torah ordain animal sacrifices because that was the nature of Divine worship known and understood within the religions of the world at that time. If Torah did not ordain a ritualized form of animal sacrifice, the people of those days would not have understood how their God was to be worshipped. YHWH gave the Torah to the Children of Israel conforming to a form of religious worship that would make sense to them at the time.

Centuries have passed. Not just one, but two Temples were built and destroyed. Animal sacrifices ceased with the destruction of the Solomon's Temple in 586 B.C.E. For many decades no animal sacrifice to YHWH was made. Under Torah law sacrifices to YHWH had to be made upon the altar chosen by YHWH. This was the Temple. No other legitimate sacrifices were permitted under Torah Law. Thus, during the decades of the Babylonian Exile, no sacrifices were offered.

Later, the Second Temple was built. There was no new prophecy instituting any new form of sacrifice. Rather, the prophecies that we do have (ref. Malakhi 1:6-10) indicates that the nature of Temple Service animal sacrifice had rather quickly become corrupted. YHWH spoke through the prophet indicating that the animal sacrificial system was no longer a pleasing thing. These sentiments were indeed echoed by many previous prophets all during the First Temple period.

The Second Temple quickly became corrupt. The Priesthood was compromised, and the High Priesthood was often sold due to political corruption. Large groups of Kohanim (Aaronic/Zadokite priests) abandoned the Temple and Jerusalem and sought to serve YHWH by themselves alone in their private, often rural communities. Yet, one thing about these groups is that they never sought to establish an alternative altar and to offer animal sacrifice based upon their own interpretations of Torah Law. Instead, these groups originated the concept that prayers were to be recited in place of sacrifices.

With the destruction of Herod's Temple and Jerusalem in 68 C.E. animal sacrifices again came to a halt, this time permanently. The tradition of the break-away group to offer prayers instead of animals soon became the norm of the entire Torah observant community. According to Maimonides and others, this evolution of the forms of Divine worship was a good thing, one that was indeed, ordained by Heaven itself.

Torah speaks in the language of man. Torah was given at Sinai in the ways and means understandable to the people then. What was written down for us we know as the Written Torah. Yet, as is well known, so much of what is written in the Written Torah defies a common sense observation.

For example, one of the strangest proclamations of Torah Law ordained that one was not to seethe (Bishul) a kid (Gedi) in its mother's milk. This commandment must have carried some importance in that it is repeated in the Written Torah three times! (Ref. Exodus 23:19, 34:26, and Deut. 14:21). Some of the most fundamental moral laws, such as the Ten Commandments, are not repeated that often. This law must have some significant value to have it repeated so often.

Is this law to be understood at face value? Does the law only mean what it says literally: not to seethe a kid in its mother's milk? What if one wished to cook the kid in its mother's milk by some form other than seething (Bishul)? Does this law also apply to other species whose babies are not called kids (Gedi)? What about other animals? Does this apply equally to them? Who has the answers to these questions, and from where did those answers come from?

It is from this Law (amongst many others) that we discover evidence of the existence of the Oral Law. Essentially, the language of the Torah was ordained in a way that it made sense to the generation that received it. But Torah is not of this Earth. Torah comes from YHWH, and YHWH exists in a quantum state of spacetime flux, where the fabric of reality is fluid, not rigid. As YHWH is quantum in nature, so too is Torah. And this explains why an Oral Torah was necessary. For as circumstances and consciousness changed in spacetime, so too did the Torah need to adapt to these changes.

While the Written Torah proclaims to us not to seethe a kid in its mother's milk, the Oral Torah that was passed down also from Sinai reveals to us the inner meanings of this strange (for us) choice of wording. For the record, the three times indicate to us three separate prohibitions, (1) not to cook meat and dairy products together, (2) not to eat a combination of meat and dairy products that have been cooked together, and (3) not to benefit from such a forbidden mixture. (Ref. T.B. Hulin 115b, S. A. Yoreh Deah 87:1).

The Laws of Meat and Dairy (Basar b'Halav) has since evolved (expanded) considerably because of the changing needs of the public over many centuries. All these expanded laws are not included in the Written Torah, but they all have their source in the Oral Torah. If not for the Oral Torah, the Written Torah would be for us a closed book, a text subject to interpretation without any authoritative guidance. Torah Law is able to evolve simply because the Oral Torah is both rock-solid and fluid at the same time. Oral Torah guides the Way for Torah evolution.

Through the many centuries, and very prominently today, there are always those who come forward to condemn the Torah in general, and to specifically target the Oral Torah for their venomous rejection. Such expressions, needless to say, do not express valid and legitimate forms of evolving religious expression. On the contrary, these voices of rejection are nothing more than the voices of rebellion, rejection, and hate. For good reasons have the Sages of old (and of today) encouraged that there be no dialogue or discussion with those who reject both Written and Oral Torah.

And yet, with this being said, Torah does evolve! Yes, Torah evolves all the time. But this evolution is not random and haphazard like the secularists loudly proclaims is the way of biological evolution. No! Evolution is real, this is true. But all evolution, religious and biological alike is directed by the Higher Hand of Heaven. There is absolutely nothing random and haphazard in any evolutionary progression!

In 68 C.E. the Temple in Jerusalem was destroyed and it has not been rebuilt since. Temple based Judaism evolved into Synagogue based Rabbinic Judaism. Everyday Torah observant Jews pray for the rebuilding of the Temple, and the restoration of the sacrifices. Every day the Torah portions that speak about the daily offerings are read with the intent that the words of one's mouth may be acceptable in place of the blood of animals. This is the evolution of Torah observance.

The Torah faithful proclaim as an integral part of our faith, that in the future a new Temple is to be established upon the site of the previous two Temples, on the Temple Mount in Jerusalem. However, both the rationalist Talmud and the mystical Zohar concur on one point: the future Temple is not to be built by human hands, but rather it is destined to descend from Heaven already built.

More than this, the Kabbalists teach that the purpose of the sacrifices of old was to serve as acts of spiritual rectification (Tikkunim). What was once done with blood is now accomplished with prayer. When the Mashiah comes, and the new Temple established, all rectifications will have been completed. If this is indeed the case, then there will no longer be any need for either prayers of the sort previously offered, or for the return of the antiquated and outdated slaughter of animals.

According to the Kabbalah, when Mashiah comes the original blemish of Adam will be rectified. Thus, rectified humanity will be restored to the idyllic state that was originally enjoyed in Eden. If this is the case, then all humanity will revert to vegetarianism, because Adam and all humanity were originally vegetarians. It seems that the evolution away from animal sacrifice will be maintained. Any step in the opposite direction could be interpreted as a devolution, instead of an evolution. And this would contradict the Divine plan.

It thus only seems both natural, and Kabbalistic, for there to be no animal sacrifices in the Third Temple to come With this being said, however, we must mention that not everyone agrees with this naturalistic, Kabbalistic conclusion. Indeed, even some Kabbalists disagree. But these Kabbalists are from a time period before the revelations of the Ari'zal school. They do not address the issues of the rectification of the "sin of Adam." Therefore, their views on the matter are subjective, not objective.

As for what the actual future holds, who can tell? Both the rationalist tradition recorded in the Talmud, and the mystical tradition recorded in the Zohar equally proclaim that the future Messianic Temple will descend from Heven fully built and operational. The rectified souls of those then living, the Kabbalah teaches, will have bodies of light, similar to that of Adam prior to the "fall in Eden." As such, they will have no need for animal sacrifices. So then, who would future animal sacrifices be for? With the promised absence of the Evil Inclination during Messianic times, again the need for animal sacrifices becomes a moot point.

As best as we can ascertain from Halakhic, Midrashic and Kabbalistic sources, while today the laws of animal sacrifice remain intact, this obligation would only apply if the Temple were still in existence today. And needless to say, the Temple cannot be rebuilt in modern times because the laws of ritual purity prohibit it.

In order for a modern Temple to be legitimate under Torah Law it would be, needless to say, have to be built by those individuals who were in a state of ritual purity as mandated by Torah Law. And today, without the ashes of the Red Heifer, no one today can become ritually pure, in accordance to Temple standards.

No one today can even offer a Red Heifer sacrifice because the one doing so must be ritually pure by Temple standards. Thus no one today can qualify. So, until a ritually pure, bonafide descendant of the bloodline of Aaron shows up and proves both his lineage and his state of ritual purity, we can have no one to offer any sacrifice. And to make matters more difficult, the only body that can recognize and authorize such an Aaronic priest would be a reconstituted Sanhedrin (High Court).

So, here we are today, with no Temple, no Court, no authorized Priest, and no ability to offer any proper, Torah ordained animal sacrifices of any kind. Not only can there not be any animal sacrifices in any future Temple built by human hands, but there can also equally not be animal sacrifices of any kind today, with or without the Temple.

Torah Law is adamant about the requirements of ritual purity. Wisely and rightly so were these Laws ordained in the way and fashion that they were. Wisely and rightly did Heaven ordain and execute the course of human and Jewish history.

The development of Rabbinic Judaism to replace Temple Judaism was the natural and normal evolution of Torah. So, the more one remains faithful to the sacred Rabbinic tradition, the greater one's bond is to both Torah and to our blessed Divine Creator. In the Way of God, we always look forward and move forward, in faithful allegiance to our past, and in rigid unshakable faithfulness to our Torah.

We await the times of the promised Messianic future and look forward to seeing what, in actuality, the Third Temple will be. But until then, we observe the Torah and its sacred commandments as we have received them from our Sages and ancestors. We rest assured that while we recall the daily offerings of animal sacrifices, we no longer have need for the actual shedding of animal blood.

Like, Maimonides revealed to us centuries ago, it is God who directs us, and evolves our understanding of His sacred Torah to bring us to the point where we can stand as mature, spiritual beings, even as was our first ancestor Adam long ago. We await the day for the fulfillment of this grand spiritual goal, amen.

SECTION FIVE

OPENING THE PSYCHIC MIND

Chapter 1

Divine Judgment in Light of Relative Time Perception

Parallel realities are right here next to us all the time. They are not far away as some might think. We experience parallel realities all the time without even realizing it. The most common parallel reality is the relative perception of time.

Time is truly relative. Time is felt to pass differently for different people. Some feel time is moving fast, others feel that time is moving slow. How one feels about time is what makes its movement relative.

We think that the movement of time is a constant. How long is an hour? We all know that it is 60 minutes. How long is a minute? We all know that it is 60 seconds. How long is a second? Normally, we don't measure this, but science has measurements to the smallest fractions of a second. But these speed by too fast for the average human being to notice. Time is, after all, experienced relatively. Whether time is moving fast or slow is ultimately only a point of view.

Now, with this said, we need to understand that we human beings measure time as we do, and that there are other races of beings that measure time in a very different way!

The Bible says that God created the Heavens and the Earth in six days. This is, of course, literally true. But we need to understand that how God measures a day, and how we humans measure a day is as different as is the Divine from the human. In other words, there is a big difference. Even the Bible (Psalms 90:4) says that a day to God is like 1000 human years. And this itself is a metaphor, and not an exact measurement.

Science has shown us that our planet and universe is billions of years old as we measure time by our human standards here on Earth. This is no way contradicts the Bible simply because we cannot compare human measurements with Divine measurements, regardless of whether or not we wish to use similar words or terms, such as the word, "day."

We humans measure time differently than does God. We must also understand that we humans measure time differently than does the various species of angels, and other life forms that exist in our universe, and elsewhere on our planet.

We measure a year as one orbit of the Earth moving around the Sun. This movement is an objective fact. Whether one is on Earth, or observing Earth from outer space, one will see the movement of the Earth around the Sun. The question is this. When observing the Earth orbiting around the Sun, is the Earth moving slow, or is it moving very, very fast? The answer to this depends upon one's point of view.

A human being may live 100 years. Other forms of life may live for only 2 weeks. Yet, from the point of view of the insect that lives for only 2 weeks, its 2 weeks feels to be for it like 100 years feels for us. As this is true in comparing humans to insects, so too is it when comparing human beings to angels, or even to Shedim/Jinn.

The life spans of higher-dimensional beings are far longer than are human life spans. And these higher-dimensional beings look upon the 100 years of a human life span in the same way that we would look at the 2 week life span of an insect. Just like we think a 2 week lifespan is very short, so too do the higher-dimensional beings consider a 100 year life span to very short.

This relativity of time experience is very important for us to understand in order for us to comprehend how angelic Watchers and the Dominions under them operate here on Earth by Divine design. Time passage for angels is very different than for humans. In human eyes, what might be considered a decade (of ten years) or a generation (of 25-40) years, in angelic eyes might be considered only a few hours, or a few days. While we might think that time is moving fast or slow, angelic entities see time moving very differently than from us.

When angels act to intervene in human affairs, from their point of view, their intervention may be considered to be immediate, yet, from our human point of view, it will appear as if their intervention has taken years to manifest.

Perception of the passage of time is very much related to the length and depth of one's personal attention span. For those with patience, time can be seen to be moving at a very different pace from those who lack patience. From our human point of view, higher dimensional beings (of all kinds) are far more patient, than are we.

I need to digress for a moment to help expand our understanding with regards to relative time perception.

Science has shown us that when something moves closer and closer to the speed of light, the slower and slower time appears. At the threshold of the speed of light, it appears as if time stops. We must understand this perception when we discuss higher-dimensional beings who themselves are beings of light, and whose very nature places them in a very different relationship with time than what we (here in physical matter) experience.

Beings of light, and those human beings who through meditative trances shift their consciousness outside of physical matter, and into the energetic parallel realities of higher-dimensional beings, experience time as if it is non-existent. This is how such a human being, while in such a trance can see the future, as easily as one can see the past (or the present). This is how prophecy and clairvoyance work.

The human mind that is trained to experience higher parallel realities can indeed do so. Time for such individuals can be observed, as if, from the outside. One can watch the passage of thousands of years, as if they are single moments. This is why and how visionaries see the future.

Now, what happens when the human mind is trained in the reverse? What happens when instead of seeking trance consciousness to expand out to experience higher-dimensions, one is instead trained (or programmed) to only focus more and more on the immediate here and now? What we then create is a human mind that views time more like the short-lived insect, as opposed to a normal human being who can patiently experience the flow of time differently.

It is thus very much to our personal detriment that we human beings have been conditioned by societal norms to demand instant gratification. We demand what we want, and we want it now! Our craving for instant gratification goes hand in hand with an attention span which itself grows shorter and shorter.

Human beings have been conditioned to think and to experience time more like animals, and less like higher-dimensional beings. And thus it is no wonder that our relationships with higher-dimensional beings suffer because of this. The further human consciousness shifts away from calibration with higher-dimensional beings, the more and more their higher-dimensional activities seem to us to be foreign, or even non-existent.

Today, one needs almost constant stimulation to remain interested in a continuous engagement. With a loss of such stimulation, one quickly loses interest in one thing, and seeks stimulation in another. Essentially, society has conditioned its members to become stimulation addicts, who demand their instant gratifications. Perceptions of time are speeding up (like the insect), instead of slowing down (like the angels).

Individuals addicted to this mental imprisonment have extremely limited attention spans. For them, time moves at a very quick pace. Any attempt to expand their attention span, or to teach them patience, is for them a very painful experience.

These stimulation addicts are quick to take in their stimulations and equally quick to move on to others, often forgetting entirely their own past experiences. They have been trained (programmed/brainwashed?) to demand fast-paced action. For them, life is short, and thus life needs to be filled with high stimulations, just like an insect.

The stimulation addicts never take the tedious time to pause and contemplate what they are experiencing and to learn from it life experience. As such all their learning is superficial and shallow. Without any depth of mind and thought, these modern day people more and more lose human consciousness, and embrace the consciousness level and attention span of lower life-forms. As such, human beings of this type become easy to control. They pay no mind to their own past. And as the old saying goes, those who do not learn from their previous mistakes are destined to repeat them. And the lives of the shallow are scared with repeated mistakes from lessons never learned.

So, as we see, the passage of time, as a concept within the mind is a very real, relevant, and important thing. One should not dismiss a discussion about relative time considering it to be only of momentary interest.

Entities of higher dimensions, and this may include a good number of physically incarnate human beings, understand to gaze out upon life and reality with a perception that seeks to see grander pictures, ones that encapsulate large amounts of time, space and even ideas.

One does not see time passing by the minute. One instead looks at time by the century, or even longer, so as to see, recognize, and understand the greater movements that those without such attention spans cannot see, or even imagine. One of the great differences between the enlightened mind, and the ignorant is with regards to how one perceives the passage of time. All things are relative, time included. The enlightened know this, see this, and live by its reality, regardless of any other perceptions held by those who cannot see.

The higher entities whose job it is to corral human beings, and to direct their history in order to bring them to higher states of consciousness, know well how humans miss seeing their hands at work simply because their actions are far slower than human minds are accustomed to see.

An angelic entity might take months or years to perform a certain task. To the entity, and to God who ordained the actions of the entity, the speed of the movement of what it is doing is normal and natural, but normal and natural is being defined by its own standards, and not by ours. Thus, we fail to see what is going on around us, all because we are out of sync with the reality of the movement of natural time.

When one begins a path towards expanded consciousness, one of the first steps that one must take is the practice of meditation. This practice is designed towards realigning an individual's consciousness, from focus on the quick movements in the outside world, and on to the much slower movements within one's own internal world. Needless to say, the stimulation junkies of today have a very hard time making any movement along this path.

Behind the scenes our angelic Watchers direct humanity, implementing plans that unfold over a period of centuries. Thus those who can gaze over a period of history that consists of decades and centuries will be able to recognize the movements of their invisible hands. And those with this insight will not only be able to see what the invisible hands have done up to this point, they will also recognize the trajectory of those hands, and thus recognize that which will inevitably unfold in the future. This type of future gazing is not prophecy, but it is clairvoyant, and as such, it is still very certain! Nature always takes its course under the singular guidance of a very patient Creator.

Think about this (if you can). The lifespan of an average housefly can be measured in single days. We think this to be intensely short. But the housefly will consider its life, based upon its life cycle to be complete. The fly does not view time beyond its own context.

We human beings share this self-centered perception of time with the housefly. Just as the fly does not consider what life must be like beyond its limitations and perceptions, so too do we. And this is where entities of higher consciousness are so different from us. They see past, present, and future as one concentric whole. We do not even see and understand our own present, all the more so our past and our future.

This is why so many people walk forward today into a dark unknown oblivious to the mistakes and hardships that they will suffer. For many, they do not know, and equally there are many who do not care! And so the work of the Watchers continues, to guide blind humanity back to sight, and to teach the lame how to walk again.

Divine Judgement occurs in accordance with Divine Time. God does not act in accordance with human speed. Therefore, for us, we often think that God is long-suffering, and slow to anger. But this may very well only be true from a human perspective, but not from the Divine one! Divine Judgement may be immediate by Heaven's standards, but by human standards, Divine Judgement may appear to take years and decades in order to manifest.

One who lives exclusively by human standards of consciousness will not be aware of the subtle movements of the Divine Hand. As such, when Divine intervention does not occur within the framework of human expectations, many human beings conclude that there is no Divine Justice or Judgement to come. With such beliefs, many continue to behave in wanton ways with conviction that there is no One and no Thing that is willing or able to stop them.

Those with faith in Heaven, and those who have learned to sense the movement of the Moving Living Hand recognize that while Judgement may be slow in coming by our human standards, there is no such slowness from the Divine perspective. Thus when Judgment does make contact with the Earth, it is very pent up and explodes with unusual fury and destruction. Human history has shown this to us many times over. And still the foolish and the blind demand to march to the beat of their own drums, oblivious to the definitive fact that God is watching through His Watchers.

When Divine Judgement makes contact with Earth, the first area to be so affected is the human ability to think clearly and rationally. The greatest Divine punishment is the loss of one's mind and independent thinking. We see a number of Biblical examples of this kind, and we are left to wonder how many examples of this are on-going even now in present times.

The further that human consciousness shifts away from the higher-dimensional realities that slow down time, the more consciousness becomes entrapped in the relative dimensions of perceived fast-paced moving spacetime. This narrowness of attention is what blinds the mind from seeing beyond the immediate moment. Such entrapped minds do not see what is coming. And so, judgement overtakes the blind, always with terrible consequences.

There is no other way to say this other than to be blunt. This is the time where human society is presently at. Those individuals who want to see need to slow down and get back in touch with natural time. As for those who want to maintain their fast-paced, action-filled virtual/artificial realities, they will soon face the consequences of their choices. This is the edict of the Watchers, as ordained by the Divine Hand. And as we say, Barukh Dayan HaEmet, Blessed be the True Judge, amen.

Chapter 2

Freedom of the Mind, Beyond Returning Home

Freedom begins with a war for independence. It is always this way. One may not be enslaved by any external power, but, nevertheless, we are all imprisoned to a domineering, abusive power within ourselves.

Freedom for the people must always begin with freedom of the individual. For the individual who does not free one's mind from its internal prison, will remain enslaved to the ways of this world, without or without an external force seeking one's submission.

External forces that seek to dominate others can only succeed because there is an element in the human mind that makes it susceptible to domination.

In order for the mind to be free it must be able to independently think both rationally and intuitively. Without independent critical thought, minds are easily convinced to accept that which should not be accepted. Thus, the individual can end up doing actions to oneself and to others that ought not be done. Slaves have no control over themselves, they are not their own masters.

Freedom is a state of mind long before it manifests as a state of being.

Thought always precedes action. If there is no thought, then correspondingly there will be no action. On the other hand, the enlightened thought will lead one to enlightened action. All depends upon the individual.

One who sets one mind free will always be free, even if one is bound and locked up in a prison. A prison is meant to lock up one's mind. This is why one's body is incarcerated. Yet, once the mind is free, the condition of the body becomes less relevant to the point of being almost entirely irrelevant.

The free mind is the godly mind. The enslaved mind belongs to the proverbial devil.

The war of independence is fought to set free the mind from its submission to the many twisted thoughts that confuse and distract it.

In order to set the mind free, one must begin by understanding the nature of one's slavery, and equally understand how it is that we all became subject to this condition. Usually this is a question addressed by religion.

Religions each create a story of sorts to explain our present condition. The stories are usually never literal and take on the form of some very symbolic metaphors. While the stories, in and of themselves may be very true, due to their symbolic nature, it is very, very rare that anyone understands their actual meaning.

In the vast majority of cases, people read a story of symbolic metaphors, and mistakenly interpret them to be literal. As such stories make no sense. The rationally minded, then dismisses the story, thus losing all hope of understanding its deeply hidden message. As such, ignorance prevails, and is perpetually sustained.

Myths aside, we must begin with a basic premise. Each of us is far more than just a biological creature whose existence is due to happenstance, and coincidence. This view fundamentally denies the very essence of identity and seeks to enslave the human mind the most.

We are each conscious, sentient life-forms that far transcend the limits of our biological bodies. The proof of this is simple; take note of our feelings, our thoughts, and our imagination. Only the most disconnected among us denies the reality of our internal existence that is very much separate (and different) from our external existence. In other words, we do have, what we call, a soul. Essentially, our true identity is that of our souls, and not the identity that we associate with our bodies.

We exist. We think. We feel. We know, and we are known. These realities do not come from a biological source. They come from us, and they are what define us.

We are souls. We are beings that transcend the limitations of our present biological encasements. That which we know as the mind, the mind that is enslaved, and is in need of emancipation is the soul. Thus, it is always correct to refer to the mind-soul when referring to our true selves.

So, where does mind-soul come from? How did it get here? Why is it here? And where will it go after its association with the present biological body is terminated? These are the questions that the many religions attempt to answer with their metaphors. In order for us to set the mind-soul free from its entrapment, like I said above, we need to understand the nature of this entrapment.

First, let me state, that which we understand as our mind-soul, by definition, is itself not something physical. All that we know is that we can call it something energetic. But this energy that we call our mind-soul is conscious and sentient. It is thus not a type of energy that we presently understand. Mind-soul energy is not like other energies that we know of, such as electromagnetism or gravity. As for its relationship to these other force, this too, we do not know.

We are beings of energy, sentience, conscious, thinking and feeling. We presently exist in our biological bodies, which we all know are born, live for a while, and then ultimately die. Religions always propagate their view as to where the soul goes after the death of the body. We are all familiar with general religious teachings about the after-life and its domains of heaven and hell.

We do not need to elaborate on these stories here. So much for talk about the after-life. What we need to focus on is not what comes after this lifetime, but rather, what came before it?

As energetic beings, our mind-souls exist in a state outside of time. From our present perspective we may state that our mind-souls are immortal. They were not born together with the biological body any more than they die along with it. So, where did we come from? What was the before-life like?

The before-life is a subject of inquiry that few bother to investigate. Some will mention the idea of reincarnation, that before we were the person who we are today, we were someone else in the past. This is very true, but at the same time, many use this idea to fantasize and dream about past-lives that never really happened. Reincarnation is not our topic of discussion right now. I acknowledge its existence and its prevalence, but with this said, we still did not address our question; where do mind-souls come from? What is their true home?

In an after-life we return to the domain from which we came. We existed as non-human energetic beings before our birth into our present bodies, and we will return to our non-human energetic forms once we depart company with our present bodies. So, what is the place from which we came, and to what we shall return? Freedom of the mind-soul can only be defined as our not being entrapped; entrapped in our present consciousness that denies us access to the reality of our own personal greater reality that transcend our temporary biological identities.

Essentially, freedom of the mind-soul means to remember who we are, and from where we truly come from. Essentially, freedom of the mind-soul means the dawning of consciousness that reconnects us with our knowing that place we can truly call home.

We are not indigenous creatures of this Earth. Our bodies belong here. They come from the Earth and return to the Earth. But this is not the case of the mind-soul. We come here, and then we leave here. The free-mind soul leaves and returns home. The enslaved mind-soul is stuck, is trapped, and cannot leave to go home. This is the enslavement of the mind from which we need emancipation.

Our mind-souls come and incarnate as humans on Earth for many different reasons. Who knows what a full list of these reasons entails? All that we know is that we are here on Earth to be taught certain lessons. Earth is our schoolhouse. We come here to learn, and we stay here until our lessons are complete. This may take many lifetimes, but in one way or another, no one leaves Schoolhouse Earth until they "graduate." With this being said, not all souls incarnate here to learn. Some stay in our home (energetic) dimension and serve us as teachers, and guides.

Freedom of the mind-soul means that the individual soul learns its lessons, one of the most important being to not forget that we are energetic beings only temporarily encased in biological containers.

Upon the termination of our connection with our biological forms, our conscious mind-soul returns to its energetic domain of origin. Yet, after a lifetime here on Earth, with such intense identity with one's biological form, many who awaken in our home dimension fail to recognize it, and thus do not know where to go, or how to get there. Remember, living in an energetic domain must be very different from living in a biological one. The fundamental concepts of space, and time themselves are very different. The energetic domain of our origins is far different from the temporary domain of the physical.

For those so entrenched in physical matter, the reality of our original energetic domain is completely forgotten. Indeed, memory of it is repressed. This is how the mind-soul is enslaved. For once we forget our true home, we come to accept another place that is not our true home to actually be it. Thus mind-souls become disconnected and lost. Freedom of the mind-soul is to remember our true home.

Yet, once we remember our true home, our purpose is not to return there! We must remember that we are now mind-souls incarnate in physical bodies here in Schoolhouse Earth. Why did we choose to come here in the first place?

Choice: we do have choice! We each chose to leave our higher-dimensional home to place that part of us that we recognize as ourselves here in Schoolhouse Earth. What is it about Schoolhouse Earth that enticed us to leave home and to come here? No one leaves the comfort of home without good reason. If our higher-dimensional home was so wonderful, and we spend all of our time here on Earth craving to return there, then what motivated us in the first place to leave?

Maybe the answer is evolution? Maybe our mind-souls are not as "grown-up" as we would consider them to be? Maybe our original higher-dimensional home, as vast, and as different as it is from this reality, was not enough for the needs of our souls? Maybe our souls need to grow, to evolve, to essentially "grow-up."

If this is indeed the case, then the purpose of our sojourn here on Earth is not to crave to leave it and to return to the home which we chose to leave. Rather, our purpose here must be to learn. And as we learn and grow, maybe we are meant to not return to the home from which we came, but rather move on, and move into a new home, one more fitting for our now "grown-up" status.

So, what was the nature of the higher-dimensional home from which we came? And what is the nature of the higher-dimensional home to which we shall go? This and this, no one can speak about with clarity and certainty. All the while that we inhabit these physical bodies, Schoolhouse Earth acts like a filter over the mind to block out from conscious experience any actual experience of the higher-dimensions, from both before and after our sojourn in our present bodies.

Yes, mind-soul can be trained to experience and remember the greater reality of the higher dimensions within which we are living right now. But the purpose of such training is not for us to return "up there." Rather, our purpose here in Schoolhouse Earth is to bring "up-there" "down here."

We come to Earth to raise up its dimensional frequencies, along with our own. We come to Earth to learn how to live here, and not to become influenced by the natural pull of animalistic natural forces. The natural animalistic forces present in this dimensional plane are simply lower forms of consciousness that themselves need to "grow up." Our mind-souls come to Earth with the intent to learn the lessons that we need to learn in order to enable us to elevate the Earth consciousness. We ourselves, learn, grow, and mature. And as we do so, we manifest an energetic signature of maturation that itself influences all around us.

Eventually, the mind-souls of humanity will accomplish the collective goal of growth, and maturity. Our mind-souls will thus have no more to learn in Schoolhouse Earth. We will graduate, and our mind-souls will move on to other places in the universe to perform whatever function that will be right for us to perform there, at that time.

As we ascend to the stars, other lower life forms here on Earth will themselves evolve. They will become the vessels for the next set of mind-souls to incarnate here in Schoolhouse Earth to learn those lessons that will be right for them. This is not only what will happen to us in the future, but this is also what has already happened in the distant past. We are not the first here in Schoolhouse Earth, and we will not be the last.

Freedom of the mind-soul means freedom from the out-of-control compulsions that are brought about through our incarnation into physical bodies. Freedom of the mind comes about by taming the body by controlling its passion and desires.

Once we can control the influence of physicality placed upon our mind-souls, we will have learned our lessons about how to incarnate into these physical domains without being adversely influenced by them. Once we have learned this series of lessons our mind-souls are greatly enriched through the experience. Our old homes did not enable us the "space" to embrace this new-found reality. Our new homes will be ready-made for our new-found expanded consciousness.

Freedom of the mind-soul requires of us a lot more than just an awakening, remembering our past. Freedom of the mind-soul requires of us that each individual live a lifestyle of appropriate freedom all the while that one inhabits a physical body here on Schoolhouse Earth. Detachment from Earthly living is no goal. Such a stoic life path may indeed contradict the interactions necessary for growth.

Life and death in physical bodies are nothing more than temporary states. There is nothing to praise or to mourn about either state. All of us come to and go from Schoolhouse Earth multiple times. The coming and the going does not matter. What matters is what one does while here.

Freedom of the mind-soul means a self-identity that is not limited to identity with one's temporary physical body. One knows that one is more than just a temporary body of flesh and blood. One recognizes that one is actually an energetic mind-soul presently inhabiting a physical form for the purpose of learning certain lessons, as well as to accomplish certain deeds while here.

To acknowledge this concept as an academic idea is not enough, indeed all such academic ideas and learning is superficial and hollow at best. Expanding consciousness is not the acquisition of information, rather it is the personal, internal experience of such things, and the integration of such lessons into oneself, thus making oneself to be a wiser, and better soul.

Freedom of the mind transcends freedom of the body. Sometimes, due to whatever circumstances in life, one is not free to live as one would wish to live. Political, social, and economic powers all seek to enslave the bodies and the minds of others in order to usurp their psychic power. These lost souls seek their own freedom by taking it away from others. They believe that as long as they lord over others, then others will not lord over them. This is a very juvenile outlook on life, and it is also a very dangerous one.

Before one can consider political, social, and economic freedom for oneself, one must first emancipate and set free one's mind-soul from the many entrapments that political, social, and economic forces use to entrap them. Remember, slavery begins as a state of mind long before it becomes a state of being. One who has set one's mind-soul free sees through the facades used to entice others into slavery. And as simple as it might sound, only the free mind is a happy mind. All others are living in the various degrees of forgetfulness and misery.

Freedom of the mind-soul begins with the contemplative efforts not to look forward, but rather to look into the pre-birth past into the before-life, where and when one existed as the luminescent being of light that one truly still is. One who can remember this, and feel, sense, and know its reality will discover the emancipation of mind from all its earthy attachments.

There is nothing wrong with having attachments; they are after all, part of this present temporary life. But just as this life is temporary, so too are our attachments to everything within it. The free mind lets go without having to physically let go.

Freedom for the mind-soul is the imperative of life. It will be accomplished by each of us, regardless of however many painful reincarnations that we endure due to our slow learning pace. Freedom of your mind-soul, it is your destiny; embrace it!

Chapter 3

Expanded & Contracted Consciousness
The Mohin of Gadlut & Katnut

There are always fluctuations in consciousness. Sometimes one can be aware of surrounding higher realities. Sometimes one is caused to be focused exclusively on the perceived here and now. This focus on physicality is often felt by one to be a loss of higher perceptions. In this state of mind, one feels less, disconnected, and even lost. But these negative states of mind are as much an illusion and delusion as is the physical world around us.

What we see and sense we are so convinced is the ultimate truth of our reality. If one were to be emersed into a virtual reality computer simulation, wherein which everything that one senses comes from the computer program, one will be convinced by one's sensory reception that what one is experiencing in virtual reality, is itself objective, true reality. Just as the virtual reality is just a program of a computer, so too is our reality a virtual creation of a Higher Source.

Just as one enters and exits the virtual reality of the computer world, so too does one enter and exit this world in similar fashion. What we know as life in this world, and what we think of as death from this world are both parts of a higher virtual (subjective) reality in which we all exist. This is a fact of what we call creation.

One who contemplates the big picture may glean insight into the true relative nature of our being here in the present reality of this world. Others simply focus on getting through the ups and downs of this world day by day. Whatever one's focus, the reality of what *is* does not change.

Expanding consciousness is not an emotionally based process. It even transcends thought and intellect, and enters into the domain of the psychic, into the reality of one just knowing what is, and living within the context of this insight.

The objective reality is, that on a day to day basis we are oblivious to the presence of the greater world surrounding us. Our own minds seem to sabotage our perceptions by attempting to lock them in focus on the physical that we see. But there is far more to reality than this minor spectrum of present human perception.

Even modern science has discovered that the physical universe, all that we see and know makes up less than 5% of the reality that they themselves know is there, but as yet cannot fully comprehend. Scientists call this 95% of reality that is unknown to us Dark Matter and Dark Energy. As for what it is, we are told that modern science does not know. They call it Dark because they cannot yet see into it.

While modern science has its limitations, human consciousness shares no such boundaries.

The human mind, consciousness, us, we are presently living in the other 95% of reality as much as we are living in the 5% seen by the eye. Being that we are already there, it is not like we have to travel to get there. When we talk about expanding consciousness, we are talking about expanding our minds and our perceptions to begin to recognize our present presence in some form and way in this greater 95% of reality.

We call this greater 95% of reality, incorporeal. In religion we call the 95% the realm of the spiritual. Regardless of what it is called the higher reality surrounds us, and embraces us in every way, and at every moment. This is a reality that one may choose to deny, but one may never be free from it, regardless of one's denials.

We touch this greater reality by the expansion of our minds and consciousness. We too delve into the dark recesses of the mind that we call the unconscious. Dark matter, dark energy, and dark (unconscious) mind; they all share the same domain in similar fashion as our present conscious mind embraces reality based upon the limitations and parameters of the 5% of reality that we call the visible universe.

When we delve into the unconscious and draw up from it experiences and insights, we are reaching out into the Dark Universe, not dark in any evil sense, but dark in the sense of it not being seen or known. As we experience periodic moments of connection with these domains, we call this expanded consciousness. These moments of experience usually happen to everyone from time to time. But most do not pay attention. Most do not even care. And this is why most people remain the dark, simply because they do not want to see the Light.

Regardless of any individual or personal desire on behalf of the part of us that resides locked into this present state of consciousness, the higher parts of our being do not tolerate being completely cut off. Although the individual unconscious is safely out of sight, and thus out of mind, it still nevertheless exerts its powerful influence upon the conscious mind in many unseen ways. No matter how convincing our present virtual reality may be, the greater part of our higher Selves always intrudes to remind us of its presence.

The nature of such intrusions, of course, are not conscious. As such, these intrusions of the unconscious into the conscious mind usually take the form of deeply felt impressions, which often express themselves as emotions. Many times, we find ourselves feeling very strongly about something for no apparent rational reason. The unconscious imposes itself into consciousness, regardless of however much we may seek to repress it. Like I said above, most people don't want to know the Light.

The normal state of everyday consciousness is what we call restricted consciousness. It is restricted due to our own imposed limitations upon expansion. Most times, these restrictions are self-imposed, but not always. Circumstances in this virtual reality of ours almost always contributes to keep us restricted into the 5% or so of our perceived perceptions of the world. In most case, one must make efforts in order to broaden the limits beyond the 5%.

The efforts of which I speak are the tools and techniques used to train the mind to sense, to feel, and to eventually see beyond the 5%. These tools and techniques have for the most part throughout history been found in the schools of meditative religions. It was not until modern times, that the ancient techniques were extracted from their religious garments and laid bare in the light of scientific secularism.

This development has both its advantages and its drawbacks. The advantage is that finally it can be shown and proven that higher states of consciousness do exist, and are not just religious fantasies, or imagination. Proper analysis of the outside world has granted us discoveries of the realities of our existence. Continued proper analysis of the internal world of the unconscious will continue to grant us even more discoveries of the realities of our existence. These are definitely advantageous.

However, the drawback is that most researchers in consciousness do not have full access to the religious, spiritual, meditative tools and techniques that have been passed down through the centuries. Many secular researchers bear a prejudice against the old and often refuse to examine the ancient teachings with any sort of open mind sincerely looking to discover their secrets. As such, the secular researcher often overlooks much, and dismisses the ancient as being unworthy of his pursuits.

Even in the science of the exploration of consciousness, there exists some residual resistance to actually experience higher consciousness, regardless of understanding the why's and how's of it. It is due to these drawbacks that those who pursue higher consciousness still resort to the ancient ways found in religious and meditative experiences.

Religions, by definition have always declared that we live in a greater universe, unseen by the limited eye. Indeed, it has always been the religions, especially those which are meditative in nature who have experienced the greater reality outside this virtual reality first hand. The practitioners of these paths are the ones who have cracked holes in their virtual reality helmets and peak through those holes to gaze upon the real world that most everyone else denies existing.

The first step of contact with the greater reality is that emotional sense, which one just feels and knows that there is 'something" else out there. One may not be able to explain it, but one senses deep within that the greater reality is somehow real, and indeed, close. This is the first step in expanding consciousness. Unfortunately, this may be the only step that many take.

In order to expand consciousness beyond this most basic sense of just internal knowing requires that one engage in practices that step by step enables consciousness to expand beyond the prison of present virtual reality. Religions developed entire systems of meditations and visualizations in order to accomplish just this.

One of these meditative systems was developed by the Prophets of the Bible. We see examples of their expanded consciousness in their recorded visions of realities invisible to the untrained eye. Throughout the centuries the methods of the Prophets were passed down and are still practiced to this day.

The practitioners of the Prophetic School today faithfully follow in the footsteps of their predecessors. And because of this, the practitioners recognize the fluid and fluctuating nature of subjective psychic vision. In other words, expanded consciousness always flows through the restricted consciousness of the individual. Therefore, what one sees and experiences today is indeed the same as it was in the past, but what is seen is seen in an entirely different way. Only the one trained in intuitive wisdom is able to see through the facades and to penetrate into the true underlying psychic reality.

The Prophetic system gave birth to the Merkava system and the system of the Prophetic Kabbalah. We do not need to waste time to academically elaborate on the history of these systems, how they are similar or different, or what they do or do not mean. What we need to focus on is experience outside the present virtual reality, and not on further experiences inside it.

Expanded consciousness means experiencing reality outside of our present virtual reality. This type of consciousness is called in the Kabbalah, Mohin of Gadlut, which literally translates as "brains of bigness." Yes, I know many desire more elaborate academic definitions, but like I said above, such an approach only takes one in the opposite direction of what one needs to experience. In other words, it is not the academic learning that counts. What counts is the experience beyond the academic, beyond rational thinking.

The Kabbalah refers to states of consciousness by the term Mohin, brains. This term was adopted centuries ago. Indeed, in modern times we can think of many other terms to maybe better describe consciousness. But the ancient term is the one that has been used for centuries. Those who embrace the system see no need to change it. It is only the outsider who wants to come in on one's own terms that seeks change. The one who wishes to embrace a system has to embrace the system the way it is, and not seek to make changes without valid experiential reasons.

The term Gadlut means "bigness." The term Katnut means "smallness." Consciousness is described in one of these two ways. Most people, most times live in the state of Mohin of Katnut. This is the term for the consciousness of this 5% virtual reality. The Prophetic system endeavors to train individuals to receive spurts of Mohin of Gadlut, which again is expanded consciousness. These insights come in spurts. In other words, they come and they go, like flashes of lighting. Nevertheless, regardless of the short experience, the Mohin of Gadlut leave behind a deep impression which itself is often life-changing.

Meditative practices have been designed to cultivate the experience of the momentary Mohin of Gadlut. Like a spark of light, or light a bolt of lightning, higher consciousness bursts into lower consciousness, and for an instant, grants one access and insight into the greater reality around us.

Pause must then be taken to digest the experience and to integrate it into one's Mohin of Katnut. This digestion process enables the Mohin of Katnut to expand just a little bit. Multiple repetitions of these practices lead to the continued strengthening and expansion of Mohin of Katnut, enabling one greater and longer exposure to the Mohin of Gadlut. And this is how the process of enlightenment is achieved.

When it comes to daily prayers, the Kabbalists speak about how the prayer service is supposed to enable one to experience, for the moment, Mohin of Gadlut. However, today in reality, modern daily prayers in the prayer quorum (minyan) are often recited very fast, and without any deep intent. For most attendees of the quorum (minyan), there is no spiritual depths in public prayer at all. For most the experience Mohin of Gadlut is an unknown and uninteresting commodity. During prayers, many are not even focused on the words that they are saying. During prayer, many do not even have Mohin of Katnut. Their wandering thoughts are all over the place instead of in the place where they are supposed to be.

This 5% world of ours presently captures almost 100% of our focus and consciousness. It is no wonder then why so many live so obliviously to the reality through which they walk daily.

Mohin of Katnut are not the normal state which we human beings were designed and destined to embrace. Our 5% world however is so intoxicating that we pass through daily life unaware of most of the 5% around us, and even more so of 95% of the rest of reality.

Remember this, our presence here in this 5% reality itself is not 100%. We are not 100% here at all. Only the smallest part of our minds is entrapped here, in the temporary identity that we have had assigned to ourselves, and to which we contribute to create. That which we call the individual self of this world, the Nefesh soul in Kabbalah, is merely a fraction of the whole "us." The reason why we lose focus of higher external realities is because we have already formerly been disconnected from the higher 95% of our Selves, the central core of which is what the Kabbalah calls, the Neshama higher Self soul.

Each of us presently has Mohin of Gadlut We are operating in it and experiencing it at every moment. So, why do we not sense it, or feel it? This is because it is the higher 95% of our Selves that is in Gadlut. Our lower self, the identity of which is what we think and believe about ourselves is the part of "us" stuck in the 5%, and thus stuck in the Mohin of Katnut.

Only when the lower part of the individual reconnects with the upper part of one's own Self can one attain a glimpse of the Mohin of Gadlut. While not everyone can integrate 100% of one's higher Self here in this mundane, mortal world, nevertheless, many can and do incorporate portions of their higher Selves to various degrees.

So, in conclusion, there is one question left to ask. What are the revelations and insights that one receives in a state of Mohin of Gadlut? Aside from insights into the deeper meanings one may discover in religious teachings and practices, one gains a heightened sense of the necessity for moral and righteous behavior.

Our souls incarnate here on Earth for a reason. Often our life's purpose is never, or only partially, realized because of our many daily distractions. We often forget who we are, where we come from, and why we are here. This is the state of Mohin of Katnut.

Mohin of Gadlut may indeed fill one with the emotional zeal to act and perform in certain ways. These ways are how our purpose on Earth is manifested and accomplished. One of the most important revelations is that all life is sacred. All life forms are part of a greater whole. All of us must come to know and embrace this reality as the internal truth that it is. Insights into righteousness and even holiness are common in the state of Mohin of Gadlut.

All expanded consciousness is not for the purpose of granting us access to the higher dimensions for no reason. There is a reason for all things. Knowing what is above is fine. But to acquire such knowledge is not why we are here on Earth. Earth is our collective schoolroom. We are all here to learn, we are all here to grow.

Mohin of Gadlut enables us to better see this, and to act accordingly.

To act in accordance with the Mohin of Gadlut means the refinement of personal character, and to improve one's behavior. One sees the wisdom in embracing the highest moral caliber. One acts with lovingkindness towards all. Yet, at the same time, the enlightened soul recognizes evil (and evil doers) and treats them as need be. This, of course, is decided by the circumstances at hand.

Mohin of Gadlut (greatness) makes one to be great, great in wisdom, great in righteousness, and great in lovingkindness. Anyone who pursues these, wisdom, righteousness, and lovingkindness will discover that actions of these kinds will themselves fill one with higher consciousness.

One who acts with wisdom, righteousness, and lovingkindness in general, in all walks of life, will discover that their performance of the rituals of Divine service (mitzvot) will become a richer, more fulfilling experience.

There are many ways to expand consciousness. Meditation is only one of them. What one does, and how one behaves defines the person, and brings one back in touch with the greater 95% of one's Self. Schoolhouse Earth is here to teach us these lessons.

Chapter 4

The Art of Identity:
Bonding with Members of One's Soul Family
Kavanot to Unite with the Soul of a Tzadik

Identity is not what most imagine it to be. Who and what you are far transcends the identity of the person that you are today, here on Earth, in a body of flesh and blood.

What we really are, we call souls. In Hebrew, there are five different names for soul, with each one being given separate and different attributes according to the Kabbalah. What the Kabbalah outlines is important academic information, but it does not lead one to experiencing the nature of soul on a personal basis.

Rather than digress to discuss the different attributes of the Nefesh, Ruah, Neshama, Hayah and Yehida, let us instead deal with the reality of identity. We can then use Kabbalah terminology to assist our understanding.

That which we call soul, the essential Self, is the level of soul that the Kabbalists call Neshama. You are your Neshama. Within your Neshama there are deeper levels of consciousness, these are your higher souls, the Hayah and Yehida.

You exist, period! Before you incarnated into your present human form, you existed. You existed then (and in a way still do) in an entirely non-human form. This original form of your essential being is some kind of higher dimensional energy body. We cannot say for sure what its composition is. All we can say is that we call it one's body of light. This is not to be mistaken for one's astral body; the two are very significantly different.

Consciousness is the realization of one's personal existence, the realization of one's surroundings, and the relationship between the two. Consciousness can be summed up in two words: "I am." However, existence can be summed up in one word: "I." Existence must come before one can become conscious of one's existence. What comes next is identity, which can be summarized by saying: "I am what I am." In other words, one is, one is aware that one is, and one is aware of what one is. This defines identity.

Now that we have defined what identity is, we must understand that our true identity is something far more than just our present association with our present surroundings, with focused consciousness on our bodies of flesh and blood. There is far more to identity, and far more to consciousness that our present narrow focus on the flesh and blood body.

Our true identity cloaks itself inside of the identity associated with the body. In Kabbalah terms, we say that the Neshama soul is cloaked within the Nefesh soul. In psychology terms, we say that the unconscious resides at levels deep beneath the conscious mind. Thus, our true identity, one's Inner Self, the Neshama soul, and the unconscious are all one and the same.

Our true identity chooses to cloak itself within physical flesh and to create a temporary alternate identity. This alternative is the present identity of our flesh and blood bodies. It is as if a part of the Neshama soul splits off and forms for itself a physical form through which it enters this world temporarily.

The reason why we send parts of ourselves into different forms and bodies in different worlds is so that a part of ourselves can learn from the experiences experienced within that temporary interaction, for the sake of the greater good of the whole Self.

Compare this to a virtual reality machine, the kind that is growing in popularity today in many shopping malls. One puts on the virtual reality headset, which controls both audio and visual input. One then enjoys the program. One of the popular programs run today in these mall shops is the roller coaster ride. The seat in which one sits shakes, bumps and jumps. Combined with the virtual reality headset one receives the impression of the experience of a real roller coaster ride. One then disengages from the machine and goes about one's business having now the enjoyment and the memory of a roller coaster ride that, in reality, never happened.

This experience best describes why the Neshama comes to Earth, creating a Nefesh identity for itself, dwelling within it, and serving as the Nefesh's higher/inner mind, its unconscious. We come here to learn, not to stay. We come here for a short period of time (in the cosmic scheme of things). We accomplish a task or learn a lesson. We then return to where we have come from, richer for the experience learned here in this incarnation. One can then evolve and grow and become more than what one was.

A normal Neshama can come and go back and forth to Earth, and to other places, planets, and domains many, many times. We can place our Neshama selves into any form through which we need to learn. Thus, one can incarnate as human, or as another other life form, regardless of its form or dimension.

Of course, the obvious danger in all this soul travel is what if someone gets caught up in a Nefesh identity and refuses to let it go? This is when we see individual Neshamot becoming entangled in a relationship to a single form, and thus seeking numerous repetitive incarnations into that form. Our group of Neshamot presently has this attachment problem with the present physical human form.

We do not need to be here on Earth, but somehow, we got stuck here. This is the underlying message that we receive from the Biblical stories about Adam and Eve, and the eating of the forbidden fruit. Due to the lengthy nature of these teachings, this is not the time nor place to elaborate on it.

We also need to be made aware of the reality that our Neshama selves may indeed create multiple Nefesh smaller-selves simultaneously. In other words, there are what we can call soulmates and even soul families. The entirety of Nefesh souls of a single Neshama Self are all soul mates and are a soul family. All Nefesh smaller-selves of a specific Neshama higher Self are essentially one.

All individual Nefesh souls, upon their departure from their present Nefesh form, and their return into the greater consciousness of the higher Neshama Self bring to the higher Self all memories and experiences from all the different Nefesh incarnations. Thus, one Nefesh soul living today has the potential, upon restoring consciousness of the higher Neshama Self within itself, to tap into the memories and experiences of all other Nefesh incarnations of the source Neshama.

This is how one can connect with the Nefesh souls of others regardless of where those others are in space and in time. Theoretically, one can tap into the memories and experiences of those others, and communicate with them, as if one was thinking inside one's head to oneself. Most often, a Nefesh incarnation does not achieve sufficient consciousness to become aware of one's inner higher Neshama Self. Thus, connection with other kindred souls is recognized more so by external clues rather than by internal ones.

Being that Nefesh identity is only a temporary shell for Neshama consciousness, it is only natural for it to not immediately see or recognize its own greater reality. Normally, this would not be too much of a problem. For the Nefesh identity, if properly trained in the ways of mind and psychic communication, would naturally grow in awareness until such a point where Neshama consciousness could stream through it fully, as a natural course of events.

This was the intended first state of Adam in the garden of Eden. It was this state of natural integration between Nefesh and Neshama consciousness that was lost with the metaphorical eating of the forbidden fruit. Essentially this act provoked the formation and crystallization of Nefesh consciousness prior to becoming fully aware of Neshama consciousness.

Thus, the Nefesh instead on serving as a conduit and a Merkava through which the Neshama could enter into this physical domain and interact with it, succumbed to the delusion of illusion of thinking itself to be a separate independent entity disconnected from, or even devoid of Neshama. The Art of Identity means that one learns how not to divest of Nefesh consciousness but rather how to integrate the seemingly disconnected Neshama.

The Art of Identity, of exploring and discovering one's Self is accomplished in a number of different ways. The Kabbalah teaches two fundamental forms of meditation, one very different from the other, but both still being focused on the same accomplishment: expanded consciousness. However, these methods are usually focused on grander, more lofty goals, such as to bond with the spirit of Torah, or to seek direct communion with God. These go far beyond the Art of Identity.

Another Kabbalistic method used to expand consciousness along the way back to fully integrating the Nefesh with the greater Neshama, is to psychically explore one's Nefesh mind to seek out other soul family Nefashot. Remember, there are many other parts of your greater Neshama soul out there, spread around through space and time. Any contact with any one of them helps an isolated Nefesh soul reconnected with others parts of its greater whole.

So, how does one recognize a kindred soul of one's greater Neshama soul family? One can sense a feeling of attachment or connection to another, but in order for this to be developed one must know who it is that one feels such an attachment. In other words, the attraction has to be felt deeply on a very personal basis. Mere intellectual considerations or curiosities do not generate enough psychic energy to enable a connection to occur. Also, such connections are most often focused upon members of one's greater soul family. If one were to choose to try to bond with someone outside the soul family, while it can very well happen, it is, needless to say, much more difficult and complicated.

To bond with one from one's soul family, one needs to identify who the other Nefesh soul is. Remember, we are not seeking to actually meet and greet this other soul in the flesh. This is not the procedure of operations for one to find a spouse. This is the procedure for one finding a kindred soul who can serve as a "spirit" guide providing one with greater revelations and insights into one's chosen form of higher dimensional expression (be it a religion or some other form of "spirituality").

One may peruse literature and discover an emotional connection with an author or other long-past teacher. In the Kabbalah tradition, students are encouraged to pore through Rabbinic literature and to seek out who among the great Sages of the past does one feel an attraction towards. Being that one is a student of these Sages, and that souls reincarnate as families, it stands to reason that a student of the Sages most likely is a kindred-soul to at least one of them.

Once one identifies such a kindred soul, and one feels the special connection to him, one can then proceed to perform specific visualization meditations that are designed for one Nefesh soul to connect with another within one's soul group.

When, however, one feels the desire to connect with a soul that is not from one's soul family, this too can be accomplished. However, the nature of the attachment will be of a different, lower intensity. R. Hayim Vital, the redactor of the Kabbalah of the Ari'zal discusses these matters and visualizations in his writings. He renumerates a set of terms that can assist us in understanding the different types of soul connections.

R. Hayim uses three words to describe soul connections. These are Hevel (breath), Kol (voice), and Dibur (speech). R. Hayim often uses the terms Kol and Dibur when discussing matters of psychic (prophetic) contact. We will follow his example in using these two terms, Kol and Dibur, in describing the different types of soul connections.

Remember, each Nefesh soul that lives here on Earth, upon departure (death) leaves this world, and ascends into a different dimensional plane to continue one's journey and mission. During this period, if a Nefesh soul merits it, it can return to the Neshama and be absorbed back into its wholeness. As we have said above, most do not accomplish this.

The Nefesh identity nevertheless is shaken off, in similar manner to how one would awaken from a dream. The Nefesh identity does not forget who it was in its previous incarnation on Earth but realizes that it is so much more than what it was. So, if we were to conjure the real and authentic Nefesh soul of the dearly departed, and ask them, are you so-and-so the recently departed? The soul would answer saying, that he was such-and-such a person, but that now he is so much more.

But if we were to conjure the dearly departed, is not our call to them a disruption of their repose in the after-life? In most cases, it most certainly is!

Think about this. Let's say that one feels a strong attachment to the soul of a dearly departed Sage from Biblical or Talmudic times, and one wants to attach with the soul of that Sage. One then performs the appropriate meditations and Kavanot in the attempt to make contact. Now, let us say that contact is indeed made. One feels as if the soul of the great Sage is indeed connected to one's soul. Let us dismiss all skeptical arguments of this not being the case, and equally dismiss any psychological concerns of this connection being some form of mental aberration. Let us say that real contact is made. And thus, we are left with a big question, which is this: if indeed real contact has been made with the soul, what exactly are we in contact with?

The soul of the departed that we seek to connect with is its Nefesh soul, which bears the identity and memories of the individual as it lived the life that it did. But have we not already learned that the Nefesh soul, upon passing from the body is either reabsorbed into the Neshama or reincarnates in order to continue its journey. How then can it be available for one to make contact with it now?

Here is where we use the Kabbalistic distinction between Kol and Dibur. We will also introduce here the concept of psychological archetype. This is important for our understanding because we see a clear example of what we will be discussing in the Biblical book of Samuel, with regards to the episode of King Saul using a witch/medium to contact the soul of the recently departed prophet Samuel.

When the Nefesh departs the body and ascends upon its journey, the residual of the Nefesh remains intact. This residual is the sum of its memories and emotions. Remember that at every moment all of us emanate brain waves, which includes all our thoughts and feelings. These energy waves never die. They continue around in the ether (the higher dimension of our atmosphere) forever. Thus, when one calls upon the Nefesh of another, it is most often the case that one is making contact with this ethereal residual of the Nefesh soul and not the actual Nefesh soul itself, which as we have already explained may be occupied elsewhere. The collection of all these residual memories has been given a modern name, they are called the Akashic Records.

This residual element of the Nefesh soul is the level of connection called Dibur, speech. For it is at this level that one is tapping into the idea and concept of the Nefesh soul, while not actually making contact with its present state. And now things can get more interesting!

What if someone wishes to connect with the Nefesh soul of someone who really never existed? We would think that if there was no Nefesh soul, then there cannot be a residual soul, and therefore there would be nothing to contact. All such efforts would be in vain. Is this not so?

The answer is that no, this is not so, not so at all! It is very possible to connect with what appears to be a residual soul, even though it is not. For as groups of people believe in an identity, even if it is they themselves that create that identity, their self-made creation takes on a life of its own in the psychological arena. We call this manifestation, an Archetype.

This understanding explains for us how a Protestant Christian can see, experience, and interact with a blond hair, blue eyed Jesus Christ who never existed. The historical Jew Yeshu would not have had blond hair or blue eyes but would have rather looked like every other Jew of his day with black hair and brown eyes. And yet, many modern-day Protestant Christians still see their imagined form of Jesus, and not the real historical residual soul. The Protestant has his idea and image of who Jesus was, and the combined thoughts of like-minded Christians serves to manifest the archetype for all believers.

There are many voices that can be heard. They do not have to be historical. The voices are real because people believe in them. Therefore, even a fictional character can have a voice and serve as a source of inspiration and insight within one's personal psyche. This is the power of a human generated archetype created by the minds and thoughts of a group of people who think alike.

While the existence of archetypes is real, this does not mean that there is any real spiritual or psychic element within such revelations. Usually, all such interactions are mere psychological projections of the individual. In other words, one hears from the archetypal image just what one wants to hear, or what one expects to hear. Nothing more! Yet, one is convinced that "the Image" has spoken. This type of experience often confirms an individual's false beliefs and may even be interpreted by one as being touched by God. This is a form of megalomania, and it is the foundation of what the Bible called false prophecy and idolatry.

Now, that we have covered the negative aspect of the Dibur experience, let us review the positive side of it before we proceed to discuss the Kol experience.

One can indeed receive positive inspiration from connection with a Nefesh soul not from one's own source. But such a connection can only be at the Dibur level. Such an experience would be with the archetype (residual image) of the person, and not with the person himself.

For example, many desire to connect with the souls of great Sages from the past. But regardless of one's desires or feelings, one might not be connected to such a Sage, and thus, connection cannot be established with any ease or clarity. What one can connect with, and does connect with, is the archetypal image of that Sage, which is the image of that Sage, which resides in one's mind.

The image within one's mind can and does take on a life of its own (autonomy). As such it serves as a cloak through which one's own higher Self communicates with one's conscious mind. This type of communication is very common.

Many believe that they hear or sense the Voice of God, or of some angel, or Sage. The image in their thoughts is strong, and thus any real communication from the unconscious is pushed through that image form, giving rise in one's thoughts that the image is alive and real. In many cases, this is benign and not a problem. We have already discussed how this experience is on the negative side the foundation of idolatry. So, when dealing with any kind of bonding with an archetype, as opposed to a real soul, these dangers are present, but they can be avoided by one with an open mind.

As for the bond with the Kol (voice), this is the true union. This level of connection with another Nefesh soul of your general Neshama soul group is a real psychic, telepathic experience. It is just that the nature of this type of experience is so often misunderstood.

When one does make actual contact with another Nefesh soul from one's greater Neshama soul group, one begins the contact at the Dibur (speech) level. In other words, one seeks contact with the truly connected in the same way that one would pursue contact with an archetype.

While the archetype contact seems real emotionally, it is in the rational and intellectual realm that one is able to spot the lack of true depth, and to thus recognize its limitations. With an authentic Kol (voice) experience, it is not overwhelming as the Dibur (speech) experience might appear. For when the Dibur experience occurs, its shallowness is usually offset by the intensity of one's emotions believing the experience to be more than what it really is.

With regards to the Kol (voice) experience, making contact is much more subtle, more refined, more subconscious, than conscious.

The Kol (voice) experience is an actual psychic connection, first with the archetype (Dibur) level of the soul sibling, and then with the essence (Kol) of that soul sibling. The Kol level gives one access to the actual reabsorbed Nefesh soul in the Neshama whole. Thus, tapping into one's higher Self, can lead one into discovering connections to one's soul family.

At the same time, one who follows his intense feeling of bond with another Nefesh, may indeed discover an inner-knowing about things related to the kindred Nefesh not found in any book. One can indeed proceed with this kind of inner dialogue, maybe at first not believing it to be an actual other with whom one is internally dialoging. But in time, one can continue to, as if, feel the presence of the one with whom one wishes to make contact. When one contemplates, say for example, the words of Torah spoken by the kindred soul, that kindred soul, through the singularity of the Neshama that you both share, can tap into your thoughts as easy as you can tap into his.

Tapping into a real member of one's soul family, like I said, is not an easy task, but it still is a doable one. R. Hayim Vital outlined a special meditative practice that is meant to help guide one in establishing and maintaining such a connection. The Rabbis' meditative practice involves calling upon YHWH and seeking the classical union of YHWH with His Shekhina. One then proceeds to visualize certain holy Names that represent union at each level of the four worlds, Atzilut, Beriah, Yetzirah and Asiyah.

This is R. Hayim's meditative practice, the Kavanot to unite with a Tzadik.

First, meditate upon Shem Havaya, יהוה

contemplate uniting the Holy One blessed be He
and the Shekhina represented by the letters Vav Hey (love) ו"ה with Yod Hey (awe). י"ה

Then contemplate Shem Havaya in Hokhma with the vowel Patah יְהֹוָה בחכמה
and the name Ehyeh in Binah. אהיה בבינה

Afterwards unite the two names together: י"א ה"ה ו"י ה"ה

by the power of Shem Havaya of Yodin. יוד הי ויו הי

This union comes about by power of the Neshama of the Neshama of the Tzadik,
which comes from Hokhma, which corresponds to the first letter Yod י
of Shem Havaya.

Meditate upon Shem SAG יוד הי ואו הי

in order to raise up from Binah MahN (mayim nokbin), which is the power of desire from below.

This meditation comes about by power of the Neshama of the Tzadik,
which comes from Binah, which corresponds to the first letter Hey ה of Shem Havaya.

After this, meditate upon Shema Havaya in Tiferet with the vowel Holam: יְהֹוָה

and the Name Adonai in Malkhut אדנ"י

Then join them together יאהדונהי

by the Shem Havaya of Alefs (MAH) יוד הא ואו הא

This union comes about by power of the Ruah of the Tzadik,
which comes from Tiferet, which corresponds to the letter Vav ו of Shem Havaya.

Meditate upon Shem BEN יוד הה וו הה

in order to raise up from Malkhut MahN (mayim nokbin), which is the power of desire from below

This union comes about by power of the Nefesh of the Tzadik,
which comes from Malkhut, which corresponds to the final Hey ה of Shem Havaya.

The image here is taken from my Shiviti for the Kavnot to Unite with a Tzadik. The terms and concepts related here are standard for R. Hayim Vital. Let us review each level.

A standard meditative practice performed all the time, and especially during prayers is called the Yihud Kudsha Brikh Hu u'Shekhinteh (the union of God with His Shekhina). There are numerous meanings applied to this statement, We will focus only on one. This is the union of God (the Holy One, blessed be He – Kudsha Brikh Hu), and the higher Neshama Self, which becomes a vessel for the Divine Presence, the Shekhina. One begins all meditative bonds first with one uniting with one's personal higher Neshama Self and by contemplating its attachment to God.

One then proceeds to meditate upon the chosen Nefesh soul that one is trying to contact. Aside from using all our standard Prophetic Kabbalah meditation techniques, one should recite words, or the teachings of the Nefesh soul (the Tzadik) that one wishes to contact.

One then proceeds to create a visualization of merging with the Nefesh of the Tzadik, step by step, one level of consciousness at a time. We begin with the most unconscious, sublime level, the Haya level of soul, the source of the Neshama itself.

One visualizes the Name YHWH with its associate vowel (patah). One then visualizes the Name AHYH (Ehyeh). These two Names represent the two forces (sefirot) of mind Hokhma (psychic mind) and Binah (intellectual mind). One visualizes the Name of YHWH of AB (72) as if acting to bring together and to merge these two Names, as described above in the diagram. This visualization is designed to connect your Nefesh soul, with that of the Tzadik at the deepest level of connection, represented by the letter Yod of YHWH.

To commune with the Neshama level of the Tzadik, one visualizes the Name YHWH of SAG (63), corresponding to the first letter Hey of YHWH. One should contemplate how intense one's desire is to bond with the Neshama level of the Tzadik in question. Essentially, being that YHWH of SAG corresponds to Binah and the rational mind, the contemplation here is a strong emotional cry (MahN) telepathically calling out to the Tzadik with all one's desire and heart.

One proceeds to seek communion with the Ruah of the Tzadik. This is his level of personal passion that inhabited his Nefesh soul, with its source in his essence in the greater Neshama soul that you two share. Again, one visualizes the Name YHWH, this time in Tiferet, with its assigned vowel Holam. One then visualizes this Name merging with the Name ADNY (Adonai), forging a union of the Nefesh of the Tzadik with your Nefesh. Visualize this being brought about by the Name YHWH of MAH (45), corresponding to the Wav of YHWH.

Finally, one contemplates the Name YHWH of BEN (52), corresponding to the final letter Hey of YHWH. Again, one telepathically cries out to the Tzadik to please come to you. Visualize your mind, conscious and unconscious become a vessel for communion with the Tzadik.

If this is successful, you will sense, feel, and see absolutely nothing! This type of contact is not subject to instant gratification.

Contact with another Nefesh soul from your Neshama higher Self is a subtle thing. You may begin to feel a process of thought in your mind giving you news insights, revelations, and entirely new perspectives on things. These thoughts, you are sure are your own, but being that they are so different from what you normally think, they may well indeed be coming from your Tzadik of choice. Continue to read the words of you chosen Tzadik and maybe you will receive some form of confirmation.

This mediative practice can take some time to produce results. And even when results are forthcoming, like I said, they may not even be recognizable as such. Nevertheless, the influence of another Nefesh soul from your Neshama source Self is very possible.

Indeed, this level of connection and influence between Nefesh souls of a singular source may actually be very common, felt at the deepest levels of the unconscious mind, and thus oblivious to the conscious mind.

We tend to think of ourselves as isolated souls, separate from everyone else. But this is never the case. Although we do not see the connection of souls with our physical eyes, our internal psychic eye sees and knows.

Did you ever meet a total stranger and just have a feeling that you have known this person for a very long time? Maybe, indeed you have known one another since the beginning of time, in many different forms, throughout many different lifetimes. This is a level of reality unseen by most, but present nevertheless!

One chooses which Tzadik with which to bond not based on academic curiosity, but rather on a deep emotional conviction that this is the right one, and that this is the right thing to do. It may very well be that the soul of the Tzadik (at the Kol level) is already reaching out to you, and this may explain why you feel an attraction to the Tzadik (be it at the Dibur level).

Follow YHWH and allow YHWH to guide your heart and mind. Seek the experience, and if and when other, profound, righteous, and holy thoughts start popping into your head, it is very possible that you have made contact.

Continue reading the words spoken (written) by your chosen Tzadik. If you have an authentic image of him, you may gaze upon his face. One way or another, to read sacred words of Torah, and to gaze upon the faces of holy Sages is itself its own reward and blessing.

Chapter 5

The Kabbalistic Purpose of Prayer
How what We Do Influences Higher Dimensions of Being
A Lesson from Sefer Olat HaTamid by Rabbi Hayim Vital

Prayer is one of the most important practices that one can perform. But why is this so? What is so important about prayer?

Proper praying is very important in the Kabbalah. Before I proceed to explain why, I will begin here with the words of R. Hayim Vital, and only then proceed to explain all the underlying concepts upon which his words are based.

I believe it is important for the reader to become familiar with the actual words of the ancient Kabbalistic text before we divulge their true meanings. Let the reader take time to contemplate R. Hayim's words, and then proceed to my explanation of them.

Sefer Olat Tamid of R. Hayim Vital, Pages 4b-5a

[This then is] the general matter of the need for prayer, what it is all about. Know that there is nothing that is not from the aspect of the Seven Kings who died in the Land of Edom. All the worlds, all of them are from this aspect of these Kings.

Now, if these Kings did not die, were not nullified, and [thus did not become] the source of the Klipot, then they by themselves would already be sifted and rectified; there would have been no need for a sifting or for a rectification.

However, being that they did die and were nullified, they [thus] became the source of the aspect of the Klipot. Therefore the [sparks of] holiness [are trapped within them, and they] need to be rectified, sifted, refined, and cleansed.

[Once the holy sparks are removed] the remaining waste matter will [naturally sink] to the bottom [of the worlds] to [the place of] the Klipot. When the sifting and refining are completely finished, with not even a single spark of holiness remaining below, for all the sparks of holiness will have ascended above, then the remaining waste, which are the Klipot themselves [will remain] below without any life whatsoever. Then will the verse (Isaiah 25:8) which states, "death will be swallowed up forever" be fulfilled. This will be after the coming of Mashiah, with the help of God.

And now, it is impossible for the [fallen] sparks [of holiness] to be sifted by themselves, rather this [needs to be done] by the power of [the one] who sifts them. This [sifting] is [performed] by the prayers and the observances of human beings below [who] perform this sifting by the [power of the] Ten Supernal Sefirot of Atzilut. For the [powers] below need the supernal support in order to do these things that are performed with their hands. Also, the [powers] above need the actions from below, even as it is written, "give strength to God," (Psalm 68:35).

The matter, as mentioned previously, is this, there is nothing in the world that is not made up from [the shattered vessels] of the [metaphorical] Kings [who reigned in Edom before there was a King in Israel]. There is within them a sifting that is needed for [the sake of] the four worlds A'Be'Y'A by themselves.

There is also a sifting for the sake of the lower souls. What remains after the sifting that is needed by the worlds, as mentioned previously, [goes forth] from there [to] the foundations of [human] souls, and not just this, but [it also goes to] every [life-form] of this lower mundane world, [which includes] all vegetation, all animals and every [other] created thing. They come from the sifting of the Kings after the sifting of [human] souls, as mentioned.

All of this is done through the prayers and observances of those here in the lower world. And this [comes about] because of help from Above, as mentioned.

The matter is this, [it is] through [the power] of ritual observances (mitzvot) performed by people in this world, and most specifically with [the recitation of] prayer, [that the sifting here below is accomplished], for [praying] is the essence and source of all this.

There is nothing greater [that accomplishes the sifting more so] than prayer. Therefore did our Sages (in B. Berakhot 6b) say with regards to praying that this action is one of the greatest things in the world.

It is by the act of praying that a human being can cause the supernal union. This then is how the sifting of the Kings [is performed], they then ascend above as an aspect of MahN (Mayim Nokbin). And there they are rectified and completely sifted, as we have mentioned in the lesson on the Rectification of the Kings, and in the lessons on MahN (Mayim Nokbin). (ref. Etz Hayim 10:1, 39:1-2,4, Sha'ar HaHakdamot 33).

General Commentary

In order for us to understand why we human beings need to pray, there are some preliminary lessons that we need to learn about ourselves. For how can be understand what it is that we do, prior to our understanding of the self who is doing the action?

First of all, we must understand that we human beings are composite entities. Only a fractional part of our full selves is incarnate in our present human form.

Our true selves, which are our souls is also a composite reality comprising multiple functions. We refer to these differing functions as separate souls, each with a given name, these being the Nefesh, Ruah, Neshama, Hayah, and Yehidah. Collectively, we call these the NaRaNHaY.

What we must understand is that these five are not separate or independent entities that gather together to serve a single function,

234

rather these five are merely five different aspect of function of one's single soul. Names can be distracting, so don't worry about naming this or that thing; just merely refer to the soul by the generic term Neshama and be done with names.

Our soul has different functions because our multi-faceted soul exists simultaneously in parallel dimensions. In each of these parallel dimensions the soul takes on a function of operation that is unique to that dimension. Thus, in Asiyah the soul acts as the Nefesh, in Yetzirah it acts as the Ruah, and in Beriah it acts as the Neshama. Beyond this into Atzilut and higher, the soul enters the domain of the supernal unconscious. Just like our human unconscious is unknown to us, so too is the higher unconscious concealed from our own higher selves.

The source dimension which defines for us reality as we experience it is the realm called Atzilut. In this dimension we have the initial revelation of the Supernal "Man" who in Zoharic/Lurianic Kabbalah is called Zeir Anpin (Z.A.), the Short Face of God (based in the Tiferet of the Ten Sefirot of Atzilut). Above Z.A. in the center column of the Sefirot are the multiple Partzufim within the Sefirah Keter. The one Partzuf that deals most directly with Z.A. is Arikh Anpin, the Long Face. Consider the relationship between Zeir Anpin and Arikh Anpin as the relationship between the Supernal Conscious Mind (Z.A.) and the Supernal Unconscious Mind (Arikh). The language of Kabbalah does not use the psychological terms of conscious verses unconscious. Rather it uses the terms revealed to describe the conscious and concealed to describe the unconscious.

Human beings are created in the image of Supernal Man, Z.A. Z.A. is the source of all human souls. Z.A. is the pattern which is the source of the human psyche. Thus what a human being does here below in this mundane world in our present mortal state directly connects to, and has an influence upon the source pattern of collective humanity, which is Z.A.

Therefore, when the finite human on Earth wishes to arouse a Force of influence to act, that human being uses the Force of Mind to imagine and contemplate the movement of supernal Sefirotic

Forces. As one contemplates these things within one's mind, the Force of one's thoughts connects to the supernal reality of these things and influences the occurrences of the actual supernal operations that one is projecting in one's thoughts.

When one recites actual verbal words that are coupled with these supernal thoughts, one's words become impregnated with one's thoughts, transforming one's words from being mere vibrations of sounds waves, and turns them into a Force of power that generates the manifestation of the physical reality that one's words (of prayer) are requesting.

Essentially, true prayer is not the asking for something to come about, rather it is the creation itself of that which one desire to come about. Prayer, therefore, is far more than just a list of requests. Prayer, with proper concentration upon the psychic elements therein (Kavanot) creates realities that the mere words simply request.

Kabbalistic prayer focuses on the use of Kavanot, the directions of the energetic flow of Sefirotic energies in the source dimension of Atzilut.

The Kabbalistic system explains in significant depth the relationship of the different dimensions (A'Be'Y'A) and how human consciousness can have an influence upon them all. The Kabbalah teaches how the order of the universe today requires of us focus and concentration upon sifting out Forces of Good that become ensnared and entrapped within vessels of the Forces of Evil. The Forces of Evil cling to these entrapped sparks of holiness and surround them like a hard shell surrounds some sorts of fruits. These shells are the Klipot.

The major responsibility of human consciousness is for the individual to recognize the difference between the sparks of holiness and the vessels of evil that seek to subvert their power. Once such a recognition is made, one uses the power of thought, and visualizes by using the great metaphors of the Kabbalah, the separation of the Force of holiness from the Force of the unclean. This mental concentration exercise influences the mind, from the conscious mind of the individual all the way up to the collective source, Z.A.

One places mental concentration upon sifting out the sparks of holiness from the corrupted vessels within which they are entrapped. Once all sparks of holiness have been sifted, then there will no longer be reason to life to continue on this world in its present form. The order of Kabbalistic prayer is designed to sifts out the entrapped holy sparks. The contemplative exercises found in books like the Sha'ar HaKavanot and the Siddur of the Rashash guide the mind of the Kabbalist.

The conscious mind is the Nefesh of Asiyah. Upon contemplating the words of prayer in accordance to the Kabbalistic Kavanot, the Nefesh arouses the Yetziratic Ruah and the Beriatic Neshama to elevate these lofty thoughts of Sefirotic interactions up to the source dimension Atzilut. This is the ascent of desire, that the Kabbalists call the ascent of MahN, Mayim Nokbin, (feminine waters).

As the mortal man below contemplates these thoughts in prayer, Supernal Man, Z.A. actually makes these Sefirotic interactions to occur in the higher realms. As they occur above, their radiance and influence trickles down below to all the lower dimensions. This is the descent of MahD, Mayim Dukhrin (masculine waters).

Essentially, the desire from below arouses activity from above. This interaction is what promotes the sifting and enables the entrapped sparks of holiness to be freed from their shells of entrapment. Needless to say, this activity is how we repair and elevate our perception of our universe. Thus, prayer activity is considered one of the most important endeavors of them all.

Chapter 6

Yihud Ya'aqob & Leah, the Easier Way
Unleashing the Power of YHWH Within

There is a great secret concealed within the sacred Name YHWH. This is the secret of the actual and real usage of its power, here in this physical world. This secret can be exposed and even taught, but few are those willing to receive its message. Few are those willing to puts its great power to practical use.

It is well known in the Kabbalah that the secret of Yihud (communion with the higher worlds) is not through limited and finite human intellectual contemplations. Such methods, however widely used, lead to nothing more than unsubstantiated speculations, which lead to debate, argument, division, and strife. This is not the path walked by those who know YHWH.

Those who know YHWH understand the Divine through vision and experience. Wisdom pours into their souls, into their unconscious, giving them deep inner convictions that no words can express, and no rational thought can comprehend. They gaze upon YHWH within. They see, they understand and they know!

One who gazes upon YHWH knows that the Image seen is only that, an Image, however sublime and profound it is, it is nevertheless only a representative of a thing, and not the thing itself. The essence of YHWH cannot be perceived by the human mind. We can only see what Torah calls "the backside," for no man can see the Face.

Thus, we know that there is a symbolic backside, just as there is a symbolic face. Those who gazed Above saw this, understood this, and knew this. Yet, as centuries past, fewer were those who made contact and who could see for themselves with their own eyes.

Heaven thus intervened and directed that the secrets of Above be written down. However, they were to be buried under layer upon layer of metaphor and symbol, so as to distract and dissuade those not yet ready to receive the true message.

In the writings of the Kabbalah, the great secret is told, and exposed, but only to those few who pay well enough attention to recognize that which others do not (and may not) see.

The Kabbalah knows well that YHWH is only the Zeir Anpin (the "small" Face of God). They expound on this meaning in great detail. It is also well known that Zeir Anpin has both a "face" and a "back." These two are called respectively Yisrael and Ya'aqob.

Words and symbols are just that! They are a way to describe something; they are not the something itself. With regards to the activity, and movement of the higher-dimensional energy forces, we do not even have an accurate vocabulary to describe them. Therefore, the Kabbalah created a language of metaphor to at least enable us to dialogue about what we do know in a language that can be taught to those so inclined.

Thus, we have YHWH, Zeir Anpin (the Small Face), Yisrael and Ya'aqob. Four names to describe the same reality, but yet, a reality that has within it subtle nuances of differences. Different names for different nuances. YHWH is the general Name that we know for God. Yet, the Torah that teaches us about the Name YHWH, also teaches us about other Divine Names. The other Names of God are said to be associated with the different levels of energy modulation.

There are levels of the Divine above Zeir Anpin (Arikh in Keter), and there are levels of the Divine below Zeir Anpin (Nok in Malkhut). ZA, who is YHWH (in Tiferet) interacts with each in its own proper way. Zeir Anpin interacts with Arikh Anpin through Abba and Imma. Zeir Anpin bonds directly with Nok, who like ZA has "two faces."

Yisrael bonds with Rahel. Ya'aqob bonds with Leah. These are the coded terms used throughout Kabbalistic literature. It is easy to read the words, and to repeat them, it is something very different to understand them, and know how to put them into practice.

We will not focus on Zeir and Arikh, nor will we focus on Zeir with Abba and Imma. We will not even focus on Yisrael bonding with Rahel. We will focus exclusively on the bond between Ya'aqob and Leah, for herein is the power to accomplish great things.

YHWH is Zeir Anpin, the "small" Face of God. Within YHWH, there is Yisrael above, and Ya'aqob below. However mysterious this might sound, it's really rather simple.

The Yisrael "face" of YHWH is that which we know as objective God, the Creator of all reality, ever-present, and all knowing.

The Ya'aqob "face" of YHWH is all these things, but in the subjective sense, within the psyche of the individual. Ya'aqob is YHWH within us (subjective). Yisrael is YHWH outside us (objective). Both Yisrael and Ya'aqob are the two "faces" of Zeir Anpin, YHWH, the God of Israel.

No human being can manipulate or maneuver the Sefirotic face of Yisrael, but one can influence the relationship between oneself and the Sefirotic face of Ya'aqob.

The human unconscious mind is given the symbolic name of the Sefirotic face of Leah, wife of Ya'aqob. Our higher Self that is accessed through one's unconscious, is often experienced in visions as a numinous being. This is the experience of God within, the subjective face of God, Ya'aqob. This is the level of Divine revelation and insight that one can receive in these times.

Ya'aqob is the inner face of God with which one can commune. Throughout Kabbalistic prayer meditations (Kavanot), there is mention of the daily yihud (communion) between Ya'aqob and Leah. This is the unity of the individual mind with the subjective Presence of God that can be experienced from within.

It is the daily communion of Ya'aqob and Leah that we seek to accomplish. For this union elevates one's consciousness and grants one insights and revelations about matters in this mundane world.

In traditional Torah Judaism, this is accomplished daily through the recitation of the Shaharit morning prayers when accompanied with the Kavanot meditations as outlined by R. Hayim Vital and R. Shalom Sharabi (in the Siddur HaRashash).

Using the Kabbalistic siddur tends to be a terribly difficult task that literally takes one years to master. Indeed, the majority of those who do use this system rarely understand the actual depths of what it is that they are doing. Most are only going through the most superficial motions, noting the Kavanot, but without any idea as to how to internalize them, in order to actualize them. Indeed, the daily Yihud (communion) of Ya'aqob and Leah does not require such efforts and elaborate ritualistic Kavanot.

The reality of the communion is an internal psychological, psychic, spiritual transformation of one's individual psyche. By understanding the reality of the union and performing it within, gives one access to the Power of YHWH as it can be revealed here within this material world. This union is what the Kabbalists call the Unity of the Holy One, Blessed be He, and His Shekhina.

The actual communion of the symbolic aspects called Ya'aqob and Leah is a psychic, psychological transformation of the mind. Through visualization and affirmation, one accepts the psychic reality that the limitations of the natural world, ruled by the Divine Name Elohim, can indeed be bent, and manipulated. This is accomplished by bringing YHWH down to Earth, meaning that one embraces the conviction that this can be done.

One does not seek to bend or break natural laws. We do not seek, nor do we rely upon supernatural miracles. Nevertheless, one can still work within the confines of natural law, bending them to will, if and when one's will is in subservience to YHWH.

The Name Ya'aqob is numerically equal to 182, which is 7 x 26, seven times the Name YHWH. This is only a symbolic reference for us to know that YHWH resides within Ya'aqob. Thus, when we realize that God is with us, and indeed is within us. We equally realize that through the power of God within us, we can make miracles happen, even though that they manifest though natural ways.

We must open up our inner minds, symbolized as Leah, to receive profound revelations, and insights from the deepest recesses of our being, where God within, the face of Ya'aqob is accessed.

We receive the imagination to dream that we can overcome the problems presently before us. We embrace the image and congeal it into form. This is symbolized by the penetration of the Yesod of Ya'aqob into the Yesod of Leah, impregnating her. Our minds are thus transformed, and we know for sure that we can accomplish the impossible, all within the realms of possibilities.

We also know that while we can and will do everything that we can, God will intervene to accomplish that which we cannot.

Remember, Zeir Anpin is one. Yisrael and Ya'aqob are one. It's just that Yisrael is concealed, and its movements are not noticed or noticeable by us. Yisrael acts through Ya'aqob, and Ya'aqob acts through Leah, and Leah acts through us.

One who understands these metaphors will understand the secret power hidden in YHWH, waiting to be unleashed by us!

Some need to perform elaborate meditations in order to grasp this simple psychic truth. But now you know how to do it with ease. Put it into practice. Change your world, and ours!

Chapter 7

The Power in Our Hands
A Hasidic Teaching about the Power of the Force

"And Enoch walked with God, and he was not, for God had taken him."
(Genesis 5:24)

"Our Sages of blessed memory have said, (quoting Yalkut Reuveni, in the name of the Aserah Ma'amarot) that Enoch was a shoe cobbler. And every time that he stitched together [the upper and lower parts of a shoe] he would unite the Holy One, blessed be He, and His Shekhina (reference there).

I have heard in the name of my Rabbi (the Ba'al Shem Tov} the meaning of the verse, "Whatever it is that is in your power to do, do it with all your might." (Ecclesiastes 9:10).

Thought is called Ayn Sof [which in this case, is associated with the name] YHWH. Action is ADNY (Adonai). When one joins together the action with [proper] thought at the time of performance, this is called the union of the Holy One, blessed be He and His Shekhina.

This is what the verse means, "Whatever it is that is in your power to do, do it with all your might." Your might [in Hebrew] is KoHha'kha. What this means is that thought is called Hokhma (wisdom) [which can be broken into two words] Koah Mah [the power of Mah]. You perform the action with all your might, which [in this case] means [all your proper] thought, for the sake of the unity of the Holy One blessed be He and His Shekhina."

Sefer Ba'al Shem Tov (Genesis 179), from Sefer Toldot Ya'aqob Yosef, Vayera 2a

Whatever you can do, do it with all the might that you have! Don't hold back! This about sums up the teaching above. There is no real need for elaborate commentary, but like the teaching itself says, I do have the power to elaborate, and to thus compliment this teaching with more information, so as to reinforce its message to the reader. So, being that I can do it, it is within my hands to do, I will proceed with gusto!

First, let us quickly review the sources for this teaching. The text itself is from the collection of writings culled together under the title, Sefer Ba'al Shem Tov. This book is considered to be the first-generation direct teachings of the Ba'al Shem himself. Thus, many consider this text to be a primary source for the teachings of Hasidut.

The book itself, which is a compendium, takes this teaching from the book, Sefer Toldot Ya'aqob Yosef, which is another text renown for being primary source material for Hasidut. Thus, we conclude that this teaching is as authentically Hasidic as it can get. But, as the text itself makes clear, this teaching does not have its source in Hasidut, but rather it can be dated to centuries earlier.

The text quotes another earlier compendium called Yalkut Reuveni. This book is an interesting collection of teachings, some of which are today very controversial. Yalkut Reuveni regularly references sources that speak about the Pre-Adamic civilizations. And this is a topic that many religious extremists today do not want the public to know about. Nevertheless, Yalkut Reuveni and the sources that its author quotes are impeccable, and are of the highest authority in Judaism.

One of these authorities is the book Aserah Ma'amarot by R. Menahem Azariah da Fano, a Kabbalist contemporary of R. Hayim Vital. R. Azariah de Fano offers a rich selection of older teachings which often is not found in many later texts.

We see from this minor digression into the history of literary sources that the Ba'al Shem Tov did not invent the teachings of Hasidut, but rather culled them from many older authoritative sources. Awareness of this, especially in his own times, was an important fact, so as to offset much of the criticism that was being directed against the budding Hasidic movement.

We learn from this a very important lesson. Some teachings in traditional Torah sources may indeed be very controversial today simply because they are not part-and-parcel of the mainstream approach. Some today will try to cover up these controversial teachings in an attempt to have them disappear from Judaism. This type of behavior is nothing new. We have seen this before, for example with the censored Part 4 of R. Hayim Vital's meditative manual, Sha'arei Kedusha. Actual meditative practice was considered taboo in the early 1600's when R. Vital wrote this text. It was not until the early 1990's that it was published for the very first time.

Censorship is never the right thing to do! Just like the Ba'al Shem Tov stood up and taught controversial teachings in his day, quoting all the authoritative sources to prove their Judaic validity, so too should we follow in his footsteps.

The text quoted above begins with an interesting story. Enoch, the man who was taken to Heaven, and transformed into the archangel Metatron is portrayed as being a simple shoe cobbler. Needless to say, this reference is most certainly not historical, but this is of no matter. Historical facts have no place, and no relevance when telling a moralistic story!

The story offers a detail about how each and every action that Enoch did, even something as simple as sewing together a shoe, he elevated that simple task into being a reflection of the highest of spiritual teachings and practices. And due to his intense devotion in the simple things, Enoch was rewarded by being taking up into Heaven and placed in charge over greater things.

This is a lovely and inspirational story. However, I do believe that it would be somewhat unrealistic for any of us to have aspirations of being translated into an angelic being because of our Earthly devotion to spiritual matters. But be this as it may, our attention to spiritual matters, even in the most mundane of things, is exactly what our text is here to teach us to do.

The message of the text is again simple, but this time, let me put its simplicity into other words. Our text is teaching us that one whose actions are completely focused on manifesting the thoughts that are within one's mind, these are actions that will be established and be successful, (just like Enoch).

Mental focus, and emotional passion are powerful ingredients when added to one's actions. Such inner force has the ability to transform one's actions from being simple things and into powerfully meaningful things, (just like Enoch).

The technique offered in the text about how to actually do this, comes from earlier Kabbalistic sources. The technique is a contemplative visualization meditation which one can perform on a regular on-going basis. This is called the Yihud Havaya Adnoot, the (unity meditation) of the Names YHWH (Havaya/HaShem) and ADNY (Adnoot/Adonai).

As the text says, YHWH is used to represent the focus of one's thoughts. Just as thoughts are invisible things, so too is the Presence of YHWH. Our text states to correlate the Name YHWH with the Ayn Sof, which is God's Unknowable Essence. Now, Kabbalistic literature does not associate the Name YHWH with the Ayn Sof at all. But just as we leave out history from an embellished story, so too can we leave out rigid Kabbalistic terminologies when we wish to be a little bit more flexible with their usage. So, while the Name YHWH usually is not associated with the Ayn Sof, for the purpose of this teaching, we do not need to differentiate them.

The Ayn Sof is God concealed; and the Name YHWH is equally God concealed. Therefore, we can put the two together to represent God's Unknowable Essence. These two concealed aspects correlate with human thought, which is concealed in the mind. The Name ADNY (Adonai) on the other hand, is the Name of God that we know and use on a regular basis. Being that this is a Name that is clearly seen (heard) and known, it is correlated to one's actions which are also clearly seen, and known.

Just as there are aspects of God that are concealed and revealed, so too are there similar aspects within human beings. God is both, present in the natural world, and is equally concealed in the natural world. Our spiritual purpose is to discover the concealed and to reveal it. In order for us to do this, we need to symbolically unite the revealed aspect of God represented by ADNY, with the concealed aspect YHWH.

In traditional Jewish prayers, when the Name of God is written YHWH, we always recite it as ADNY (Adonai). The Kabbalists correspond these Names to Sefirotic attributes. YHWH corresponds to Tiferet, whereas ADNY corresponds with Malkhut. We human beings live here on Earth, which is in the domain of the Malkhut of the world of Asiyah. We know that God is YHWH (as revealed in the Torah), however we refer to God by the manifestation of Him that is right and fitting for this world, at this time. Thus we call God by His Name in Malkhut, ADNY (Adonai), and recognize that this Name of Adonai is associated with physical actions, ours, and those of the world.

A simple verse from the Bile teaches the enlightened how one can manifest thought into deed and thus unite all the Sefirot. When one contemplates the diagram of the Sefirotic Tree of Life, one will see how the Sefirot originate with Will (Keter), proceed to insight (Hokhma), and then cognition (Binah), moving forward to motivation (HaGaT, NaHiY), and finalizing in accomplished deed (Malkhut). When Ecclesiastes 9:10 tells us to act with gusto, with regards to everything that we can, this pretty much sums up the passage of Divine Light along the Sefirotic Tree.

Let me briefly explain. In order for the Divine Light to manifest, there must first be ready for it an appropriate vessel wherein which it can shine its Light. The first step then to manifest such a vessel is to want for it to be. There must rise a desire for something to be that is not yet manifest into being.

The desire (Keter) for such and such a thing arises deep within one's unconscious for reasons unknown and unfathomable. The desire sparks a revelation and insight (Hokhma) in the mind, just at the place where the unconscious meets the conscious mind. This is experienced as a deep state of inner knowledge. One then proceeds to contemplate the matter until one derives at a clear and precise understanding (Binah) of it. Once this mental process is complete one must now become fired-up emotionally (HaGaT NaHiY) in order to be motivated to stop thinking about the matter at hand, and to actually go out and do it (Malkhut).

Thus when one feels so charged up about a thing to do it, one must act upon such feelings. Or, in other words, whatever you are capable of doing, do it with vigor, and do it now! For when the inner pattern of the Sefirot is connected within one, one feels the conviction and even the compulsion to act. It is this inner conviction and compulsion to act with righteousness and with zeal that we call Ruah HaKodesh, Divine inspiration.

Ruah HaKodesh needs to be understood as the psychological phenomena that it really is, as opposed to the fantasy and mythology that is usually applied to it. Ruah HaKodesh is not magical. No Voice of God is heard, or even felt. Rather, what one feels is a sense of compulsion, of absolute conviction that what one must do is the right thing to do. Needless to say, in order for such a spirit (Ruah) to be Ruah HaKodesh (holy), it will never inspire or compel anyone to act in any way which violates either law or moral boundaries. There are many "spirits." Most of them are not holy!

Usually, when "the spirit" comes upon one, one is not conscious of it, and thus one does not act in a way as if one is implementing a well thought-out plan. One "in the spirit" is in Higher Hands who guides one's actions, ofttimes overriding one's own thoughts. "The spirit" has taken over, and it is guiding one.

Some may consider such a loss of control to be a very negative thing. Indeed, there is much truth in such a consideration. Nevertheless, when the time is right to act for YHWH, then as we see from such Biblical examples as Pinhas and Shimshon, the "Spirit" does not fail one. Both Biblical examples reference each man receiving incredible physical strength and courage to act with zeal on behalf of a higher cause. Today, we are very concerned about the mental health of one who expresses such zeal to act for any cause, especially one associated with God and religion.

Not every act of zeal needs to be an expression of violent behavior as was with Pinhas and Shimshon. Zeal can be expressed even in the smallest of things, like with something as innocent as the benign making of shoes, as with our legendary story about Enoch.

Always beware of the Ruah HaTumah (the unclean spirit). This is the one that will seek to compel one to actions which are immoral, harmful, or even criminal. Only one truly devoted to YHWH will be able to seek shelter in the Holy Name. This is why we regularly perform the Yihud Havaya-Adnoot, so as to purify one's mind, and thereby hopefully to refine one's behavior.

What we learn from our lesson is that zeal and passion, when properly grounded in God's holy Name, are good things. They can be expressions of one's inner strength and spiritual duty. While such expressions can clearly have their dark sides, those who are righteous, like Enoch, would never entertain such negative thoughts. And so Enoch becomes our role model of sorts to teach us how to focus absolutely on the Presence of God everywhere, and in everything, such as with the making of a shoe.

Each of us has the potential of serving as a conduit for the Ruah HaKodesh, even as did the legendary Enoch referred to in our text. To become such a conduit, one must unite YHWH with ADNY in a perfect union. Contemplation upon this act of spiritual unity is performed every time that one prays the traditional Jewish prayers, and one recites the Name Adonai. For every time that the Name YHWH is written in the prayer book, it is the Name ADNY that is recited.

When one recites Adonai, one should have in mind that the Name and the reality of YHWH is therein concealed. This brings the awareness of the invisible into the visible. By doing such a simple mental exercise, one can cultivate from it a tremendous amount of motivational energy. This is how one can muster the passion to do great things.

So, when there is something, anything, that a person can do, no matter what it is, one should strive to do it, whatever "it" is with passion, gusto, devotion, and with total dedication to God. One who acts in this way will find that there is a power within that motivates, encourages, and brings to manifestations to many blessings that come from the holy Name of God.

Chapter 8

The Coming Cleansing

Let me be blunt. Your life is a lie! Everything that you know and that think you know is but a shadowy reflection of truth.

Neither you, nor I knows the actual truth about life, the universe and everything. All we have are small fractions of information, none of which add up to any real whole number of objective truth.

How many of us remember the rules of adding fractions? Math rules state that when adding fractions of unequal denominators, that a common denominator must first be found. In math, finding a common denominator is easy. In life, however, finding the proper common denominator is an arduous and sometimes impossible task.

This is why, when we penetrate deep enough to contemplate the truth of anything, nothing in life makes any real sense. Thus, in the end, we are forced to acknowledge that in reality we know nothing and everything that we think that we know doesn't add up.

In math, if the numbers don't add up, then the answer is wrong. This is also how it is with everything else in life. Being that we do not have the proper common denominator to add things up together, every answer that we derive at is by definition only partially true at best!

The mind of every human being is somehow infected by what the Bible calls the forbidden fruit of the Tree of Knowledge, Good and Evil. This is the usage of the rational, intellectual side of the mind, in the absence of the psychic, telepathic side of the mind (the Tree of Life).

Knowledge is what we think, instead of what we intuitively know. Thus, what we think is blemished, contaminated as it is by the confusion between truth and falsehood, right and wrong, and good and evil. Without the clarity of the inner compass to reflect higher truths, human intellect comes to embrace all kinds of bad thinking as being good.

Many people believe ideas to be true, right, and good which are in actuality false, wrong, and evil. Of course, the opposite is also true, some people consider certain things to be false, wrong, and evil, that are in fact true, right, and good.

The human mind is easily deceived and confused. The forbidden fruit of the Tree of Knowledge, Good and Evil has done its share of harm.

While the mind of man, individually and collectively is blemished and confused, the human heart (our inner psychic, telepathic side) can still partake of the fruit of the Tree of Life and be reborn, revived and resurrected.

Although there is an angel waving a sword of fire blocking access to the sacred Tree, nevertheless, access is granted to those of "pure heart and clean hands."

The blemished mind may not understand this. Then again, the blemished mind rarely understands anything. Yet, deep within, the heart knows.

Deep within, those who silence the objections and chaos of the mind are entitled and enabled to hear the Still, Soft Voice that arises from within and directs one along the paths of God and life.

Many people talk about God and claim to represent Him and His truth. Many are willing to act in many inhumane ways to prove this. Yet, God's Word is the Word of Life. The Word of Life does not bring death and darkness, it brings Light!

Those who live by Light embrace a life that seeks to unite God's creation under the banner of the true common denominator. No human mind limited by rational intellect can figure this out on one's own. No idea, belief or doctrine can figure all this out in all its wonder and truth, and then explain it to others. There is a mystery here.

The human mind, collectively and individually, is confused, but the psychic, intuitive human heart that embraces Light and Life can be made to understand that which the rational, intellectual mind cannot.

In such a case, words cannot describe truth. But even without words, what is known is known. It is embraced and lived. The mind cannot solve the mystery, but the heart can.

There is a time and a purpose for all things under Heaven. There is a time for illness and there is a time for healing. Today we are in the days of illness. But in not too many tomorrows, the time of healing will come. Those who are sick will be healed. But the illness itself, will cease to exist. The illness will die, so that we can live.

All we must do now is chose. Which are we? Are we part of the illness, or part of the cure?

Our minds and thoughts cannot answer this correctly because there is no common denominator upon which to form an answer. If we chose to contemplate the question, then we must let the answer arise from within our hearts.

Individually speaking, who is part of the illness and who is part of the cure?

In our arrogance, we are each convinced that our way is right and that our views, beliefs, and doctrines are the correct ones. We are convinced that God is on our side, and that equally God is not on the side of any who oppose us, or dissent from us. Such elitism is arrogance.

The mind embraces this arrogance and the heart is taken along for the ride. When this happens, hope for change is lost and the fate of said individuals is sealed.

One who has succeeded in corrupting one's heart, silencing it from hearing the still soft inner voice, is doomed. Such a one is part of the illness and the illness will soon be removed. The time of healing is coming and the ill amongst us will not survive. This is, in the end, their own choice. It is not like they have not been warned.

Collective humanity today is heading towards a global disaster. It will not be avoided because it is only natural that it comes.

The illness must be healed. This is the natural order of things. Therefore, the closer we get to the destruction of the illness, the greater becomes the arrogance in the hearts of those slated for destruction.

Deep within them, their own hearts rise up against them and allow their minds to embrace deception. The more the mind embraces deception the faster that individual runs towards his own doom. Deep within, the blemished are led towards their cleansing, even though this cleansing means the death of their bodies and the release of their souls.

Honor awaits those who are humble. Humility is the acknowledgment of truth. This truth is that we lack the common denominator of life. As such, we follow Heaven and seek to unify all things in our best understanding of truth.

Lacking the common denominator in life we do not leave this precious work to the activity of our rational minds and our intellectual thoughts. On the contrary, we silence the mind, we remove question and doubt. We allow the heart to open to hear the still soft inner voice, and in faith we follow its directives.

The directives of Life take us to life and light. This is how we recognize the fractions of truth that we can indeed embrace in our present blemished state.

Humility is simplicity of thought. We do not try to make sense out of that which cannot be rationally understood. We cannot overcome the blemish of the forbidden fruit, at least not yet, not now in the time of illness.

But when the time of healing dawns upon us very soon, we will see how our healing will take place. For now, how this will be done must remain a secret. The blemished mind is not able to handle such information, so as not to be a further stumbling block before those already blind. Certain knowledge is reserved for the "pure of heart and clean of hands."

There is only one guaranteed safe haven for today and anytime in the future. This safe haven is God's holy Name YHWH. This Name alone is the One that God, the Creator revealed Himself. God Himself said this is His Name when He said, *"I am YHWH,"* (Ex. 20:2).

This Name alone contains the promise of salvation. *"And it shall be, in all the land, says God (YHWH) two parts in it shall be cut off, and die, but the third shall be left in it. And I will bring the third part through the fire, and will refine them as silver is refined, and will try them as gold is tried, he shall* CALL UPON MY NAME *and I will answer him. I will say, this is My people, he will say YHWH is my G-D."* Zechariah 13:8-9

For those seeking more practical directions about how to walk this sacred path, the **Wheels of the Merkava** await you. Also, my books, **Let There Be... Knowing**, and **Using The Holy Names of God** are available for you.

Chapter 9

The Prophecy:
The Secret of what Will Be on the Day
that The Mashiah Comes to the Land of Israel

Hesed L'Avraham, the Third Fountain, the Eye of the Land, River 22 (Pg. 27A) by Rabbi Avraham Azulai

"Know, that it is an accepted tradition in our hands, that on the day that King Mashiah will come with the ingathering of the exiles to the Land of Israel, there will be found in the Land only seven thousand of the children of Israel.

On this same day, the dead of the Land of Israel shall be restored to life. On that same day also, the walls of Jerusalem shall be removed, and rebuilt from precious stones and pearls.

Then, at the time, the dead of the Land of Israel shall be restored to life, they shall be new spiritual creations. Also, the seven thousand who shall be left alive at that time, they too shall be new creations, all of them with spiritual bodies, similar to the body of Adam prior to his sin, and the body of Enoch, Moses our teacher and Elijah.

They shall all float in the air, soaring like eagles. This shall be seen by all the people ingathered from the exile.

When these, their brothers, are made a new creation, soaring through the air, going to dwell in the (lower) Garden of Eden to learn Torah from the Mouth of the Holy One, Blessed be He, then all together the children of the ingathered exiles, with worry in their hearts and anguish in their souls cry out to King Mashiah.

They ask, we also are the nation of the Children of Israel, like them. Why have they merited to be spiritual beings in body and soul, and not us? Why are we less?

The Mashiah shall answer them saying, "The character of the Holy One, Blessed be He is already known and famous; He gives to each one 'measure for measure'.

These also dwelled outside of the Land, and after great effort they succeeded to come to the Land of Israel, in order to merit a purified soul.

They cared not for their physical or material wellbeing.

They came by sea and by land, and were not dissuaded by the dangers of the sea or of being robbed along their journey.

They suffered under cruel regimes, all for the sake of the essence of their spirit and soul. Therefor have they become complete spiritual beings, measure for measure.

However all of you, who had the ability to come to the Land of Israel, as they did, were discouraged over concern for your finances.

You were worried about your physical safety and your money. These, you made to be the principle things in your lives, and not your spirit and soul. Therefore have you remained physical beings."

Let this serve as a lesson and warning. In the time before the coming of Mashiah, the Holy Land will not be a safe-haven protected from all harm.

Today, over seven million Jews live in the Holy Land. If this prophecy recorded from an impeccable, unimpeachable source is correct, then this means that of all the Jews living now in Israel, only 1/10 of 1% are destined to survive. This is not a very desirable outcome.

Only God knows the truths of these things. One must follow God in pure and simple faith, doing what one knows to be true from within. Heed not modern voices and calls which are the equivalent of modern-day false prophecy.

Trust God to guide you, and do not "go with the flow" simply because it seems like the right thing to do.

May God bless and protect us all, amen!

SECTION SIX

THE WHEELS OF THE MERKAVA
SECRETS OF TORAH LIFE ACCORDING
TO THE MA'ASEH MERKAVAH
IN 68 BRIEF CONTEMPLATIONS

Also Lessons about Other Worlds, Other Realities,
Angels including Metatron & Sandalphon
Warnings about the Future, the Imminent Coming of Armilus
Living Torah with Natural Halakha
& Practical Down to Earth Direction, Wisdom & Guidance

The Wheels of the Merkava
Secrets of Torah Life According to the Ma'aseh Merkava

Introduction

In every one of these, my poetic/prose writings,
I conceal many secrets about the practices and the path of the
Ma'aseh Merkava
(the original Torah "mystical" school of the Benei Nivi'im, the
Children of the Prophets).

My words are not meant to be just read,
they are meant to be contemplated.
If you take the time to FEEL
what it is that I am saying,
you will understand far more than what the mere words say.
This is the ancient way how psychic powers are developed.

<u>**1**</u>

<u>When is Mashiah Coming?</u>

Before we ask when is Mashiah coming,
we must first ask,
what does it mean for him to come?

Does Mashiah come
as a master magician,
to magically make
all our problems disappear?
No!
There is no legitimate
prophecy or prediction
that makes any such claim.

Mashiah comes
and his role is one
of hard work.
There will be no magic,
but instead,
there will be tremendous efforts,
struggles and wars.
Mashiah will dominate
and be victorious,
but not because of any
magical interventions,
but rather because he
will do what needs to be done,
in the right way, in the right time
and in the right place.

When will this happen?
This has already been answered
over the many centuries
by our people in the wise.
Long ago, the Talmud recorded
a legend, a story
about one of the great Sages

who met the Mashiah sitting at the gates of Rome.
He asked Mashiah when we was planning to
come and redeem both Israel and the world.
He answered the great Sage and said to him,
"today."

Bewildered the Sage turned later
to the immortal prophet Elijah
and asked him what the Mashiah meant
by such a strange and seemingly
untrue response.
Elijah answered him in the words of scripture,
"today, but only if you hear His Voice."

Mashiah gave the condition for his coming.
We must learn first how to hear the Voice of God
as it speaks telepathically within our minds.
This is what the Bible calls
"God writing His Word upon our hearts,"
and what the Sages later called,
Ruah HaKodesh, Divine inspiration.
When this occurs Mashiah will come.

Many years later another Sage
stated it ever so eloquently.
He said that
each of us has a spark of Mashiah
within us,
and that it is up to each of us individually,
to bring the Mashiah
first, into our own selves,
into our minds, our psyches, and our lives.
When we can first embrace Mashiah
internally and personally,
only then can we expect Mashiah
to come into the world.

We have always been taught,
to first bring Mashiah to the individual from within,
and then the unified and transformed people

will bring Mashiah out,
from within them, to the outside world.

We are a long way off from this.
There is no wonder then
why Mashiah has not yet come,
and may not come for a very long time.
War may come
and destruction may follow,
but there is no promise
now or in the past
that Mashiah will come
to save us from such a destruction
or to rebuild us if and when
such a destruction occurs.

God has placed our fates
in our own hands.
What we chose to do with it
is up to us
and the Watcher Angels,
along with their ward,
Mashiah son of David
is watching and waiting.
Truly they must be very patient,
for we have kept them waiting for a very long time.

We can change matters,
if we please,
it all starts with one person,
YOU!
You influence collective humanity.
Your individual influence
will influence one more,
who in turn will influence another,
who in turn will influence yet another.
One after another, after another.
This is how we build,
and this is how we restore the
fallen tabernacle of David,

one stone, one soul at a time.
Today, if only we hear His Voice.

2

A year is only a matter of measure.
There is nothing new under the sun, no new year,
and no new hopes.
We are in the middle of a countdown.
Where we are heading, time will tell.
I believe that it is too late to save the world,
but, we can save the people therein,
at least, those who are willing to listen.
Party time is over, it's time to get serious.
It's time to let go, and let God!
Focus only on the Holy Name - Yod Hey Waw Hey.
This alone is the security that can have.
Remember the Name, use it, call upon it.
The Name will save you when the time comes,
but you and the Name must become one.
Start now, learn the unity, and live it.
Everything else is a lie. Ignore them.

3

When you awake in the morning, make this your first, daily prayer:
"God, how may I serve you today, enable me to shine Your Light."
When you lie down at night, make this your last, nightly prayer:
"God, I pray that I did shine Your Light today.
Show me how I can better serve You tomorrow."
Don't just say the words, mean them!
As you draw closer to God, you will become
more and more aware of the Sacred Presence.
This is the beginning phase of Ma'aseh Merkava
and the Prophetic Path.
Forget all the hype and show!
The basics are where it's at!
Stay simple, stay basic!
It is in the simplicity that you will find God

4

When two opposing forces collide, they create friction.
Friction causes heat. Heat leads to melt-down
and eventually an explosion.
This is the natural course of things.
It exists in the outer world and it exists inside each of us.
Violent extremism is growing dramatically everywhere.
Everyone sees it, everyone fears it, yet, no one seems to know
what to do about it.
Everyone has an answer, but none of the answers seem to work.
And they won't!
When continents collide, they create earthquakes and volcanoes.
When civilizations collide, it is no different.
Earthquakes and volcanoes destroy but at the same time build.
So it is with our social upheavals.
The old will continue to rumble until there is the big eruption.
Then the old will fall and the new will be born.
This is the natural order of things,
guided by the Hand of Nature, Elohim.
We can do nothing to stop it or slow it down.
Instead, we must move to the side
and allow nature (God) to take its course.

5

Be silent.
Be still.
Keep your eyes on Heaven alone,
and allow the course of nature to dominate here on Earth.
God will move you to where you need to be moved,
But, you must keep your eyes on Him.
For if in a moment He guides you,
and at that moment you were distracted by looking around you,
you will miss the Divine cue.
If you do not see because you chose at the moment not to look,
then you will move with that where your focus lies,
and not with Heaven.
Focus on Heaven, on God's Name, always! (Psalm 16:8).

This will save you when the time comes - be part of the new
and not part of the old.

6

There are yet many secrets.
Not everything can be revealed.
Reality is not what it appears to be.
There is a sinister truth concealed out in the open.
It is too horrible for most to believe, but it is nevertheless true.
Darkness comes before the dawn,
and the darkness is not yet its darkest.
The time of testing is upon us.
Evil will seek to divide and conquer.
Good will gather together under the banner of righteousness.
But be careful! Do not seek the truth unless you are ready for it!
You may not like what you find!

7

There is Heaven and there is the Earth.
There is YHWH and there is ELOHIM.
There is the spiritual and there is the physical.
There is only ONE GOD
and our eternal proclamation is:
YHWH is ELOHIM, YHWH is ELOHIM.
Everything is part of a concentric whole.
There is only ONE.
Spiritual is physical and physical is spiritual.
The two are one even as THE ONE is one.
Therefore, do not create divisions where none exist.
Fulfill your obligations and perform your duties.
And know that we exist in soul and body,
and that both serve God together.
One cannot serve Heaven all the while ignoring
one's physical or spiritual responsibilities.
Both are given to us by God YHWH ELOHIM our Creator.
We serve Heaven here on Earth
when we fulfill our Earthly responsibilities.

It is a dangerous sin to become so heavenly minded
that one becomes no earthly good.

8

Psychic development is as natural as muscle building.
And it is accomplished in the same way.
Exercise of body makes it strong.
Exercise of mind (soul) makes it strong.
When I lift weights, I push my body to go beyond what I think
are its present capabilities.
My perceptions of my physical abilities are usually
a self-induced deception.
When I lift more than I thought I could, I am made aware
of what my flesh can perform when my mind wills it.
My mental (spiritual) abilities are likewise limited
by self-induced limitations.
When I practice "no-pain, no gain" in my mental exercises,
I push my mind (soul) to grow and strengthen
beyond what I (wrongly) thought impossible.
I go forth into mental (spiritual) space
and instead of moving forward with fear,
I do so with boldness (as well as with caution,
just like in body building).
I know how to work-out my body in the gym.
I also know how to work-out my mind (soul) in the "spiritual gym."
In this way I draw close to God.
Pay attention! What I reveal here are of the secrets
of the true Ma'aseh Merkava.

9

All who seek their inner calm will first find the great storm
and then the great cloud.
Many consider the cloud to be the great calm and silence within.
Actually it is only a delusion to seduce the lazy,
to entrap them and keep them imprisoned.
Only one who has the passion will reject the silence
and calm of the cloud
and penetrate beyond it to encounter the bolts of fire.

One must overcome the fires that burn away all sense of self
and attachments.
Only then will one gain a glimpse of the Image of the One
who sits upon the Throne.
This is the proper path, it cannot be circumvented.
There are no short-cuts.
Deceptions are many. They arise by Heaven's design
to teach discernment.
We are obligated to turn away from evil (Tree of Knowledge),
before we are allowed access to the Tree of Life.
This is a long and arduous path, only the most serious will pass.
This is the path of Ma'aseh Merkava.

10

In order to trick us, magicians use "sleight of hand."
This means they distract you with one hand
all the while doing something unseen with the other.
Politics and social media use the same techniques.
Do not pay attention to what is being said,
rather, pay attention to what is not being said.
When you are told, "don't look here," that's where you need to look.
When the "choir" sings that "this or that" is nonsense,
it is that very nonsense that needs to be examined.
You will find that much that is condemned as nonsense,
truly is nonsense.
But not everything!
Hidden in that haystack is a very sharp needle.
You won't find it by looking for it.
You'll have to sit down in the hay to find it.
You'll find it sticking you right in your a**!
Then you'll know, you've found the hidden truth.
Search for the truth, find it! But when you do, keep it a secret.
Guard your tongue.
What Heaven shows you are for your eyes only.
Pay attention to what I am saying and to what what I am not saying.
These are of the secrets of the Ma'aseh Merkava.

11

Watch closely now!
The magic act is well under way.
You will not discover the truth.
It is not meant to be revealed.
Those who are bringing on what is coming,
will unexpectedly be overtaken by designs of their own creation.
This cannot be avoided.
Prepare as you will, all you do is build walls.
Walls are toppled with the greatest of ease.
It will be God alone who upholds or topples our walls.
Rather than build walls, it is time to build true spiritual faith.
DETACH!! GET OUT!! LISTEN!!
Turn within to YHWH. Learn the use of THE NAME.
Bend like a reed in the wind, or break
when the great winds (ruhot) come.
Be silent, be still, move within, and become a master,
this alone must be your kung fu.

12

I have heard it said
that one must follow "tradition."
But, just what is tradition?
And who decides what is traditional?
When one group says,
"what we accept and others like us accept, this alone is tradition,"
this is not tradition – this is a cult!
Cults are groups that follow a path,
without thinking & without inquiry.
Shutting down the mind is a dangerous thing.
Shutting down the mind makes one more like an animal
than human.
Animals travel in pacts, so too do cults!
Cults today have become accepted,
and many are today included in the mainstream.
This does not make them any less dangerous.
Cult-think will destroy anyone and anything it touches.
Anyone who tries to manipulate your thinking

and to get you to conform to cult-think
is not your friend!
Beware of him or her.
Follow God and His Word.
He will guide you – beware of cheap imitations!

13

A long time ago we were warned.
Centuries ago the Sages feared to take that which is fluid
and make it solid.
This is very dangerous.
But it was a gamble needed to be taken.
For a time, the wise could keep the newly solid properly malleable.
Yet, many fought this process and demanded solidity and rigidity.
The rigid thought that rigidity was and is the only right way.
Those who remember the original fluid state,
worked behind the scenes to neutralize the influence of the rigid.
At most times, they did succeed, but in recent times,
the rigidity is overtaking the living and killing it.
The rigid will not be allowed to destroy the living.
The fluid will always flow and will never be fully stopped
in its place and held prisoner.
This is the secret of God's Word, His teachings, the Torah.
Torah is alive and transcends the pages of every book.
The living know this, the dead cannot.
There is Torah and there is Torah,
but there is only the Word of God.
Pay attention and learn!

14

I warned you about sleight of hand.
I told you not everything is as it seems.
Sometimes we look too hard for deeper meanings
that simply are not there.
Sometimes we miss actual deeper meanings that are there.
You cannot judge a book by its cover,
nor can words and statements be judged at face value.
In an election, politicians say what they want heard,

not necessarily what they believe.
Once elected, every politician is essentially a slave
to a system much larger than themselves.
There is only so much one can do,
be it for good or for evil.
Grandiose promises of sweeping change
sound good but always ring hollow.
Sometimes, our worst enemy can turn out to be our best friend.
And the opposite is true,
sometimes one who appears to be a good friend,
turns out to actually be a terrible enemy.
Learn a lesson from my previous post.
Words can be misunderstood,
and people's imaginations can and do run wild,
with all kinds of silliness,
that they imagine to be rational and truthful.
I have told you, be silent, be still
and eventually the real truth will come out.

15

I am told that most people today do not believe in spirits.
Well, what can I say?
Just because one chooses not to believe
does not make what they deny to disappear and cease to be!
Seeing is not always believing!
Sometimes people see and deny in every way what they are seeing.
They have eyes but refuse to see,
there is nothing new under the sun with this.
Evil exists and it does possess unprotected and unprepared souls.
Many are the symptoms of possession.
This is not make-believe, this is real.
Evil knows how to conceal itself and disguises itself well.
Yet, evil is as evil does.
Evil is recognized by what it does, what it says
and by the beliefs it expresses.
Religion is no safe haven.
Many religious individuals are agents of evil
without even knowing it.

The only safe haven is to recognize evil and to confront it.
Confronting evil is frightening, but unless one faces the fear,
one cannot overcome it.
God brings us into confrontation with evil to enable us
to overcome it and to learn how to teach others to do the same.
Trust in God, serve Him with sincerity.
Confront evil, overcome it and only then
will one be able to do good.

<u>16</u>

Racism is evil, what more can I say?
You think you are better than another?
Why? Because of your religion?
You think your chosen form of religion brings you closer to God?
Yes, I'm sure you do believe that!
Everybody believes that they are better than the other guy,
and that their religion is true and everyone else is wrong!
These sentiments are not Biblical!
Anyone claiming superiority is revealing their lack of it.
God does not administer theology tests!
What you believe to be true may or may not be so.
Luckily for us, God does not judge us
based upon the beliefs in our heads.
God judges us, like the Bible says,
by how we act towards one another.
How you treat one who is different from you
is how God in turn treats you!
God hates arrogance and the arrogant!
There are many who claim to speak for God,
but while many might claim to speak for God,
I have never heard God claim that He speaks through them.
Evil is among us and it grows in the heart of the extremist.
One cannot be a racist without first being an extremist.
Watch out for elitism, racism, and hatred,
these lead down the path of separation.
United we stand, divided we fall.
God and good unite, evil seeks to tear apart.
Watch for the evil within you.

We are all different and we all have different beliefs, so what?
If God blesses us all, why should we do anything less?
Blessed be the bridge-builders, for they shall in turn
build God's Temple on Earth.

<u>17</u>

I warn you, but do you listen?
I show you, but do you see?
You say you want to learn wisdom,
you say you wish to gaze upon the Supernal Chariot.
Yet, when you are shown the way,
do you walk the path?
Can you see the difference between the Tree of Knowledge
that brings death,
and the Tree of Life that is the only true wisdom?
If you cannot instinctively discern
between the light and the darkness,
how do you ever expect to get through the darkness
and make it to the dawning light?
You live a make-believe life,
and you follow a make-believe religion.
God is truth, thus truth is God.
What lies we embrace, what lies we believe!
We live a facade, and ignore the essence.
I try to teach you to look beneath the surface,
and to search for hidden meanings.
Why can you not see this, why do you not know?
Clear your mind of questions.
Silence your tongue from speech.
Listen for the inner voice, it makes you calm, not afraid.
If the inner voice promotes fear, cast it out.
It is the voice of lies.
The inner voice of peace and harmony makes one strong,
not afraid.
The Supernal Chariot (Merkava) awaits you,
but you will not ascend to Heaven all the while
that you are still shackled to the Earth.

18

How do you expect to find silence when all you know is noise?
How do you expect to be still when you are constantly running?
When was the last time you took a long walk off trail in the woods?
When was the last time you paid attention to God's creation
and appreciated the goodness in nature?
When was the last time you breathed fresh air,
and ate natural, healthy food?
When was the last time you cared more about who you are,
instead of how you look?
When was the last time you looked within,
instead of looking in the mirror?
When was the last time you went shopping out of need,
instead of out of desire?
When was the last time you had actual peace of mind?
You seek silence and you seek stillness
and you do not know how to find either!
To find what you do not have,
you must first let go of that which you do have.
You cannot be full of something new,
all the while you are full of something old.
YHWH is renewal. If you have renewal, you have YHWH.
If you do not have renewal, you do not have YHWH.
Empty yourself so that you can become full again.

19

What if?
What if humanity survives and our scientific discoveries
continue growing, unhindered?
What if, as we explore our universe, we also explore ourselves?
What if, as we explore ourselves, we discover
the secrets of our collective humanity?
What if, as we discover ourselves, we discover
what we call today, our souls?
What if, as we discover that we are far more
than our physical bodies, that many choose to live life
beyond the confines of the physical body?
What if humanity evolves to such a point

that being in a physical body is no longer considered necessary
or even desirable?
What if living in the physical body becomes understood as infantile
and that the time has come
for humanity to mature and grow up?
What if the vast majority of humanity
transcends their physical coils and live life in a parallel dimension
here on Earth and everywhere else in the universe?
What if there was a small portion of humanity
who could not tear themselves away from their physical bodies
and instead chose to stay physical?
What if this small portion of infantile humanity
cannot bear to further interact with their more mature brethren,
and chooses instead to ignore contact with the rest of humanity,
whereas the rest of humanity does not lose contact with them?
What if the rest of humanity decides to direct the course of the last
remnant of physical humanity, to assist and guide them
to evolve as they must, as did everyone else?
What if this is the future of humanity?
What if this was humanity's past?
What if this has already happened, millions of years ago.
What if it is we who have become disconnected
and that our brethren are trying to help us reconnect and evolve?
What if humanity's childhood is at its end and our time has come
to grow up, just like our brethren did before us?
What if this is now?

20

There are many secrets in the universe.
There are many secrets within ourselves.
We know so little.

Rather than learn about the new,
how many people cling desperately to the old?
How can one move forward, all the while
that one is chained down from behind.

Only the unchained can move forward.
Only the unchained are truly free.

Chains upon the body weigh down the body.
Chains upon the mind weigh down the soul.
Freedom of the flesh is paid for with
blood, sweat and tears.

Freedom of the mind is paid for with
discipline, desire, and devotion.
One cannot be free all the while that one is still in chains.

We are beings created in the "Divine Image."
This is no mere statement, these are no mere words.
Being created in the Divine Image
is a calling, a challenge, and a responsibility.
The Divine Image alone is what makes us human.

Within us we have the ability to soar to the Heavens.
We can unshackle ourselves and fly like angels.
Of course, only the free are unshackled, only the free can fly.

The children of Heaven seek to return to Heaven.
We seek to create Heaven here on Earth.
Something deep inside us tells us to do this,
and shows us the way how to do it.

Children of the Divine Image crave freedom,
freedom of body and freedom of the mind.
The secrets of the universe and of ourselves await our discovery.
Discovering the secrets is the destiny of all those who embrace the
Divine Image within.

This is why the children of God always seek to free their bodies
and to live far away from the domains of domination,
created by other human beings.
This is why the true children of God reach out with their minds
and seek out truth, no matter where the journey takes the mind.
In this, there is freedom, this is the Path to God.

God is Truth, thus truth is God.
One cannot proclaim truth, one can only know it.
One cannot show the truth, one can only live it.
These things belong to the secrets of the soul.

Those knowing the Divine Image within, know these things well.
Those who embrace the Divine Image in deed
and not just in words,
serve as the Chariot through which the Divine moves here on Earth.
These are of the secrets of the Ma'aseh Merkava.

21

It is so easy to manipulate those who do not think.
All one has to do is to arouse the passions
in those to be manipulated.
All one has to do is to get another "pissed off,"
then the other stops to think
and starts to react with emotion and without clear thinking.
Those who react without thinking are easily swayed
with further emotionally charged influences.
People follow their hearts, even though
what they are doing is misguided and wrong.
People follow their hearts to either embrace or reject
based upon how they feel,
but seldom do they pause to think about
what it is that they are embracing,
or what specifically it is that they are responding to.
Long ago, we were advised, "be deliberating in judgment."
This means that we are supposed to pause, think, and deliberate
what is before us.
Only after careful consideration and an overall revue of the issues
should one choose how one shall respond
and how shall one interact.
Emotions and passions are strong.
Clear, lucid, calm thought is weak.
This is why most people feel their ways through life,
and by doing so cause one disaster after another,
for themselves and for others.
Those that think, pause to consider,
they contemplate, they explore, they investigate.
The wise ask the necessary questions.
What is being said, why is it being said,
why is it in the format that it is,

and why here and now, and in this way?
Answers to these questions take time, so the wise take the time
to find their answers.
Only then do they respond, with wisdom after careful deliberation.
In this way, the wise lead and are not led.
In this way, the wise recognize their emotions and their thoughts
and make the great separation between them,
choosing to follow the clarity of mind,
instead of the cloudiness of passion.
Head and heart, both serve us, and can serve us well.
Yet, as the head of the body is above the heart,
so too must one's clear, coherent, and careful thoughts
rise above one's passionate, emotional and clearly incoherent
"knee-jerk" reactions.
A mind is a terrible thing to waste.
A non-thinking emotionally led mind
is an easy thing to manipulate.
Think before you respond. Learn carefully, read properly!
Only then will you see what is, as well as what is not!
Do not allow your passions to deceive you and misguide you.

22

Where does faith come from?
Where does faith take us?
What is true faith, what is false faith?
Is faith the ideas that are the foundation of what you believe?
Or is faith the foundation that guides your actions and behavior?
The two are not the same!
People believe many different things.
Most time these thoughts and ideas give them comfort
and a sense of understanding about the world and about life.
Yet, tragedy strikes those who embrace this kind of faith,
just like it strikes those who do not embrace it.
Belief alone has never protected anyone
from harm, mishap or disaster.
Plenty of good people suffer undeservedly.
There seems to be no rhyme and reason
as to why the good suffer and the bad prosper,

yet our minds, based on faith, demands answers,
answer that make sense to us and will enable us again
to have peace-of-mind, that the world is somehow in order.
But this is not to be! This is not how it is!
Our world does have an order, an order all its own,
and this order does not fit so comfortably into what we believe,
and what we want our faith to be!
We learn faith by word of mouth and by the words of books.
Yet, the human mind does not understand faith,
how then can the human tongue speak it?
What the mind does not understand,
the hand cannot write into any book!
Faith is our life and the length of our days.
By faith alone do the righteous walk before our Creator.
Faith sums up all the commandments of God (Macot 24a).
Faith is fundamental and essential for life and continuity.
But what is it? And what is it not?
What it is not, we have already described.
As to what it is, we shall see.
We shall see, but not with eyes of flesh and blood,
but only with the eyes of the spirit.
Faith in God is true. Faith in man and in man's words is not.
Many speak for God who have not heard from God.
Their words bear false faith.
Watch and wait, and keep one's eyes upon Heaven
and one's feet firmly planted on the ground.
Those who watch for God will be watched by God.
This is true faith.
God in Heaven will teach one and guide one
how to rightly be righteous
and how to rightly live by faith.

23

Science knows that light travels in both waves and particles.
Yet, light does so because it is reflecting its surrounding reality.
Reality itself flows in both waves and particles.
This is why reality has the appearance of being set,
like a wave,

but in reality, it flows from moment to moment,
like a particle.
Space and time flow in waves and they flow in particles.
We see the wave movement and call it natural.
We do not see the particle movement and thus call it supernatural.
Wave and particles describe the ebb and flow of reality.
This reality describes the universe around us,
and it equally describes the universe within us.
Human perceptions also flow in waves and particles.
Human consciousness perceives the waves.
The human unconscious perceives the particles.
Reality flows along in waves from past, to present to future.
Reality flows along in particles, with each and every moment
being new and unattached to those before it and those after it.
Because there are no attachments, each moment in time
can give rise to something new, each place in space
can be altered and turned into something else.
One with such awareness can melt
into the nothingness between waves and particles
and even change lead into gold.
Reality is what we see.
Change how we see and we change how reality unfolds.
Pay attention! I am revealing to you great secrets
of the Chariot of God.
God will travel and move through you,
if only you allow Him to join particle to wave and to surf you.
Contemplate this deeply and unleash your inner power.
Close your mind and open your soul!

24

In Oriental Medicine, the doctor can touch one's pulse
and learn from it numerous things
about the health and illness of the human body.
This is tried and true science.
Since ancient times doctors have been taking the human pulse
and learning much from it about the human condition
and one's medical prognosis.
Just like the individual human being has a pulse,

so too does the natural world around us.
Doctors of the spirit seek to take the pulse of the world.
They seek to learn about the health and illness
of the world around them.
Doctors of the spirit can foresee the world's prognosis
and they can prescribe what is necessary to heal it
before the world, like an individual human body,
becomes sick and dies.
Doctors of the spirit speak little and do much.
They do not seek fanfare or notoriety.
Doctors of the spirit prefer to remain in the background,
remain unnoticed and undetected.
In this way they remain undisturbed
and thus better able to work their medicinal healing skills.
Today, our world is sick and in need of some serious healing.
Yet, not all healing is pleasant, not all medicine is sweet.
Indeed, healing is hard and medicine is bitter,
but if the body is to survive, then it must follow
the required regiment to restore its health.
This is true of the individual human body
as much as it is true of the body of the whole world.
Doctors train to learn how to read the pulse
to monitor health and illness.
Doctors of the spirit train to tune into nature
and foresee that which is coming upon the world.
Today, they do not like what they see!
Yet, what they see in spirit cannot be seen with the human eye.
Only those trained in the way of spirit can see the things of spirit.
Those who see the ways of spirit know the pulse of the world
and see that the world's illness is growing
and prognosis in not good.
Learn to read the world's pulse.
Stop listening to the wavering words of men.
One day, they say this and one day they say that,
but on all days, all their talk is nothing but air, and like the wind,
their air just blows away and leaves nothing behind.
Pay no heed to those who know not the pulse.
FEEL the pulse of the world, become sensitive to its subtle nuances

and you too will learn the way of spirit.
Live in nature, not outside it, in this way will you come
to know nature's Creator.
The Creator will guide His creation
and those who monitor the pulse will learn
and know what to do, how to do it and when it all should be done.
The rest are the secrets. You will learn them from within the pulse.

25

God has concealed the secrets of His universe
in the simplest of places.
We can learn the ways of the universe,
and the Divine Laws underlying it, if only we open our eyes
and understand what it is that we see.
Learn the way of truth
from the peanut, the walnut, and the pistachio.
Before one can acquire the sweet meat inside the nut,
one must first break off and discard its shell.
Like the fruit inside a nut, truth is often concealed
within a hard shell of emotional distortions
and intellectual dishonesty.
Before truth can be exposed, knowledge must be cleansed
of all emotional and intellectual distortions.
Emotional and intellectual distortions are not discarded with ease,
they have to be smashed, ripped, and broken.
Without effort, shells remain intact and the sweet meat inside
remain unconsumed.
Getting to truth is always hard.
Without efforts to discover truth, no truth is ever exposed.
Truth is not revealed, it is discovered.
Even at Mt Sinai, where God Himself spoke
directly into the minds of human beings,
some could not handle the influx of the Divine Revelation,
and insisted instead that all they heard was thunder.
Even when God Himself speaks, some refuse to accept His Voice.
As it was at Sinai, so nothing has changed to this day.
To this day, the echo of Sinai can be heard
within the mind and soul and any who chose to listen.

Yet, the shell of resistance, of emotional and intellectual distortion
and dishonesty must be removed. This requires of us effort.
Effort is hard, but the shells must be broken.
The truth lies within, waiting to be discovered.
Who is willing to explore the undiscovered universe.
Nothing is like you think! Nothing is as it appears.
The sweet meat of the nut is nothing
like the hard shell that encases it.
This is what I know by observing God's creation.
His secrets are to be found in plain sight.

26

What would you do if you ran out of money?
What would you do if there was no money to be had?
How would you survive? What would you eat?
Could you live without your house?
Can you live without all your comforts and belongings?
If you had nothing, can you survive?
Can you rebuild? And if so, how?
If there is no money to be had,
then working your chosen occupation can no longer
bring you support, so, now what?
This is where the tests of faith, skill, and survival begin.
Many have already experienced this,
they never thought it could happen to them.
We do not have to wait for the Apocalypse and Armageddon
to encounter hard times.
Hard times come to the best of us.
To every fortune, there is equal and opposite misfortune.
Is this not the natural cycle of life?
Day turns to night and back to day again.
Fortune lasts but for a while and then turns to misfortune,
before it turns to fortune again.
This is the natural cycle, it is to be found in everything, everywhere.
As it says, there is a time and a purpose for all things under Heaven
But who really knows this truth?
Who really understands the nature of the roller-coaster
that Heaven has ordained to dominate all life?

Ups and downs, fortune and misfortune, having and not having,
thriving and surviving,
this is the way of the world, and God is King over all.
One who knows the way knows when to expand
in the times of fortune and to contract in times of misfortune.
Borrowing to maintain the status of fortune in times of misfortune
is a recipe for disaster.
One cannot maintain balance at a time of imbalance.
Those who try will fail and fall farther
than those who go along with the natural flow.
Obedience to God means to go with the natural flow,
not the flow of man and society, but rather the flow of life
and the universe.
Man and life, society and the universe
never flow together in harmony.
When there is one the other is absent.
When all is lost and gone, and rebuilding is impossible,
this may not be misfortune,
but rather a whole new learning opportunity.
The old is gone, long live the new.
And now for the final secret:
The new to come is the old of the long forgotten past.
The cycle is completing and we are returning to the beginning.
And the beginning is always the most delicate of times.

27

Everything in this physical universe is in motion.
Every atom and molecule is in movement
and so too is everything made of them.
The Earth rotates around its axis, it revolves around the sun.
Our Sun revolves around the center of the Milky Way,
and the Milky Way itself revolves around a greater Core,
which itself revolves around an even greater Core.
Everything moves and travels, circle within circle within circle.
The circle is the common form of cycle
that measures both space and time.
Cycles strictly obey the natural laws that were ordained
by the Creator in the beginning.

The worlds around us and the worlds inside us move in circles.
They are each self-contained and orbit one within the other.
Yet, there exists more than one circle and one passage
from one circle to the next.
Passage from one circle to the next follows a straight line.
Straight lines do not normally exist in nature,
but they do normally exist in the minds of human beings.
So, we have the circle, which is a sphere,
and we have the straight line that is a column.
These are the two sides of reality, the sphere, and the column.
The spheres are the circles of each successive universe.
The columns are what connect them and unite them.
Consciousness ascends upon the columns from sphere to sphere.
This is not mere talk, this is the path of ascent,
the secret of the Igulim and the Yosher.
In order to rise up from one circle to the next,
one ascends the column, which can only be found in the center.
The column resides in the center, but this is no physical center,
it can only be seen where it is not.
The column appears like a raging storm,
yet it is only the first of seven doors.
One must pass through the raging storm in order to access
the path that leads Above.
The column resides inside each of us, at our very center,
at that place where the conscious mind meets the unconscious.
At this place there is tremendous movement and a turbulent storm,
yet in order to rise, the storm must be tamed.
The domain of the King is in turmoil, but the dragons maintain the
spheres and align the pillar, waiting for us to act.
It is up to us to align the spheres, first those within,
and then those outside.
In order to do this one must stop walking around the circle
and contributing to the turmoil in the Kingdom.
One must stay still in order to climb the column.
Pay attention and look within!
First tame the circling storm within,
only then will one face the deception of the cloud.

<u>28</u>

Why are we here?
We are here to shine the Light of God and to point the way
to the holy path.
One does not fulfill this because one claims to do so.
Doctrines and beliefs are empty vessels.
Thoughts and words alone cannot encase the Divine Light.
All claim to be holy to God, all claim to be the elite.
Yet, those who belong to God are not those who proclaim so,
but rather those whose actions reveal them so.
What one does reveals who one is.
Nothing else matters, there is no other criteria of judgment.
You are what you do.
What you do reveals where you come from
and to where you are going.
With this understood,
let us ask how does one come to know right action
from wrong deeds.
Are there trusted and proven words that speak to us?
Alas, everyone claims that theirs are the holy words of God
and that all others are false.
So we live in a world of accusations,
where everyone claims everyone else is false
and only they themselves are true to God.
With such confusion how can one know truth?
The answer lies along the path, for truth can never be proven
from a book,
but one can come to see with one's own eyes.
Although the mind might be forever full of hollow shells,
the heart and the hand may become full of God's Light.
Those who shine the Light in deed and not merely by proclamation,
these are the vessels through which the Divine moves.
They are the chariots (merkava) of God.
After one tames the circling storm of thoughts in one's mind,
one settles into a calm that is not a calm.
After one struggles with all that is false
and silences it from distracting the mind,

one settles into a kind of nothingness.
Some have mistaken this nothingness to be the great Nothing
from which all things come forth, but this is not to be.
This nothingness is a numbing, it is another distraction.
As the storm distracts us with mental noise,
this cloud of nothingness distracts us with mental silence.
Little do we know that this cloud also harbors a storm.
This cloud blinds the eye and silences the mind,
it prevents one from seeing the flashing lightning that waits ahead.
Unless one goes forward, one can stay lost in the cloud forever.
The dragons watch as is their mandate.
Only those who perceive the deception inherent in the cloud
are met by the dragon's thunder.
Those who harness the dragon's thunder will pass beyond
to gaze upon He who sits upon the Throne.

29

Daily, I speak to so many who claim to know so much.
Everyone can see, everyone has eyes,
everyone sees exactly what they want to.
But can one see beyond one's scope of vision?
Can one see outside the spectrum of one's self-imposed limitations?
How many can draw down the Unity of the Sacred Names
from the Supernal Crown into the place where
the Supernal Father and Mother unite in her womb?
Who can crown the Small Face and place within his head
the necessary brains to enable him to establish his kingdom?
Who can raise the fallen sparks when proclaiming
the great unknowable to be King of the universe?
Who can direct the radiance of Heaven down from above
and on to a specific place or thing here below?
Who can raise the dead? Who can heal the sick?
Tell me if you know all these things?
Be honest and confess that you do not!
You do not understand the language of the ancients,
any more than you understand the code in which they speak!
Yet so many claim to see! So many claim that they know,
and that they know better than did the ancients themselves!

There is no talking to such souls, they are so full
of themselves that there is no room for anything else to enter.
This is what happens when one gets lost in the cloud.
The cloud fills one with a heaviness that is lite
and a darkness that appears bright.
Those in the cloud have raised their heads to heaven,
and have placed their minds in the clouds,
and there it stays, forever short,
and forever cut off from true Heaven.
But who knows this to be true?
Those who look up cannot see,
and those who look down are silenced and not heard.
There is only one path out of the cloud and that is faith.
Yet, faith must be fired with passion.
If there is no passion, there will be no faith.
The King desires always to mate with the Queen,
this is the secret of the Male and Female Waters.
Unless there is passion, there is no ascent.
Passion is the heart, the center of the center.
The heart receives from all above and gathers from all below.
Know the heart and you will know God.
The heart is God's glory, His beauty (Tiferet).
Seek the heart and the passion of the search
will take you up and out beyond the cloud.
Yet, this requires faith and faith requires passion.
God says, light my fire and in turn, Heaven will light yours!

30

People with their heads in the clouds,
they are so sure of themselves.
They are so convinced that they are right,
and that you are equally wrong.
So be it! I cannot show something to those who cannot see.
I cannot speak to those who cannot hear.
But for those who still crave to see,
and for those who still yearn to hear,
for these precious ones, I will not hold back.
They will see and they will hear,

not with my eyes or my ears, but with their own.
YHWH is real and YHWH is present.
YHWH knows, YHWH sees, YHWH understands.
YHWH divides truth from falsehood,
YHWH divides light from darkness.
Those who seek YHWH will see with their own eyes the truth
and the light denied by those whose heads are in the clouds.
Those who crave to hear the Voice of YHWH
will hear it with their own ears,
unlike those in the clouds who can only hear the fleeting wind.
So many speak in the name of religion,
so many speak in the name of Torah,
so very few try to speak in the Name of YHWH.
So many lies, all surrounded in garbs of righteousness and religion!
As it was in times long ago, so it is again,
exactly as it was in the past.
There is nothing new under the sun.
Those with their heads in the clouds see everything in the world
as being either black or white.
They lack the vision and the depth to see the true colors
and beauty created by YHWH.
Their black and white monolithic vision poisons
everything within them and everything around them.
Those who embrace the black and white
will become full of their venom.
Those who embrace the black and white will by nature
reject the colors, their beauty and YHWH their Creator.
They will reject YHWH in YHWH's Name.
Little do they know that they do the opposite
of that which they claim.
They are the true wolves in sheep's clothing,
the black and white of extremes, rigidities,
false life, and false living.
YHWH removed them from before us once, twice
and soon a third time.
Will they return again? No! Three strikes and you're out.
That is what the ancients teach.
Those with their heads in the clouds can rise

if they so choose to face the cleansing fires,
but alas, most reject the fire, the cleansing and YHWH,
who is the Esh Okhla, the devouring fire.
What will be? We will each choose,
and the time of choosing draws nigh!
Separate from the black and white,
embrace the colors (SEFIROT) of YHWH.
Look to the future, and let go of the past. Torah is eternal.

<u>31</u>

I am often asked how to tell
the difference between truth and falsehood.
The answer to this is not as difficult as one might think.
However, it does require of one to study the Sacred Texts
and to know well what they are saying.
This is clearly not being done today.
A cultist cloud has arisen these days
that dictates to all what to study and how to study it.
Today, large segment of sacred study and sacred texts
are wrongly banned by the cult-mind and deemed unacceptable.
Simply put, those who ban sacred texts and teachings
seek to conceal the light that they themselves cannot handle.
If you seek truth and light,
then one must shun those who ban things,
and investigate with open eyes that which they seek to ban.
Heed not false words.
You will know them because they try to instill within one fear.
Heed not false words that begin with,
"we don't do this, or we don't accept that,
and if you want to belong with us,
then you too won't do this or accept that."
This type of manipulation is akin to mind control,
this is not the way of the Torah of God.
God desires of us to think,
this is why he gave each of us a brain.
Our Sages want us to be deliberating,
therefore their first words to us (in Pirkei Avot)
are to be deliberating in our judgments.

We think, we contemplate, we discriminate, we investigate,
and only after we look at something from all sides
do we draw conclusions and decide
what it is that we embrace and what it is that we reject.
And one person's conclusions will be different from the next.
This too is the way of Torah.
This is not the way of the black and white today.
Their narrow thoughts are reflected in all they do,
even down to how they dress.
God's Torah is not black and white, not the Laws,
not the beliefs and not the Kabbalah.
There are always many shades, many colors,
and as we say, elu v'elu divrei Elohim Hayim,
these are all the words of the Living God.
Thus we live in a world of color.
We see. We discriminate. We study, We learn and we grow.
When learning stops and fear sets in,
growth stops and darkness dominates.
This is what we see all around us.
And as we see it, so too does God. And He is not pleased!
Study all! Learn! Grow! Mature!
Do not be intimidated by the black and white.
Do not fear them or be afraid of what they say.
They will be erased in short time,
with a wonderful brush of red color and blue.

32

Secrets of Sandalphon

The fog/cloud of silence and sleep must be traversed
in order to see the flashing fire on the other side.
This fire is the flame of cleansing.
It is the final stage one must pass
before one can gaze upon the Supernal Image.
This fire is the flaming sword that guards the way to Eden.
This fire is the chariot upon which Elijah ascended to Heaven.
This fire is the cloak of Sandalphon,
the great Seraph, the angel of fire.

Sandalphon is the twin of Metatron.
Sandalphon ascends and Metatron descends.
Sandalphon is the fire surrounding the Supernal Throne.
Only one who embraces this fire
will be able to handle the Supernal Fire.
YHWH is the Supernal Devouring Fire.
One cannot embrace the Devouring Fire
unless one is first cloaked in the fire of Sandalphon.

But who understands these things?
Who is willing to learn the secrets of the sacred path?

Truth cries out into the mainstream of human consciousness,
but (truth) EMET – Alef, Mem, Tav, is rejected and despised!
Alef is the beginning of all things, Heaven above.
Tav is the end of all things, Earth below.
Mem, is in the middle. Mem is the womb of the Mother,
the source of the mind/soul of human beings.
YHWH is Alef.
Metatron is Mem.
Sandalphon is Tav.
It is the sign of Sandalphon (the Tav) that is placed
upon the foreheads of the righteous.
The mark upon the righteous is the scar of fire
that has singed and burned away the dross of the mind,
enabling the soul to be set free.
Sandalphon burns and Metatron waters.
There is not one without the other.
No one can gaze upon the Supernal Throne
and gaze upon the Image of the Small Face
unless one is first burned by the fires of Sandalphon
and watered with the water of life from Metatron.

Seek, therefore, the fires of purification.
Allow them to penetrate your mind and
to cleanse your thoughts, both conscious and unconscious.
Only when you are so cleansed
at the conscious and unconscious level
will the Supernal Image of He who sit upon the Throne
begin to become clear to you.

Embrace the flame, embrace the pursuit of truth.
Destroy all your inner idols and embrace the Only True One.
The path is long and arduous.
Many run in fear from the stormy mind.
Many more are lost in the fog/cloud on mental sleep.
Only those with the passion to preserve
merit to be burned by the sacred fire.
Only those who merit the sacred fire,
will ever drink of the waters of life, the hidden well of Miriam.

<u>33</u>

Silence the mouth from speech.
Silence the mind from questions.
Still the body from movement.
Breathe shallowly.
Deafen your ears from sound.
Close your eyes to sight.
Let go of this world.
Go within the recesses of your mind,
and find your soul.
I cannot be more direct, I cannot be simpler.
The path of ascent is the way of descent.
One does not go up to gaze upon the Supernal Throne,
one goes down.
One goes down into the deepest recesses of the mind/soul,
where the individual ceases and the collective begins.
I am teaching you step by baby step what you need to do.
But are you listening?
Unless you awaken your mind to the passion,
forever will you try in vain!
Passion is the foundation (Yesod)
that nourishes the body (Malkhut).
Passion is the passageway (Yesod)
that enables ascent to the upper worlds/Sefirot.
If you do not start the right way and "follow the yellow brick road,"
you will never arrive at your destination.
The road is paved with yellow/golden bricks,
not silver ones, or ones of any other color.

Gold is precious, the steps along the path are precious.
Miss one step and you'll drift off course.
FOCUS! FOCUS YOUR PASSION – FIRST!
THEN FOCUS YOUR MIND.
The path is always from below to above.
We begin in the Kingdom (Malkhut)
and unite it with passion (Yesod).
Only then can we conquer (Netzah)
and experience the glory (Hod) therein.
This is the path through the seven doors,
the domain where prophecy begins.
PAY ATTENTION!
I will not reveal to you more now.
Review what I have already shared with you,
and when you are ready, we will proceed.
Welcome, all children of the ascent (benei aliyah).

34

Is it all in the imagination, or it is real?
Is the imagination itself something real or not?
Doubters say, "it's all in your head."
And indeed, they are right!
Everything that you think, that you dream,
and that you experience is all in your head.
Essentially the entire universe and all of reality is in our heads.
This being so, our heads must be far bigger
than that big lump on top of our shoulders.
And indeed it is!
For the head is the seat of the mind,
and the mind is just the sheath for the soul.
Thus the head is the vessel for the soul.

Indeed, everything is perceived through the mind
and through the soul.
All reality emanates from and returns to the mind/soul.
Soul is to mind as sword is to sheath.
The soul is sharp and its pierce can kill.
To protect the outside world,
the soul is sheathed in the conscious mind.

The conscious mind protects the world around us
from the piercing gaze and awesome powers of the soul.
The mind contains the soul and keeps it safe
in the sheath of the unconscious.
The soul is the only true consciousness,
it sees and knows far beyond that of physical flesh.
The soul travels in space and time
and thus sees beyond eyes and knows beyond knowledge.
What the soul knows is stored in the mind.

Only one who can access the mind
can see what the soul sees.
Thus to expand into the surrounding outside world,
one must penetrate first within, in order to catch a ride
aboard the penetrating gaze of the expanding soul.
The eyes of the soul see that
which the eyes in the head cannot.
Thus when the doubter says that he cannot see,
and therefore you too cannot, remind him,
that indeed he cannot see, but that his blindness
does not make you equally blind.
The doubter may not want to see and deny sight even if seen.
So be it!
The soul of the doubter limits his mind and restricts
what there is to know and what there is to see.
Perhaps such a doubter is fated to doubt, to be blind,
to stumble and to fall.

Who are we to question the Higher Ways?
What can we possibly understand about them?
What we can understand will come to us
only upon our explorations within.
We may indeed see without eyes
and know without knowledge.
It may indeed all be in our heads.
And that is what makes it most real of all.

35

You say you want to see, but no you don't!
You lie to yourself. You say one thing but you do another.
I am often asked for words of advice and direction,
yet, while I provide that which is asked of me,
I discover that so few read what they have asked me to write,
and of those who do read,
even fewer are willing to follow the direction
that they themselves have asked me to lay out for them.
I have discovered that so many claim
that they want something,
but their actions clearly show they have no such true desire.
So, why continue? Why go on?
The answer to this is the secret of the path to God.

We do not do what is right for the sake of others.
We do what is right for its own sake!
Service and righteousness are performed for their own end.
This is the proper path, what the Bible calls Tzedaka.

Tzedaka is translated today as charity,
but its true meaning is righteousness.
For there is no righteousness that is not charitable
and there is no charity that is not essentially righteous.
Charity and righteousness are both the path of Tzedaka,
and the one who walks this path is called a Tzadik,
a righteous individual.
So, we do what is right, simply because it is right.
This is the Torah Code of Honor.

In order to walk among the angels
and be given passage through the dragons,
each individual must embrace Tzadik Yesod HaOlam,
this is the Righteous Foundation of the World.

But beware!
The misguided and blind fool thinks Tzadik Yesod HaOlam
to be a fellow human being
which one must follow as a slave does a master.
This is falsehood, a lie, and an evil deception.

Those in black and white perpetuate this myth.
Last generation, their blindness led a continent into flames.
Today, they try to engulf the whole world in their blindness.
Indeed, they will succeed to fall again
into the fires of their own making.
Yet not all who cling to them, must follow their path
into the fires of destruction.

Tzedaka requires that the truth be told, for its own sake,
and for yours!
Tzedaka requires that the true path of Torah
be distinguished between the sacred and profane,
between the light and the darkness.
There is no righteousness that is not charitable
and there is no charity that is not essentially righteous.
This is the secret of Tzadik Yesod HaOlam.

The angels await the children of Tzedaka.
Tzedaka will save one from death.
Tzedaka alone can influence the Watchers,
and grant one passage through the dragons.

Once the Kingdom is firmly anchored,
one must embrace the Yesod, hold tight,
and pull oneself up into the higher world.
How can you not understand this?

Enough for now, deal with the truth.
How can more be forthcoming,
when even this is not firmly embraced?

36

The purpose of one is two.
The purpose of two is three.
This is why in the real world one plus one does equal three.
This is the purpose of uniting the one with the other.
Ask any man and woman,
when together, they will understand this.
In the beginning there was only one.
Yet, one unto itself can only be known unto itself.

Thus does the one truly know itself if there is no other to know it?
One can be and not know, but can one know and not be?
In the beginning, the One was and knew
It knew it wanted to be what it is.
In order for it to be what it is, there had to be another.
Only in the eye of the other can the One be seen for what it is.
Thus the One made way for the other.
Now, here lies the mystery of existence.
For the other also became many,
the one other became many others.
An infinite amount of others came forth from the first other.
Yet, all others are not truly other,
they are merely reflections of the original One.
In the beginning was the One,
and today all that really exists is the One.
All others are mere reflections created by the One.
Reflections are mirrors, one mirror reflects many things.
Being that there are so many things to reflect,
there has arisen so many mirrors.
All ultimately reflect back to the original One,
who is beyond all reflection.
Life is all about mirrors.
Everything is merely a reflection of something else.
When we gaze upon reflections,
all we see are other reflections.
When we live looking into mirrors
all we see are the reflections of others.
In order not to be distracted by mirrors,
one must not look at them.
While mirrors can show one many things,
they forever distract one from seeing the One
from which all things come forth.
Thus we are taught to close the eyes to outside sight.
We are to silence the mind from questions.
When we calm the storm within and navigate the fog cloud,
and then face the fires that burn the mirrors,
we can gain a glimpse of the original One.
But I must warn you,

what you see when you gaze will change you forever.
Once upon a time, a person was punished.
He was taken to Paradise to experience the wonder
and beauty of the world of truth.
After a while, he was returned to Earth.
From then forward, even the most beautiful things here on Earth
seemed ugly and meaningless.
Once one gazes upon the One of all,
the all is seen for what it is, just reflections in the mirror.
Learn to see, learn to understand.
Words can limit, but your imagination can set you unbound.
Be free - - and see!

37

Bounded as one, separate as points,
joined together in the never ending line of life
that circles the universe.
This is the order of evolution, how the One became many,
and how the many become One again.
This is the way of the world.
Words can describe it on a page,
but no mind can fathom it from the words.
Words only hint to the meanings of truth,
but they can never substitute for truth itself.
Words are vessel for light, but not the light itself.
One must never mistake the vessel for the light therein.
When I point to the sun to teach you a lesson about light,
pay attention to what I am saying,
and not to where my finger is pointing.
Do not look at my finger, instead, look beyond it.
Look to that to which I point.
I point to the invisible and to the wordless.
You can see it only when your eyes are closed,
and your mind is open.
You will be able to read the invisible
only when you have cleared your mind of the words
written in the many books.
That which is bound, that which is pointed,

and that which when joined together form the great line
from one end of the universe to the other,
cannot be seen with eyes of flesh
or understood with a mind encased in a prison of limitations.
The bound are known within the Almighty breath,
they can be heard only when the mouth breathes in silence.
The points are seen when gazed upon with the supernal eyes,
yet the eyes must see from above the heart and from below it,
and know the difference between the two.
When the two become one,
they form the line that lasts forever.
The one become two, the two become three,
the three become nine and the nine return into the one.
Thus one and zero become the form of all, above and below.
Seek this not from the pages of any book,
Rather, gaze within, past the storm, the fog, and the fire,
and see that Sandalphon will guide you to understand
the visage of Metatron.
And in Metatron will you see YHWH,
and see the line that forms the square and the circle.
Walk the yellow brick road around the circle,
and the circle will lead you down the line that takes you
beyond the Kingdom and into the Palace of Paradise.
Close your books, open your mind.
See within, and let the path guide you.
For those who seek more, come to me, I await you.

38

From within the head, from within the very brains themselves,
a voice emanates outward,
It is not heard in the ears, but comes forth from the ears.
And how is this?
This is because that which emanates outwards
belongs to the upper worlds.
It is the perennial giver.
That which absorbs and takes in belongs to the lower worlds.
It is the perennial receiver.

Right ear, left ear, the secret of soul and body.
But what body can a sound have?
What form does a sound take if it cannot be heard?
Yet, the voice emanates out and surrounds us.
It vibrates our very being and touches the heart itself.
Yet, once the voice touches the heart, it goes no further,
for once the heart hears the voice, the heart then arises
to give birth to the lower worlds.

The unheard voice emanates forth out of the ears,
from the very essence of the mind.
It is not heard, it can hardly even be felt.
But yet, its presence is detectable.
The sensitive know, they can sense it, they can smell the voice
as its pleasant fragrance ascends into their nostrils.
Not for naught are the ears and nose connected.
One gives forth, the other receives, this is the secret of above
and below, for those who can grasp a whiff of it.

The fragrance goes forth out of the nose
to create the aroma for birthing life.
There is in and there is out.
There is the sound of mind and the fragrance of thought.
Both come forth from within the upper worlds.
The fragrance of life comes forth from the two nostrils,
one baring the soul, and the other, the body.
There is no life without both body and soul.

Yet, the sound of the ear and the fragrance of smell
both lack a solid form though which to give below.
So the sound of thought and the fragrance of mind merge
and unite in the mouth, the place of breath.
Here is the birth of life.
For as we breathe in, we speak out.
Breath goes in, words come out.
The words of the mouth build all that which is thought of.
Pay heed and know, there is no creation and no birth
unless there first comes forth the voice from within the ears,
and the fragrance of the mind from one's nostrils.
The nostrils are the receptacle for the breath of life.

In the breath is life, in the word there is form and structure.
We think, we feel and then we combine them to speak
and thus create the universe.
As we speak so we create,
Avra K'davra, I create what I speak.
This is the secret of the ears, the nose, and the mouth.
Together the source of life is bound up within them.
Together they are the domain of the bound, the Akudim.

<u>39</u>

Why don't we learn from that which we see?
We live in a reverse world,
this we know to us from our own anatomy.
Left controls right and right controls left.
This is not without reason or precedent.
There is in and there is out,
there is above and there is below.
The way of one reflects the way of the other.
That which is above is the opposite of that which is below.
Upper and lower realities are reflections of one another.
It is not Above that operates backwards to us,
rather it is us that operates backwards with regards to them.
For us time marches forward, for them,
(from our point of view), time marches backwards.
We go from past to future, they go from future to past.
When the two meet, the Active Present is created,
then a vortex will be opened, as it was at the "big bang."
The two universes will unite, Heaven and Earth will become one,
and death will be no more.
This vortex of dimensional union will not be a seeding
as it was in our past, but rather it will be the "time"
for the birth of the old-born child.

Here below, we breathe in and exhale to speak.
But Above inhales and speaks and exhales in silence.
We cannot fathom this. All we can do is gaze upon
the wondrous realities in amazement.
With the first Divine breath came forth the beginning of all form,
undivided, undifferentiated.

There was no separation of light from darkness
or right from left, or above from below.
As such there could be no universe.
Thus the breathing had to continue,
and in the breaths that followed
came forth life and the lower universes.

Yet, as the breath withdrew within, not all came forth back out.
The crown remained concealed
and wisdom reigned over all that was to come.
Wisdom was crowned and became the new master.
It gazed out over its new kingdom
and saw what needed to be seen.
Then the supernal gaze of the wise crown gazed below.
When it did new worlds came forth.
The pointed vision of the wise master
saw as we too shall soon see.

40

Turn around, and look at what you see.
Behind you there is a mirror into your soul.
Look into your dreams
and there you will see reality looking back at you.
But can see you the vision in your dreams?
Can you understand the message not spoken in words
but rather in pictures.
The ears hear and the eyes see.
Not for naught did Heaven design us in this way.
We reflect the supernal pattern,
we are created in the Image of God.
Ears are to the sides, this is the domain of the extremes.
We hear one way or another,
seldom do we ever hear that which is in the middle.
The eyes are in the middle,
they eyes see that which is directly in front of us.
Although our vision can be turned to either side,
it is still designed primarily to see that which is in front.
Ears hear words, eyes see images.
Ears hear words which can swing a soul

from one extreme to another.
Eyes see pictures and a picture is worth a thousand words.
More is seen than can be heard.
The eyes know what the ears can only try to understand.
After the supernal ears emanate forth the sound
which is to be heard below,
the time has come for the eyes to see.
First the ears hear and create the most basic of ideas,
then the eyes see and ideas take on more concrete form.

The eyes Above gaze below.
They see the words of the ears spoken by the mouth.
The eyes see that wisdom reigns over the bound kingdom
and sets out to release those who are imprisoned.
The eyes gaze upon the bound, the heard, spoken ideas,
and understands what needs to be to set them free.
Yet, freedom comes at a price.
No freedom is free.
Freedom is purchased for a price and is maintained at a price.
Anyone with eyes can see this,
although words can be spoken to confuse this truth
and block it from being understood in the mind.
But the eyes see! The eyes know!
What the eyes see, leads the eyes to act upon what is seen.

The eyes embrace the heart
and begins to manifest what the heart knows best.
The crown of the heart comes forth
and reigns over what will become
the land of the free and the home of the brace.
Yet, freedom is bought through bravery,
and bravery is only shown in conflict and war.
The eyes know that freedom will only come about
through great effort.
Therefore, the eyes see what needs to be done
and sets out to enact that which it has envisioned.
Woe to the one who lacks a sense of inner vision.
Those who are blind within can never see the outside clearly.
The supernal eyes narrow in, like points (Nikudim),

and sets about to set free the bound
and prepares to bind the brokenhearted.

<u>41</u>

You know that we are not alone.
You know that we are all being watched.
Big brother might be watching us,
but THEY are watching big brother.
THEY work in accordance to the Heavenly plan.
THEY are meticulous, and thorough.
THEY know what THEY are doing.
We do not know THEM, but THEY know us.
Many of us do not even believe that THEY exist.
But there are those of us who know better.

THEY are there, although we are oblivious to their presence.
Yet even the oblivious can be taught to see.
All one has to do is to learn to see.
Yet, learning to see is not that hard.
What is hard is wanting to continue to see,
once sight is achieved.
For what there is to see is very frightening.
THEY are watching and THEY are legion.
THEY are here, right now.
THEY are here with me right now.
THEY are there with you, right now!
You do not see THEM with your physical eyes,
but you do feel them,
you can sense their presence, even now.

THEY are Watchers, that is what THEY do.
THEY rarely intervene, but THEY are always there.
THEY whisper into your ear and you hear
their voice inside your head and you mistake their voice
to be your own.
THEY guide us as Heaven guides them to do so.
We are all subject to the Guidance of the Higher Hand.
Good and evil both are creations of Heaven.
Both serve the Divine Purpose.

If you wish to tune into this, you must learn to listen,
and you must learn to see.

Silence your surroundings, calm your mind and body.
Focus on the sacred, call out to God.
Sit in stillness and silence, and wait, and wait.
Your eyes will become heavy and your mind will become dull.
Allow yourself to doze as you call out within yourself:

Watcher, Watcher, let me see your face.
Watcher, Watcher, let me know your place.
Watcher, Watcher, I am not meek, I seek to see.
Watcher, Watcher, I am not weak, reveal to me.
Elohim Adonai open my eyes.
Shadai, El Hai let me be wise.
Watcher, Watcher, let me see your face.
Watcher, Watcher, open to me your space.

Over and over again, round and round.
All change comes slowly.
But changes do come, and they are frightening.
Once you overcome the fear,
THEY will allow you insight, passage, and access.
Now!
Because there is no later.
Why hear me?
Instead, listen to THEM!

42

Dangerous Messianic Speculations

Many words have been spoken by many sources.
Yet so few of them are prophecy,
and just as few are actual secrets revealed from Heaven.
The rest are the words of men, the personal opinions
of flesh, blood, and human imagination.
While there is a great difference between the two,
all are presented equally, all are thought to be the same,
all are thought to be equally valid revelations
of the word of God.

But this is not so!
There is that which comes from Heaven,
and there is that which comes from Earth,
and more so, there is that which comes
from an even more nefarious source.
Not all that is spoken or written is to be believed.

The word of God is just that.
It stands on its own merits as found in the Bible.
The Sages of old spoke with Angels.
The Angels revealed to the Sages of old many things.
Their words are recorded in Talmud and Midrash.
Later came the words of the Mystics, they too heard from Above,
and recorded their words in Zohar and Kabbalah.
Thus we have the records,
these form the body of the Tradition (Mesorah).
Together these spell out to us
what to expect and what signs we are to watch for.
Together, these have guided us for centuries,
and those with eyes have used these ancient words
to enable us to see that which cannot otherwise be seen.
And see, we do! And what we see, is what there is to see.

Now, in recent years, there has come a darkening cloud,
and it is spreading confusion, deception, and misdirection
over the words of the ancients.
Many false words are propagating,
being told over and over again,
by many people in many places.
Yet, no one bothers to question, no one dares to ask,
are the words popularly spoken today true and real?
Who bothers to check, who bothers to investigate?
When the popular words of today contradict
the ancient teachings of Bible, Sage, and Mystic,
does anyone notice, does anyone care?

Today, the voices from Hell
outnumber and out-shout the voices from Heaven.
Heaven allows this, as it did with Pharaoh in ancient Egypt,
to punish the blind with more blindness.

Isaiah the prophet warned us long ago that this would come.
Yet, who today reads Isaiah, when they can instead
entertain themselves with the popular
modern teachers of darkness.

The ancients have spoken, but many ignore their words.
They instead embrace a false teaching, a dangerous teaching.
They proclaim, against every word of prophecy,
against every word of Sage, Talmud, Zohar, and Kabbalah,
they claim that in the war to come,
that the physical Holy Land will be the only safe haven
for the righteous, and that all others are doomed to perish
as punishment for not coming to live in the Holy Land.
It is truly beautiful to live in the Holy Land,
to many it is a religious obligation.
Yet still those who say so, must also know
that not all religious views agree with them.
The Bible is clear that when the Mashiah comes,
it will be he that gathers in the exiles.
They must be there outside the Holy Land
for prophecy to be fulfilled.
Who can deny this?
Who dares challenge the living word of God?

There is a terrible war to come, this is true.
What is also true is that the Bible, Talmud, Midrash,
Zohar and Kabbalah speak in one voice and proclaim,
the Holy Land will not be a safe haven
in the days before Mashiah comes.
On the contrary, the cleansing in the Holy Land
will leave few in this world, some say as few as 7000.
This is an ancient tradition
passed down for hundreds of years.
It elucidates what the Bible says.
Yet, there are those in religious garb who come along
to mislead the masses to believe that which contradicts
all that has been revealed in the past.

Study for yourselves.
See what the Bible, the Talmud, the Midrash, the Sages,

the Zohar, and the Kabbalists have taught.
Their books, their words are still with us today.
And who is to say that all the ancient teachings
of thousands of years are wrong, and what is said today is right?
I am stunned and silenced by such a question!
Those who dare question the foundations of faith,
by challenging the ancients,
have created for themselves a new faith,
one that the true faithful children of Torah
cannot recognize and will not embrace.

God's Torah is in living color,
those who embrace only black and white
deny the living color of Torah and the God who gave it.
So let it be. Isaiah 29 told us that this would be so.
This sad state today fulfills the prophecy that was recorded
in Isaiah so long ago. We were warned!

The great war is coming.
The Holy Land will not be a special safe haven.
No place outside the Land will be a special safe haven.
There is now, and forever will be, only one safe haven!
"He who sits in the concealment of the Most High,
will reside in the shadow of the Almighty." (Ps. 91:1)
Do not embrace false hopes,
reject false words and false teachings.
Return to the sources of ancient truth, as revealed by Heaven,
know them and you will know those who spoke them.
Then will you know the One
from whom these words of truth came forth.
Know the One and you will discover
the true safe haven that He alone prepares for you.

43

In order to create that which the eye can foresee,
it must first look into the heart
and bring forth from there the crown of creation.
The eyes within look forth from within the heart.
They look up into the mind, and see what was,

they look down into imagination, and foresee what is to be.
Once the eyes can see within,
they gaze outside and see only that which is already there.
Once the eyes gaze outside, they again close to gaze within.
This makes external reality to disappear,
and the reality within the mind to again become
alive and dominant.
Once inside the mind, the eyes can gaze upon the dream.
The dream of what can be takes shape.
What can be is first seen in a dream
and then the dream is contemplated in conscious thought.
Conscious thought is like the small breath
that blows ever so softly upon burning embers
causing them to ignite into a great flame.
Dreams combine with thought
and once the internal vision becomes clear in the mind,
the eyes reopen.
The eyes now open, see that which is there,
as well as that which is not there yet.
What is not there outside, is first seen within,
it is then taken out from within the mind
and its place is defined in the outside world.
The eyes look out to the place
where it will guide the building of that which is to come.
Time has now come into being.
At first, we had what was.
Now, we have what is.
In the future, we will have what will be.
The eyes see that not all things that can be, will be.
In order to bring forth that which will be,
there must be more than the eye's vision.
The eye turns towards the heart,
and from the heart comes forth the vision of the eyes.
The eyes in the heart create,
with motivation and with passion,
for thus is the nature of the heart.
Yet, when the eyes gaze down to bring about what is to be,
it is imperative that what the eyes saw above be not forgotten,

for that which is forgotten cannot be remembered
and brought to be as it needs to be.
When memory fails the eyes
because of the nature of the heart,
what comes forth starts off right, but finishes up wrong.
The sparks of light end up entrapped in vessels of darkness.

44

When the inner eye unites with the outer eye
a plan develops that leads to creation.
The inner eye communes with the heart,
the outer eye communes with the mind,
together the One becomes four
and the four create the next one.
This is the secret of Yod Hay Waw Hey.
This is the secret of the unity between God and His Name.
His Name is being in action.
His Name comes into being when the eyes gaze out,
and sees and create.
Yet, the eyes must be merged inner and outer,
and the heart united with mind,
for if the inner eye loses sight of what the mind tells the heart,
herein lies the genesis of forgetfulness.
When forgetfulness unites with the passion to create,
that which is created does not properly reflect
the Supernal pattern wherein which everything
is properly united and everything is in proper balance.
When creation occurs, its begins with clarity,
yet, when forgetfulness comes into the heart,
at the point of knowing, which unites mind and heart,
the creation becomes blurred, and that which comes forth
unites that which is to be with that which is not meant to be.
This creation is a combination,
a mixture of things good and things bad,
this is where darkness has its genesis in the world of light.
Darkness and light come forth together,
two halves of a united whole.
Yet, in order for the one to be complete, the other must be,

not what it is, but rather that which it was meant to be.
In the beginning, the great separations occurred,
this was meant to be.
Yet, there are separations guided by the light
and then there are those guided by the darkness.
Those created by the light seek to build.
Those created by the darkness seek to destroy.
Those divisions created by darkness seek to destroy,
for this is their nature.
They cannot change, but they can be exchanged.
Forgetfulness is allowed to manifest
to teach us the value of remembrance.
Remembrance is of the heart and mind,
of the inner eye united with the outer eye.
Yod Hay Waw Hay, only in the unity of the four that is One
is there remembrance, is there redemption,
rectification and healing.
Before there was a wound, there was the cure for the wound.
The wound came forth to teach us how to use the cure.
Yod Hay Waw Hay is that cure,
but only for those who unite the four into One.
Know this, inside, in that place where the heart meets the mind.
This is called Knowledge,
and it shows the way to the Tree of Life.

45

Who is a true leader? What does a true leader do?
A leader is one who leads by example, not by proclamation.
A leader is a wise man who teaches others
how to recognize wisdom.
A leader leads through inspiration,
not through fear and intimidation.
A true leader, says follow my example,
but that example is exemplary and is worth following.
A true leader sets such an example
that the light of which shines through all darkness of doubt.

One is not a leader because he is called such by others.
A true leader is not one that is proclaimed.

A true leader rejects any who would follow blindly.
A true leader demands his/her followers to follow in wisdom,
in knowledge, with questions and inquiries.
A true leader welcomes challenge and debate
when these are done in the spirit to pursue knowledge and truth.
A true leader does not need to speak,
his/her deeds alone are inspiration.

The path of the leader leads to righteousness.
The path of the leader leads to being responsible,
self-reliant, and independent.
The path of the leader leads to being normal.

What does the future hold? No one knows!
All who prophesy for you doom and gloom,
may be right and they may be wrong.
We have no prophets today,
no one can honestly say, "Thus says God."
True we have today many wise Sages,
and unfortunately all too many unwise leaders.

46

The Sons of Light & Metatron

The war between the sons of light
and the sons of darkness continue.
It is inevitable that in the end
the sons of light are destined to win.
But we are from the end,
and the inevitable is not yet plain to see.
As it says, it is always
darkest before the dawn,
and as the dawn approaches,
the present darkness tightens its grasp.
This is the way of things.
One must know and understand the darkness,
if one is ever to recognize its many deceptions,
and defeat its many faces.

The war for righteous continues,
and the forces of the righteous
are continually and overwhelmingly assaulted.
Were it not for the Hand of Heaven,
the righteous would have long ago
succumbed to the enemy darkness.
And true, many of the mighty have indeed fallen.
Nevertheless, there remains and always shall remain
the righteous remnant, those chosen by themselves,
and embraced by Heaven to fight the good fight,
to win the righteous battle,
and to be victorious in the sacred war.
The righteous are tested daily,
yet, they are battled-hardened trained soldiers of
the Lord of Armies, YHWH Adonay Tz'vaot.
All good soldiers are honed to obey orders
and to carry out said orders
above and beyond the call of duty.
The sons of light are the special human forces
in the battle with the sons of darkness.

It has been prophesied, it has been told long ago,
that in this great war, and through its many battles,
the sons of light shall wage war like the Angel of the Lord.
We know him, we know his many names,
the 72 that are actually 91.
He is Metatron, the general/captain of the armies of YHWH.
Metatron fights with the flames of his words.
He speaks and brings into reality
the words that pass forth from his lips of fire.
Metatron can kill with a glance.
Those who fight like Metatron
also kill with a glace and a word.
And their word shall bring death eternal
to those who stand against the righteous.
The sons of light are the disciples of Metatron.
The sons of light study his Torah today,
even as it was taught to the father of all the sons of light,

315

Moses, when he ascended into Heaven from Mt Sinai.
The sword of Metatron comes forth from his lips of fire.
In the final battle, the sons of light shall call upon
the many names of Metatron,
and bring forth his words from his lips of fire,
and by doing so,
they will bury the sons of darkness under walls of fire,
even as the ancient Egyptians
were buried under walls of water,
when the Sea fell back down upon their heads.
Moses became Metatron,
and he, the angel of YHWH, guided Israel through the wilderness
to bring them to the Promised Land.
He still guides the sons of light today,
even as he always has in the past.
Those who know his secret call upon him,
for YHWH is within him.
One cannot gaze upon the sun
other than through a filter to shade the eyes.
Metatron is YHWH's shade.
Know the servant and he will bring you to the Master.

Long live the sons of light, the fighters for righteousness!

47

Life is always in movement,
but there can be no stability without central balance.
The universe operates in accordance to its own laws.
We cannot change this, we cannot even understand this.
Natural law dominates and dictates.
Surely, we can influence some things
and maybe redirect the course of yet others,
but in the end, nature's course will reign supreme,
regardless of the best laid plans of not-so-mighty men.

All reality follows higher laws.
We should never deceive ourselves
from knowing and seeing the obvious.
Laws do not create themselves.

For every set of laws, there must by definition exist
the Law Giver, who has ordained such laws in the first place.
Natural law cannot exist outside the framework
of natural common sense.
If there is a way to things, then such a way exists for a reason.
It came to be because of something greater than it,
and that which is greater also came into being
by something greater than it, and so on, and so on.
Knowledge and discovery are infinite pursuits.
No one will ever fathom them.
No matter how far we go, there will always be farther to go.

Just as human laws are enforced by a body of police,
so too must natural law have its enforcers.
Yet, the enforcers of natural law,
in order to accomplish their mandate
must by definition themselves be intelligent and thinking.
They regulate the flow and course of nature.
They do so in accordance to the laws of things
that govern them and those above them.
Now, just who are the "THEM" of whom I speak?
It would be safe and comfortable to say
that I speak of angels or other spiritual beings.
Yet, just what is an angel?
The original Hebrew term for angel
in the Bible is Malakh and means "messenger."
So, while we may understand the job of the messenger,
at the same time, we know nothing about the actual nature
of the messenger(s) themselves.

These messengers are entrusted with the daily operations
and enforcements of natural law.
Yet, these messengers are not like you and me.
Certainly they are not in any way
like what we fantasize angels to be.
There are no actual beings who look human,
wear long white robes
and have actual wings growing out their backs.
This image is a made-up fairy tale.

Yet, while we may not know or understand
their true nature and their true appearance,
nevertheless, they are here among us.
They are watching, as is their right and is their duty.

We are being watched by a power
far beyond our feeble human comprehensions to imagine.
THEY are the Watchers, the ancient ones.
THEY have been here for a very long time,
and in a time coming soon they will be exposed.
The Watchers have many names,
but we know them as the SANDALPHON.
They are the messengers (angels) for the METATRONS.
The METATRONS are the messengers for the YHWH.
And thus is the cycle complete.
Many secrets have I revealed to you now.
Pay attention, contemplate, and learn!

In a time, not too far away, you will be called
to give account for what you know,
what you don't know,
what you don't want to know,
and what you willingly deny.
The Watchers are doing their jobs,
and we are being recorded!

<u>48</u>

Wheels go round and round,
but wheels do not turn on their own power.
The wheels of destiny are also subject to this natural law.
The wheels that control our fate
are turned by the supernal animals,
those with the faces of lions and eagles, bulls, and men.
These animals turn the wheels and the wheels direct our fate.
One world on top of another, on top of another,
three-fold that is united, united in purpose and united in destiny.
The three worlds of Heaven, Earth and the Divine
that rules over them all, are all united, all ultimately one,
all subject to the direction of the Unknown.

Even the animals and those on fire
ask where is the place where the Unknown dwells.
Even they cannot know, even they cannot delve
into the supernal mysteries,
nor see that which lies hidden in the Supernal Holy of Holies,
the domain which only the One may enter.
As it is above, so is it below.
Should I be a revealer of secrets?
Should I say that the Sandalphon be wheels,
that the Metatrons be animals,
with their heads engulfed in the flames.
Should I speak of the unspeakable
and expose that which is ordained to be concealed?
Far be it for me to do such a thing!
Suffice with what you now can know, what you now can see,
if only you willingly open your eyes and allow the wheels of fate
to turn unhindered and you go where they go,
for the spirit of the animals is within the wheels.

Knowing the path of Heaven on Earth is no hard matter.
It is as simple as watching and observing the natural world.
The natural world was brought about through natural law.
And there is no law other than the Torah, therefore,
as one learns from nature, one comes to see nature's Creator.
When one lives in accordance to nature,
one is by definition living in accordance to Torah.
This is true religion, this was the revelation of Sinai,
and the essential purpose underlying all the commandments.
On Sinai, the wheels came down to Earth,
and then rolled on back up to Heaven,
bringing along with it
all those who sought to ascend.
The wheels still go round and round,
and those who embrace the wheel ascend,
and once ascended, they often chose to descend again,
to help elevate others.
This is after all the natural way,
natural law and the Torah of the universe.

Return to nature is to return to nature's Creator, God.
Elohim is in the Teva, and the Teva is in Elohim.
One knows one through the other,
and he who knows not the one will not discover the other.
This too is natural law and the Torah of the universe.
Contemplate the wheels and know the animals within them.
Only they can enable one to ascend,
to reach the head engulfed in flames,
cleansed, healed, and powerful!
Walking through the fire, one comes out the other side,
and into what?
That cannot be told, no words can describe the indescribable.

49

Ophanim & the Merkava

Wheels are round, they turn.
Squares are flat, they do not turn.
Those who think like wheels can turn and move.
Those who think like squares remain flat and immobile.
Nature is round, like a wheel, and thus is ever in movement.
The untrained human mind is square,
it is flat, stagnant, and forever stuck in the same, boring place.
Life is guided by higher hands
whose job it is to make a circle out of the square.
Life always rubs us against our edges,
taking with it from us a little piece by a little piece.
Those who learn from this
allow themselves to be honed into a wheel.
When one becomes a wheel,
one can be attached to the supernal chariot.
As a wheel, one becomes part of the supernal Merkava.
As the Merkava moves, so too do its wheels,
for the spirit of above is in that which is below.

The secret to accomplish this is easy.
All one has to do is to let go of one's sharp and flat edges
and learn to roll like a wheel.
This is a matter of attitude adjustment.

This is a matter of frequency modulation.
Change from being one thing and to become another.
Move from a place of stagnation to a place of reception.
In order to receive, there must first be room to receive.
If one is full of themselves,
then there is no room left to receive from Heaven.
One needs to empty oneself, before one can be filled again.
This cannot be any easier.
One simply pours out and peels away the old,
and approaches Heaven,
waiting to receive the new.
Heaven never slacks in its obligations.
One who asks, receives, but there must first be the room
to receive, or the asking is viewed to be hypocritical.
Heaven does not tolerate the hypocrite.

We make matters difficult for ourselves
when we embrace that which is sharp and that which is flat,
instead of the round and the moving.
We crave stability and security.
We mistakenly believe these to be
the constant and consistent flatness of the square.
We want to be planted and grounded.
In this we think that we are unmovable.
Yet, that which does not move is dead.
Every plant and tree knows this.
For as grounded as they are,
they still move with every breeze of wind.
We do not learn from the plants to bend in the wind.
We instead seek to stand tall against adversity,
and so we break.
Wheels turn and move.
Squares can only be pushed with the greatest of efforts.
Spiritual is circular, intellect is square.
Place the square inside the circle, and we have a wheel, that can
turn and move.
Place the circle inside the square, and we have what is flat,
and worse, we have imprisoned and contained the wheel, disabling

its natural power.
Wheels must be released, squares must be honed.
This is all a matter of attitude,
and the first step along the great work of the chariot.

We can commune with the Watchers,
the Ophanim, the Sandalphons.
But we must go to them. They will not come to us.
When we roll like a wheel
and attach ourselves to the supernal chariot,
we will naturally draw close to THEM,
and THEY, in turn, welcome us home.
Wheels rolls in harmony with one another.
Squares are left behind,
to be worked on, for however long it takes to hone them down.
Wheels fly, squares are immobile.

We learn by unlearning.
We grow lighter by getting rid of all old baggage.
Let go and let God.
When you do it, you will see what I mean.

<u>50</u>

<u>The Earth is Alive, and She is Not Happy!</u>

The Earth has a soul, knowledge, and intelligence.
She is alive and knows her Creator.
see, RaMBaM, Y.T. 3:9

Fools say in their heart, there is no God.
They seek to live life as they please,
in accordance to their own rules,
to make their own laws
and to force others to live by them as well.
The fool who says there is no God
does so for a very precise reason.
Although he/she may not want to admit it,
but in their own eyes, they themselves are a god.
The great rule of the one who denies God is that
"I" am my own god,

and I shall have no other gods before myself.
The fool denies God so that he/she
can set him/herself up as god, in their own minds.
This shows that such a one has lost more than God.
They have also lost their soul,
and that special spark within
that makes them distinctly human.

Nature is a terrible "mother" to scorn.
Nature cannot be mocked,
without serious, harsh, and widespread consequences.
Humanity is a part of nature
and is thus subject to her rules and laws.
When humanity seeks to defy "mother" nature
and make the unnatural to be natural,
"mother" intervenes.
She is not happy with her children
and she knows just how to show her displeasure.
"Mother's" displeasure is not pretty.
When "mother" gets angry
her children die.
We are part of nature and nature is a part of us.
We cannot separate the two and remain human.
The fool tries to separate the human from nature,
the fool claims to be making improvements on nature.
Science is the new god.
Technology is the new prophet.
Yet, "mother" nature is not amused.
She alone is the author of science,
She alone is the author of the laws that enable technology.
Leave her out, and in turn,
she kicks out those who would seek to kick her out.
Really, it is all quite natural.
"Mother" nature acts in complete harmony and balance
with her "husband," the Creator, God.
The fool says in his heart that there is no God.
"Mother" nature will respond with harsh reprisals

against those who have offended her "husband."
It is only natural, and one cannot mess with "mother nature."

The world is not coming to an end.
But our world most definitely is coming to its end.
There will come war, famine, disease, and natural disasters,
the likes of which we cannot possibly imagine.
These will not be avoided.
They are only natural!
They come from "Mother" nature
to cleanse her face from her blemished children.
For "Mother Earth," her wayward children
are no more than acne pimples,
needing to be removed, so the skin can be cleansed.
So, inform the fool who says in his heart that there is no God,
that both "Mother" nature and her "husband" say,
there are no "other gods,"
especially those who appoint themselves.
"Mother" will soon act
to cleanse herself of her wayward children.
So, return to nature, to our "Mother."
Reconcile with our Father in Heaven.
Cast out the false gods,
and let nature and her Creator act as they most certainly will.

51

Long ago, there was a way.
And many walked the path and followed that way.
Yet, many others corrupted themselves.
They polluted the path and combined it with others.
With many paths combined, the original way became unclear.
Instead of many walking the path and following the way,
many could no longer distinguish between one way from another.
Thus those who knew the way grew fewer and fewer,
until only a small number knew to recognize the way
and to walk its path.
The many others had come to embrace the many paths,
that led them down a different way.
In their lack of knowledge, experience, and remembrance,

they came to look at their new way as the only way!
Even the original way of the ancient ones
was not accepted now.
So, in order to protect the original way,
from those who would seek to replace it,
the descendants of the ancient ones chose to hide the way,
and many times, also chose to hide themselves.
Left alone, the children of the ancient way were free
to practice and experience as it was since the dawn of time.
From their places of concealment
they look out at the new way
and watch how it has become many new ways,
each one different and further away from the original way,
safeguarded by the ancients.
As time went by, so too did the many paths
drift further and further from the original way.
What was there to do other than watch?
What was there to say, when no one wanted to listen,
when no one cared to know?

Time marches forward, century after century,
and those along the many paths
drifted further and further away,
one more lost and misguided than another.
And so it has been.
The many paths talk, they explain and explain,
the many paths are full of many words, many ideas,
many concepts and many other things.
What all the many paths lack is clear to all with eyes to see,
they all lack the experiential contact
that the ancient original path always provided
for those who embraced it.
Talk and more talk,
sending the mind on journeys into fantasy and make-believe.
When there is no way to know the truth,
all one can say is one's view of truth,
and in order to make one's version of truth to be true,
one must impose it on others.

So, we have the blind leading the blind,
each going further and further away
from the experiential contact
that the ancient ones and their descendants
understood, embraced, and thus know so well.

Silence! Stop talking and stop thinking!
Open your heart and your mind.
Sense the Presence around you, behind you, right now!
Close your eyes, reach out into the darkness
demand that the inner light be seen,
and that you be shown the original way,
as was the ancients.
The path is open, the way is clear.
Silence your mind from questions.
Close your eyes, and open your heart.
Travel within, do not fear where you will go,
or where you will end up.
True, there are frightening stops along the way,
but once passed, their lesson is long remembered,
and the fear of the experience soon forgotten.

Now, go, close and open, be still and move out.
You will understand how the make the square a circle,
when you do it.
I cannot reveal to you more at this time.
When you do what you must, you will know, you will go,
and inside you will even glow.
When you're ready for the next step,
together we will know and we will go.
We await you!

52

There is time,
and then there is time before time,
and there is also time after time.
Know then that the three times form a triad
and the triad is the source of the human unconscious,
and it is centered in the heart.

There is right,
there is left
and then there is center.
There can be no center
if there was not first both right and left.
The right was,
the left is,
the center is that which will be.

Movement comes from Heaven,
but movement is also reflected in the mind.
Many can remember the past,
but no one can live in it.
Many dream of the future but it is not yet here.
Their dreams are but fantasy and an illusion,
that keeps them off-balance
and unfocused about the present.
We are here,
we are in the now!
This is an inescapable truth,
yet many seek to deny it,
many crave to ignore it,
many seek to flee from it.
Yet, the present will not be denied,
it cannot be ignored,
and it is impossible to flee from.
Travel in the mind all you want!
The body and its consciousness
remains here and in the now!
You cannot leave the here and now with your body.
It has to be left here in order to leave here.
Yet, while one may escape the body with its death,
there is no guarantee that THEY will not return you here,
in another body,
for you to fulfill the amount of time
your soul has destined itself to remain here.

There is no escape.
Yet, while there is no escape, there is return.

One who clings to the present
can influence it with memories of the past,
and with dreams of the future.
It is hard to change the present, but it can be done.
It must be done,
for how else do you think the future will come about?
God alone does not bring the future,
we work with Him to bring it.
This is why the future may come in its natural time,
or it may not come for a long-time after that.
In our quantum reality,
times flows at the speed of consciousness.
The more we make the future real,
the quicker it becomes.
The more we dream of the future,
the longer it takes to come.
This world is the world of actions.
Deeds are not performed with dreams,
they are performed with actions.

The pendulum always swings,
it was right, it is now left,
and it will again swing into the center.
Yet, the pendulum must be pushed into the center,
into acceptance, tolerance, honor, and heart.
For as long as the pendulum remains on the left
and is reinforced on the left,
there will remain severity, suffering, sadness, and sorrow.
The left is black, darkness, rigidity,
narrowness in mind and in deed.
Those who embrace it will always be subject to its influence.
Those who embrace black will forever remain it the dark,
this is the nature of the left.
This is ELOHIM, nature, and the Will of YHWH.
For YHWH is ELOHIM,
and YHWH ordains upon all those on the left,
to feel and know what the embrace of darkness entails.
After they have suffered enough,

their souls will swing back into the center.
This is only natural.
As for how long this will take,
that all depends upon the souls themselves,
and when they have decided they have suffered enough.
When they make this decision,
they will cast aside their blackness,
and crave the center, and the colorful.
What a glorious day, this will be,
when everything is restored again into balance.
Pay attention!
If there is no action, there will be no shift!

53

The fool says in his heart,
God will provide,
I have no need to make any personal efforts.

The fool says in his heart,
whatever happens is God's Will,
my lack of activity has no influence whatsoever.

The fool says in his heart,
give me everything,
and in return I give back nothing.

The fool makes no efforts,
does nothing to better his lot,
and expects, and demands,
that his plate and belly both be full, always.
The fool has no idea how the real world,
create by and ruled by God really works.

Long ago our Sages referred to us all
as partners with God in creation.
God does His share
and we do ours.
Yet, God only does His share,
once we do ours.
God told the patriarch Abraham

to walk before Him and to walk with simplicity.
God did not tell Abraham to follow,
God told Abraham to lead!

The children of Abraham
are those who are the natural leaders,
who rise up and like Father Abraham before them,
walk the path of life in simplicity,
honesty, integrity, charity, and sacrifice.
Children follow their fathers,
be it their father on Earth or in Heaven.
The fool is no child of Abraham or of God.
The gimme-gimme soul
that demands all but gives not in return
is no child of Abraham
and is certainly one who displeases and angers
our Heavenly Father.

God helps those who help themselves.
If you want something done,
then do it yourself.
God is not going to come down from Heaven
to do your work for you.
God gave you what to do in this life,
and you are expected to fulfill your destiny.
You are not allowed to sit back
and wait for destiny to come to you.
No! you must go out and meet your destiny
and make your destiny.

Like Abraham, God is with and blesses
the one who goes out into the world,
looks for every opportunity, makes every effort,
and is not afraid to sacrifice.
These are Abraham's children
and those with whom God is pleased.
These energetic, hardworking,
self-sacrificing souls are showered with God's blessings.
True, not all blessings come in the package
and form that we ourselves may prefer.

But remember,
we are partners with God in creation.
We are not creation's masters.
God helps those who help themselves
even more than they help themselves.

God's help is often a mystery to us.
Those with busy hands learn to see
God's invisible Hands working through theirs.
Those who sit back and rely on others,
have no hands, see no hands
and are of no benefit to themselves or others.

THINK!
WORK!
SWEAT!
Six days shall you work – is as much a commandment
as resting on the Seventh, Sabbath day.

God is already with you,
but are you already with Him?
Are you an open receptacle to receive His blessings?
For His blessings will only descend
upon the works of your hands.
So, what is in your hands?

54

The Things That I Am Not Allowed To Discuss

There are many conspiracy theories today
that are indeed real.
There are many lies out there,
but there is also much out there that is true,
and is covered-up
with mounds and mounds of false information.
It has come to the point
that unless one is somehow aware of,
or connected to, the real conspiracy
there is no way to ascertain truth from falsehood.
Everybody has their beliefs and everybody has their proofs,

this is the desired state of affairs,
because with so much conviction out there,
there is so little scrutiny, investigation
and discovery of the actual truth.
Those who are in the know
are vowed to silence.
Those who know not, speak much.
Those who know much, speak not.
Yet, while no direct information can be passed on,
we can still ask questions.
Yet, what are the right questions to ask
that will lead one to a glimpse into the hidden truths?
Even these can only be provided in a round-about way.

So, I will provide a list of questions.
You ask them.
You research them.
You pray about them.
And then, if and when,
you believe that you have made a discovery
or that you can draw conclusions
or put together the pieces of the conspiracy puzzle,
then, dear God! Keep your mouths shut!
Silence your tongue and clear your mind of questions.
Now contemplate these.

* In the beginning, Elohim created the Heavens and Earth,
yet, just who or what is Elohim?
* How do Genesis 1 and Genesis 2 differ,
 and why are they different?
* What really happened before the flood
that required its coming.
* How did Enoch fit into all this?
* How did Atlantis fit into all this?
* Who is Elohim and who are the "sons" of Elohim?
* Is there a difference between Elohim and "The Elohim"?
* From where do the Elohim come,
 and to where did they go?
* What really happened to their children, the Nephilim?

* Do any of these questions
have any relevance to anything happening today?
* Do any of these questions
have anything to do with the Holocaust?
* Do any of these questions
have anything to do with the State of Israel?
* Do any of these questions
have anything to do with the coming of Mashiah?
* Do any of these questions
have anything to do with what comes before Mashiah?
* If up is down, right is left and above is below,
then what is the proper vision, when seen right-side up?

The end is found in the beginning,
and the beginning will be found in the end.
The truth is far more terrifying
that anyone can possibly imagine!
Many simply will want to dismiss all worry,
and to lie back and trust in God.
So, let the sheep be.
They will be soon led to slaughter,
as is the destiny of sacrifices.
Remember this!
Only animals are subject to sacrifice.
Human beings are not sacrificed,
they are the ones who perform the sacrifice.

All the pieces are falling into place,
and still no one will suspect who is the puzzle-maker.
Things are not as they appear.
The truth is concealed under layers of husks and shells.
It will not be recognized by most
even if and when it be properly exposed.

No more for now.
Dismiss me for crazy if you'd like.
Draw your own conclusions,
but do not discuss any of them with others.

<u>55</u>

How do you combat the unseen?
How do you fight a ghost?
You don't know, do you?
And it is because you don't know,
that you have already lost the fight.

But even a lost cause
can still be fought!
All it takes to fight a lost cause
is a soldier, one who is willing,
ready and able,
to fight, to sacrifice,
and stop at absolutely nothing to win!

The Torah teaches that the children of Israel
went up armed when they left Egypt.
God took care of the Egyptians at the sea,
but after that the new Free Men,
had to fight to survive.
God did not defeat Israel's enemies for them,
they fought and won for themselves.
God was indeed with them,
but they still had to fight, and to die.
And indeed, they did both!
Ancient Israel was made of soldiers.
This is the legacy of the ancient people.
Wherever you find those who embrace the ancient legacy,
you will find righteous warriors,
who fight for their freedoms,
and survive because of them.

Today we are faced with a very devious enemy.
He is the enemy of freedom.
He is the enemy of truth.
He seeks to enslave all,
first, their minds, and then their bodies.
His plan is almost at its end,
He has almost finished his devious designs.

He is ready to unleash his final onslaught on truth.
Almost all have already fallen,
the rest are targeted next.
The Great War is coming,
but know now,
it is a deception!
It is a ploy.
It is a tool to gain complete control.
And nothing and no one on Earth is empowered to stop it.

The righteous are his target.
They are already identified and readied for the slaughter.
The only chance the righteous have to survive,
is the fall back on to the ancient legacy,
of a mighty Israel.
But alas, Israel is no longer mighty!
Everyday Jews, the surviving children of Israel,
have no idea about, and thus connection to,
the ancient legacy.
Because of this, they will again be like
sheep led to the slaughter.

Freedom survives only for those who fight for it.
Some remember this and live by it.
Others are too busy partying and having fun to notice,
that they are in line for the slaughter soon to come.
Warriors can defend themselves,
but they cannot defend everyone.
The righteous warrior will do what he can,
he will not do what he cannot!

The fool relies on miracles,
when our Sages warned us, that such a reliance
is misguided faith.

God helps those who help themselves.
It is time for the righteous to realize this.
GATHER!
LEARN THE WAY!
While we cannot fight ghosts and the unseen,

we can learn to see the unseen,
enter the domain of ghosts and
become as one of them.
Ghosts can fight ghosts,
and the unseen, when seen, can indeed be fought.

Human beings know these words,
and heed them.
Animals hear not, and care not.
They are all ready for the slaughter.
Our mission is to our fellow human beings.
Let the sheep face their destiny.
But human beings are Freemen!
It is our right and destiny
to learn the way of the ghost,
to see the unseen, and to face destiny,
in accordance to our ancient legacy.

The great lie is coming.
All animals will indeed follow the leader.
The sons of the legacy will follow no false leader.
The sons of the legacy will
GATHER and LEARN
how to fight the ghosts in the world of ghosts.
They will combat the unseen with the inner vision.

We will not change the course of the world.
But the righteous will survive
when they fight the right battle,
in the right way.
Long live the Freemen warriors.
Long live those who embrace the legacy of Living Israel!

56

Armilus, The War To Come – The Coming Fall & Rise

The war to come will begin to cleanse the earth,
but it will not be the final war.
The war to come will devastate almost all,

but the rebuilding will begin almost immediately.
It is, as if, it was already planned to be this way.

Rome will rise and fall only twice,
it will not be built a third time,
but not for lack of trying.

Only time will tell, only God can know.
But this we do know,
let man plan as he may,
Heaven can still intervene in a moment
and topple the best made plans of any men.
Mistakes do happen, accidents do occur.
God is really good at making accidents happen.

Let those who plot and plan continue to do so,
let them act in all their devious ways.
So what?
They themselves are nothing more
than puppets on a long string.
They themselves do not know the true puppet master.
They may lie to others to conceal their plans and actions,
but others above them lie to them.
They do not reveal to their minions
the true reasons behind their directives,
and to whom indeed they serve.
We thus have plans within plans
and conspiracies within conspiracies.
So let it be!

Our world today is in a seriously unstable state.
It will not take much to destabilize the whole.
Once the toppling begins,
there is no telling where it might end.
What are the righteous to do?
What shall the righteous do?
Nothing!
There is nothing to do to stop this.
Life and nature take their own course.
When the body becomes sick,

it activates its natural defense systems
to fight and eventually expel the invading illness.
The body of collective humanity
and the Earth herself is no different.
Sickness will grow worse and worse
until the body itself kicks in to expel the illness.
We are growing ever so close to this moment.
And most are in total oblivion and have not a clue.
The clueless are always the first to go,
They will not be missed.

The Great War to come begins the cleaning,
but it is not the end.
After the cleansing, the great plan will be implemented.
Once the old has been torn down,
the planned rebuilding will come
planned in accordance to an ancient, yet familiar agenda.
When this occurs, Heaven will take notice
and Heaven will then judge.
Rome will rise and fall only twice,
it will not be built a third time,
but not for lack of trying.
The agenda which is not Heaven's
will face off against Heaven itself.
And thus will the final battle begins.
The Third Temple is scheduled to be rebuilt
and it will be more of a hollow shell than was the Second.
Armilus is rising, like the Phoenix,
he will rise out of the ashes,
as a high-tech, super spiritual, "all- natural" messiah.
All is a pretense, it is all a show.
But he has always been a good showman.

Flee the pillars of smoke, the fire, and the blood.
Prepare for the day because it is coming soon!

57

Magic is the power of human will,
focused and directed to control the minds of others.

Magic can indeed bend, but never break, the laws of physics.
Magic can indeed bend and break
the minds and wills of weaker human beings.
As it is said, when there is will, there is a way,
and when there is no will, there is no way.

Slavery always begins in the mind.
Slavery begins when one person or one group
begins to control the minds, thoughts, and attitudes of others.
This is accomplished in all too many ways.
One can be made to be afraid,
one can be made to be complacent,
one can be made to be apathetic,
one can be made to be distracted.
The dull mind, like the weak laser can penetrate nothing.
Yet, the focused mind is like a sharp laser.
It can cut through almost anything.
Indeed, even water can be focused
with tremendous force
and harnessed like a drill to cut through steel.
If God's Word is called the Water of Life,
then so much more so can it be used by the sharp mind,
to slice through any obstacle.

The masters of magic know well
the power of the spoken word.
They use the tool of speech as their focal point of will.
Thus they actually create and bring into being,
that which they say,
for their words are no mere words,
they are sounds of raw power and creation.
Indeed, this secret is also known
to the masters of the secrets of creation.
They too know the secret, sacred sounds,
and how they are used like instruments
through which the mind is focused,
and power is expressed externally.

Do not underestimate the powers of dark magic.
They have almost completed their take-over of the world.

It is the forces of dark magic that instigate hatred,
and use hatred to provoke wars and destruction.
In this way the old is removed with all its goodness,
and the masters of the black magic remain
to rebuild another world in their own image.
This is the here and the now,
and the weak of mind, see it not, hear it not and know it not.
They will all be collectively killed
in one quick swipe of fire
and the pillar of smoke that it shall leave behind.
Long ago, the prophet Joel warned about this.

So ominous is this warning
that we recite it annually
as part of the Passover Seder service.
We pour out the wine and remove it from us.
So too will this old world,
with all its good and bad be poured out
and removed from our memories.
Rome shall fall and rise twice,
but as it is being built the third time,
Heaven will intervene,
and Rome shall be no more.

Here we are at the dawn of redemption.
Yet, no one sees it, no one is looking for it.
The darkness and the black dress
has darkened both the eyes and the heart,
leaving their minions both blind
and bereft of feeling and knowing.
The great cleansing is coming.
Again, the angel of death shall pass over
the doors of those who have prepared the offering.
But alas, the darkness has blinded all
and no offerings have been made,
no blood marks the door posts.
When the angel of death shall pass,
he shall not pass over, save the elect few.
As for the rest, they will this time

have to suffer the fate of the modern Egypt
and the modern Egyptians.

Those who are blind, can still be made to see.
All they have to do is to will it,
for when there is a will, there is a way,
and when there is no will, there is no way.
Learn the lesson of the first Passover,
and understand now,
why we are commanded
to perform these rituals year after year.
The sleeper must awaken, for time has run out.
If not now, then when?

58

Freedom is first and foremost a state of mind.
It must exist on the inside
before it can ever exist on the outside.
Freedom, however is not just what you believe,
it also must be what you do!
No one can be free in the mind alone.
One must live in accordance to the principles of freedom,
in order to be truly free.

We live in a society that seeks
to enslave its members in all too many different ways.
We become slaves to our governments,
we become slaves to our finances,
we become slaves to the opinions,
wants and needs of others, whose interests
have absolutely nothing to do with our own.

Today, we are not free.
And it has nothing to do with the fact
that we are being constantly monitored.
Even monitored people can be free.
But today, if one dares to stand up for what is right,
he can be branded a criminal,
and be held liable to
an ever growing number of penalties.

This is not true in just any one country.
This is true in them all,
including the land of the free,
and the home of the brave.

The ever-encroaching hand of Big Brother
tightens its growing grip more and more
around the throats of its citizens.
Yet, most care not about the powerful hand.
Some even welcome it and consider it comforting.
Yet, the hand of the task master
is the hand of the slave driver.
At one moment it may feel comforting,
knowing that a guiding hand is leading us,
but then it cracks its whip
against the backs of the innocent.
There is never any comfort in slavery.
Slaves are not guided, they are led,
and usually it is to the slaughter.

Today, no one is free,
and thus no one can honesty celebrate their freedom.
The only path to freedom today
is as it was in the past.
Rebellion!
One must cast off the oppressive yoke of slavery
that today enslaves us all.
Today's slave masters
have also learned their lesson from the past.
They know that slavery of the body,
without slavery of the mind
leads to rebellion,
so they first enslave the mind,
then the "pocket-book,"
and only then to severely curtail
and limit the rights of citizens,
thus enslaving them in body, as well.

One cannot take up arms against one's government.
Those who do so are hunted down and killed.

Divided, there is no strength in numbers.
United, we stand,
but today, no one is united,
therefore, divided we fall.
Today, there is no option of arms against governments,
for there is no organized form of resistance,
as there was when Moses and Israel
stood against Pharaoh,
and when the Americans united
to stand against England and its King.

Today, resistance must be in the mind,
in the pocket-book and in one's daily affairs.
One must not march to the beat of slavery.
Instead one must march
to the beat of a different drummer.
One must learn to hear the Voice of God within,
and follow it
outside of this society and its many entrapments.
Only when one distances oneself
from the main focus of Big Brother,
can one stand a chance to act in freedom,
"under the radar" of prying eyes
that seek to intervene at every opportunity.

Freedom is the right of every human being.
Freedom is an inalienable human right,
endowed upon us by our Creator.
Freedom is the message of the first
of the Ten Commandments.
One cannot proclaim God to be King,
all the while that one is still a slave
in modern day Egypts and houses of bondage.

Proclaim freedom
by living it.
Proclaim freedom by choosing a lifestyle
that enables you to live as free as possible.
Freedom was first given to us as a free gift from God.
Ever since that fateful time in ancient Egypt,

it has been our duty and our destiny
to fight for our freedom.
For freedom only endures
for those who fight for it.

Long live the fighters.
Long live the free.
Don't talk freedom, live it!

59

What path leads to life?
Action!
What path leads to death?
Complacency!
What path leads to success?
Effort!
What path defines success?
Only time and God can tell.
For that which Heaven defines as success
is different from that defined here on Earth.

What type of action leads to life?
Action which has meaning and purpose!
What type of complacency leads to death?
All kinds!
Complacency is partner to many things,
including laziness and denial.
Those who do not want to see never will.
On the other hand,
those who seek vision
will accomplish it
only after great efforts has been made.

It takes energy to awaken from sleep.
It takes nothing to remain asleep.
Those asleep never see what is coming,
they are overtaken and rudely awakened.
Only then do they complain that they had no warning,
and could not see that which was coming.
Those who are asleep see only their own dreams.

The harsh realities of the real world
are far away and foreign to them.
When the reality of the real world overtakes them,
the blind are astonished and numbed.
They never dreamed such a harsh reality ever existed.
Indeed, their dreams kept them in the dark,
and oblivious to the fate that they must then suffer.

Those who learn to commune with the angels
also hear what they hear and begin to see what they see.

Reality is what is perceived.
But not all that is perceived is real.
There is subjective reality and there is objective reality.
Is the virtual reality of the computer
different than the reality outside it?
I should say so!
So too is the reality perceived different
from the reality unseen.
Unseen, maybe not even sensed,
but ever present, ever influential,
and ever dominant.
Just because we do not see a thing
does not make it go away and cease to exist.
Just because we deny a reality
does not make it become any less real.

Communing with the Others
is not like communing with
fellow flesh and blood.
We do not commune in virtual reality
the same way we do in the outside-computer world.
Why would you expect those that exist outside our dimension
to commune with us, like we commune with each other.
Outside is outside and inside is inside.
This is true of the virtual reality of the computer
and the subjective reality that we see around us.
Essentially, the virtual reality of the computer
is a reality within a reality that itself is within a reality.
If we choose not to look

who can we blame other than ourselves
when we do not see?

Learn to see!
Then act upon what you see!
If you see not and act not,
then speak not when the moment of fate arrives!
Your fate is what you prepare for,
your fate is what you embrace.

Choose now what to embrace,
so you will be willing to welcome it
with open eyes and open arms
when the moment arrives.

Act and lead
or be complacent and be led,
but don't complain about where you end up!

60

"Magic" Circles & Prophecy

A circle is either made or drawn
around the practitioner.
He stands in the center
to perform his ritual.
He begins standing
and then reverts
to the position of the prophet.
The circle keeps him safe inside.
The circle keeps all things outside
safe from what will happen within it.
The circle is thus both protector and prison.

Once inside the circle
the practitioner creates his own reality
and his own space.
Once inside, the world outside exists only as an Other.
When the reality within the circle is complete,
the practitioner then projects

his reality outside the circle.
The inner reality collides with the outer reality.
Reality verses reality,
and the greater reality wins.
When the mind of the practitioner is stronger
than the world around him,
then we have a successful expression
of mind over matter.

The drawing of the circle is ancient
and was used by the prophets of the Bible themselves.
Elijah and Habakkuk were the masters,
many have since followed in their footsteps.

Life, mind, and the universe
are all interconnected
and form a distinct type of unity.
For although there appears to be many separations,
beneath them all there is only unity.
In order to travel from one to the other,
one does not travel upon the surface
where differences and separations are so glaringly clear,
rather one goes beneath the surface,
to the underlying structure,
and thereby travels along the submerged highways
that unite all.
Like roots of a plant,
they are not visible above the surface,
yet, the entire plant depends upon its roots.
Life, mind, and the universe is identical to this.

What looks diverse and separate above ground
is all united through its roots below ground,
below consciousness,
below the visible thresholds of modern science.
Worms make soil, in which roots grow deep.
Wormholes thus best describe
the passages through the "cosmic" soil.
The mind of the prophet and the practitioner
knows these well.

Thus he endeavors to live in the soil
"with the worms"
rather than waste his time
with the illusionary diversions of division
that permeate this world around us.

Isolation of the mind
is coupled with isolation of the body.
When the two are united within the circle,
nothing can stand before their power,
for the power is not that of the individual,
but rather it is the power of life,
the mind and the universe combined
that now alters reality.
All this is in accordance with God, pleases God,
and is God's desire for His human creation.
In this we fulfill our destiny as human beings
created in the Image of God.

As God thinks, so too must we learn to think.
Thought is not abstract, detached, and theoretical.
Real thought is like the seed,
it sparks creation, initiates pregnancy,
and leads to the birth of life.
All this is performed within THE CIRCLE,
the womb of the universe, the cradle of life.

Let the one who knows
continue to learn and thus know more.
Let those who be in darkness remain in the dark.
There is no creation in the dark, but only in the light.
Thus the first words spoken were,
"Let there be light"
and then, "There was light."
Only with light can the darkness be seen.
Only in the light can darkness be separated
from light and put in its proper place.
Only those within the circle know and understand this.
Creation is God's circle.

Our circles await our creation,
blessed as they will be by God.

61

Light and dark always exist.
They are always in struggle.
This is not the way it is supposed to be.
In the beginning God separated
light from darkness
and declared this separation
to be good.

Then along came man,
and embraced knowledge
of both good and evil.
Yet, unlike God,
who separated light from darkness,
man did not separate between
good and evil.
As such, good and evil
became unnaturally mingled.
This is what created the great mess
that we presently inhabit.

Good and evil are mixed
and intertwined.
Good influences evil,
and evil influences good.
Good seeks to be on top
and so too does evil.
Yet, this is not the natural way
that was ordained by the Creator.
Good and evil,
light and darkness
cannot exist together in the same space,
without constant conflict,
struggle and warfare.
This has been the way of humanity
since the days of Eden.

Evil seeks to root out good,
good seeks to root out evil.
Yet, as the two are opposites,
so too the way they combat is different.
Good seeks to shine its light.
Evil seeks to extinguish all light,
and to dominate, control and enslave mankind.
Good resists and sometimes fights back.
But good is by nature peaceful.
Good does not turn to war,
without great provocation.
Evil on the other hand,
seeks war for war's sake.
Evil seeks to destroy and to tear down,
just as good seeks to create and build up.

The forces of evil
seek to deceive
because this is the nature of darkness.
The forces of evil seek to destroy
because this is its nature.
The forces of good
often do not understand
the true intent and purpose of evil.
Evil seeks to destroy the good,
no matter the cost.
Thus evil seeks to corrupt
and undermine the good,
to reduce its strength and thus
remove its ability to resist evil.

This is why today the forces of good
are breaking down
and will soon be subject
to an all-out attack
by the old-enemy,
thought dead, but still very much alive!

In the last war,
evil came after the Jew.

Many were lost because the majority forgot
the right ways how to fight the ancient evil.
In the coming war,
evil will again go after the Jew,
just like the last time.
Only this time,
evil knows where it fell short before,
and it will not repeat its previous errors.

This time,
not only will the Jew be the target
but also all those
who embrace the scriptures of the Jews
and its code of righteousness.
Anyone who embraces the Bible,
the Ten Commandments and God,
in any size, shape or form,
will be treated just like the Jew.
This time,
many more will be targeted,
just like prophecy warned us
so very long ago.

We cannot get away.
We cannot escape.
There is no way out.
There is only one way, and that is through.
There is a razor's edge
to walk through the coming fire.
Knowing that the fire is coming
is the first step is preparing for its arrival.

No one will remain asleep for long.
A rude awakening is coming.
Some will awaken to life,
others will awaken to face another fate.
Awakening BEFORE the coming fire
is the way of light and good.
Remaining asleep is the way
of darkness and evil.

Good will claim its own.
Evil will do the same.

We cannot get away.
We cannot run and hide.
We must choose between
good and evil,
between light and darkness.
The separation is returning,
just as it was before our exile from Eden.
The parting will be a tearing,
it will not be easy,
but it is necessary, and it is coming Soon.

62

I want to ask you a question.
How do you receive?
How do you learn?
How do you eat and digest new knowledge
and new information?
Do you prefer words,
involved concepts and ideas,
or dramatic pictures
with involved imagery?
Do you listen to learn,
or do you see and perceive?

I am not being poetic here!
I am trying to help you both see and hear!
Can you do these things?

There are those who want things straight.
They do not want to work
for their information.
They want it straightforward, simple,
easy to understand and easy to digest.
Such a simple meal
is easily attained
and just as easily forgotten!

Then there are those
who are willing to work,
to work for their "supper,"
to gather their own food,
cook their own meals,
and then sit back and enjoy
the fruits of their labors.
These alone fulfill the meaning
and purpose of reciting
grace AFTER meals.
For how can one be truly thankful to God
before the fact.
Once one has partaken and is full
only then can one truly be thankful
for all that which God has given.

As it is with food for the body,
so too is it with food
for the soul.
The greatest food for the soul
is knowledge, understanding and wisdom.
These three come to one
through the proper acquisition
of proper information.
This can only come about
when one is open to receive them.
Reception in Hebrew is called Kabbalah.
And who today is open to receive
the true knowledge of God's Will?
Who then today
knows the true Kabbalah,
who then today
can see God's Invisible Hand
and hear God's silent, still Voice?

Sheep are animals,
because they cannot think like humans
they do not realize that
they are being led to the slaughter

before it is too late.
How many people are just like sheep?
How many allow themselves to be distracted
by so many distractions,
that they too have lost what it means
to be human, created in the Image of God.
Like sheep, these people are being led
down the path to their fate.
Just like sheep and cattle,
the blind serve the needs of others.
Like cattle and sheep,
the blind and the deaf become
the meal of life-force energy
to those entities that
blind them and deafen them,
specifically so that they can be harvested
and their souls eaten.
Everything enjoys a good meal,
including THEM.

THEIR minions are hard at work
doing what they do best,
fattening the new calves for the slaughter,
and leading the new blind and deaf sheep
to their fate.

No one sees.
No one hears.
No one wants to!
And those who say they do,
with their words,
seldom follow through,
with their deeds!
It is no wonder why THEY
look upon the blind and deaf
as nothing more than sheep and cattle.
For when a human being
chooses to act dumb like an animal,

why shouldn't THEY
treat them as they treat themselves?

Men live, animals die.
God made us all (male and female)
to be MEN.
When we fail, we fall.
This is the fallen tabernacle of David,
which God has promised to raise anew.
But who will be like David,
and fight the good fight,
as a warrior of YHWH?

Learn about King David,
and become a child of his,
a child of God,
in the Image of He,
who sits upon the Throne.

63

Many words have been spoken over many centuries.
Each speaker and each teaching
is absolutely true, in the mind of the believer.
But such beliefs do not necessarily reflect
the absolute, objective reality of anything,
other than that which is in the mind of the believer.

No one who thinks
has ever come to grasp true reality.
All thinkers manage to grasp
is that which their thoughts allow them
to understand.
Their own minds become their domain,
and their prison.
Thinkers are usually incapable of thinking
outside the box of their own minds.

When it comes to learning the teachings
and views of different schools or opinions,
it is important that we keep in the forefront of the mind,

that we are dealing only with the subjective,
individual beliefs embraced by either one,
a thousand or a million.
Yet, regardless of how many chose to believe this or that,
such beliefs do not necessarily reflect any reality
outside of the minds of those who embrace them
Therefore, as we learn, let us remember,
we are learning DEOT,
the ideas and opinions of mortal men.

We may ascribe to these ideas greatness,
we many call such ideas inspired by God,
we may claim that a belief is the proper path to God,
we may equally claim that anyone not accepting
the accepted belief is wrong,
those rejecting such beliefs are dangerous
and those of other beliefs may even be harmful.

Nonsense!

Ideas and beliefs can never be proven.
This is why we call them faith!
One person's faith is always different from another's.
Those of strong faith can tolerate the faiths of others.
Those of weak faith cannot tolerate anything different.
To the weak of faith, their ideas and beliefs are sacred,
they are from God and they are absolute truth.
Therefore any deviation from them is not to be tolerated.
Such intolerance usually leads to prejudice
and even violence.

In order to expand consciousness,
one must be able to realize
that when exploring the ideas and beliefs expressed by many,
we are delving into the minds of mortal men.
And, in spite of the beliefs of the self-convinced,
we are not dealing with the revelations of God.

Revelations of God do not come from man,
they come directly from God.
Therefore, one who does not know

how the approach God directly
and to hear His Voice in truth,
hears nothing, and knows nothing,
but at the same time, believes that everything they believe
is beyond question and is absolutely true.

We can learn the ideas, beliefs, and faith
held sacred by many.
But these will not put us in touch with God.
We can however use the words
and concepts used by many,
to describe the experiences
perceived and known to the very few.

Experience teaches that
which words cannot.
Experience teaches that
which cannot be learned in a classroom,
or from a book.
Experience enables one to see for themselves
as opposed to seeing through the eyes of others.
Experience brings one direct knowledge
instead of abstract faith.

One has faith in words and believes them true,
whether or not they are fact or true.
One with experience has knowledge,
which no faith can sway, no words can challenge,
and no self-professed faith can contradict.

Thinkers think in the minds.
Experiencers experience with their souls.
The soul transcends the mind
and includes within it the emotions.
The soul is called the Neshama
and it includes the Nefesh of the body
and the Nefesh of the brain.
The soul also includes the Ruah,
which is the swaying spirit
that motivates and drives things

either forward or back.
This is the source of human emotion.

As the dark clouds gather
so many seek to make sense out of the senseless.
So many will offer their many words,
their ideas and beliefs.
So many will follow them,
and all of them will find out in the end,
that those without experience
are the blind, and it is they who lead the blind.

The blind shepherds will lead the blind sheep,
and the voices of experience that cry out,
are drowned out by the many yelling,
"we know what's best,
we think clearly, and faithfully, follow us."
The blind shepherds are very convincing
and the blind sheep know not to see, or even how to see.
Those with experience try to teach the sheep how to see,
but the shepherds chase away those with experience,
and call them wolves.
Yet, these are not wolves in sheep's clothing,
rather those with experience are themselves innocent lambs,
thrust into the image and appearance of wolves.
The blind lead the blind and keep the blind from seeing.

The voice cries out alone from the wilderness.
You hear it daily within the recesses of your thoughts.
The blind shepherds tell you to ignore it.
Those with experience tell you to look out
and see for yourselves.

Be silent in the midst of the noise!
Be still in the midst of the constant movement!
Listen within, and hear!
Experience for yourself the Way and Word of God.
When you see you will know,
when you hear you will understand.

The shepherds will despise you for this,
but in case you haven't noticed,
they already do.

64

Standing up for what you believe,
this is courage.
Speaking out about important things,
this is courage.
Remaining silent when wisdom requires it,
this is courage.
Taking right action against what you know is wrong,
this is courage,
Making a difference, instead of being indifferent,
this is courage.

One of the great ground rules
of approaching the Heavenly realms
is to know
that your soul is examined
every time you draw near.
The Watchers read our souls telepathically.
They know us inside and out.
The Watchers can read us
because in the realms of energy,
which we call spirit and the spiritual,
all we are is vibrating, pulsating light.
The colors of our souls
reflect the nature of both
our consciousness and our actions.
When our minds and our hearts
are united as one and properly
emanate through our righteous actions,
the colors of our soul shine brightly
and are prominently noticed
by the Watchers in the air.
They see the righteous and gather around them.
This is how the Watchers know the righteous

and by God's design brands their foreheads
with the sign of His salvation, the great "X."

Courage is the power that aligns mind and heart.
Courage is the resolve to act properly
and to always do the right thing.
Courage speaks out when speech is required.
Courage is silent when such silence is appropriate.
Courage foresees and prepares for the future.
Courage leads one to do what is necessary,
regardless of the objections or doubts of others.
Courage leads because it follows God's directives.
Courage stands upon the Rock of the Word.
The Watchers take note and surround the rocks.

When all gets dark, courage remains light.
When all becomes heavy, courage bears the burden.
When all turn against you, courage alone stands for you.

Those with courage prevail.
Those without courage are already lost.
Only those with courage can be called free.
Those without courage are already slaves.
Those with courage stand strong against their oppressors.
Those without courage surrender to their oppressors,
and suffer their abuse in silence.
Those with courage move and are still,
those with courage speak out and remain silent.

Those with wisdom
know to distinguish between the times,
when to move and when to be still,
when to speak and when to be silent.
When wisdom is coupled with courage,
the united two created a soul
whose colors impress the Watchers
and bring the forces of Heaven
to surround and support,
and to conquer the age-old enemy.

We wish the courageous well!
They are in the forefront of battle,
but in the end, they will prevail.
This is ordained by the Watchers,
and it will not be overturned.
Watch closely,
for the hand of the Watchers
will soon become apparent.

65

God is the Creator of nature.
God established the laws of nature
in accordance to hidden Divine wisdom.
The laws of nature reflect the Will of God.
Therefore to follow the laws of nature
is to follow the Will of God.
This should be clear to all to see.

Nature's laws cannot be denied,
they cannot be broken.
There are natural laws
within natural laws, within natural laws.
One can explore nature
and discover previously unknown
and previously hidden knowledge
as to how these laws operate.
With this once hidden knowledge now revealed,
one can interact with natural law
and thus bend them and mold them
to serve the Will of Man.

Man too is part of nature
and is subject to natural law.
Discovering the Way of natural law
and living in harmony with it
enables one to discover the Will of God
and to live in harmony with the Creator.

Nature's Way is not learned from the mind of man.
The mind of man is not big enough

to comprehend God's Way and God's Will.
Rather than try to comprehend it,
we can instead simply follow it,
doing what we know,
understanding what we can,
and live accordingly in harmony with it.

One can observe nature
and learn from it the laws that govern it.
As one learns nature's laws,
one learns the Will of God that established them.
Thus nature's law is God's law.
God's Will and God's law are one.
This law alone is the true "Word" of God,
that was with the Creator when the universe began.

We call nature's law, God's Will, God's law, the Torah.
The Way of the Creator, God's Torah
is all around us,
it can be seen in all things,
and it can be learned by merely observing
God's Will in action
as expressed through the workings of nature,
following its laws.

Living in harmony with nature
is living in harmony with God.
Conflict with nature is conflict with God.
Man cannot conflict nature and God and win.
Nature will always move forward
and brush out of its way
anything that stands against its operations
under natural law.
This law is nature's Way
and it is the Will and Law of God.
This is Torah.

To live with Torah
means to live with nature
then one can live in harmony with nature's Way

and thus be in harmony with nature's Creator.
One in harmony with nature's Creator
is the one following Torah, the Way.
One out of sync with nature
is out of sync with God
and is out of sync with God's Will,
God's Way and God's Torah.

This is simplicity.
All can see it.
All can know it.
All can do it.

Yet, man must exit the prison of his own limited mind
and escape back to the real world of nature.
By doing this the natural world can teach one nature's Way,
and one can thereby come to embrace nature's Creator
and the Creator's Way, the Torah.

This is how we follow God.
We learn and live by Torah.
Look around you,
existence itself bears witness to this.

66

What blocks the eye from seeing?
It is only one thing.
We are gazing upon the idols of our own making,
and worship them as did the ancients long ago.
There is nothing new under the sun,
only the forms have changed,
but the forbidden essence remains.

Today we worship many false gods,
and like in ancient days, we make every effort
to proclaim and prove
that our modern idols are real.

Modern idols are not statues made of wood or stone.
Today's idols are made of flesh and blood,

and are the creations of flesh and blood.
We have made ourselves to be today's idols.

The new commandment today
proclaimed by the arrogant secularist is,
"I am the lord, my own god,
I shall have no other god before me!"
Deny this all you wish,
you still know it is true.
Selfishness is the greatest false god of all times.

For most today,
they are their own gods,
and they worship their own selves.
They look to nature as just another
servant to be conquered and to be put into service.

The soul of man needs to be filled.
It is filled with man himself
who makes himself to be a god,
or it is filled with God our blessed Creator,
who makes man to be a man.

A man who is full of himself
is full of *-*-*-*-.
But a man full of God,
is one who is full of self-sacrifice,
righteousness and giving.

Full of God
means fulfillment of responsibilities.
Full of self
means fulfillment of nothing,
other than personal desires.

When man serves himself,
others pay a horrible price.
When man serves God,
others are serviced,
instead of being placed in servitude.

Idol worship is as real today
as it ever has been.
Man's mind is confused,
and his eyes are blinded.
Even many of the religious serve themselves.
Many times they are the worse perpetrators
of the crime of self-worship.
No need to concern ourselves with them.
God knows very well how to deal with those
who proclaim his Name,
and at the same time contradict it
and disgrace it at every turn.

The only place where God is not to be found
is in the soul of the one full of self.
Idolatry is punishable by death,
but God does not carry out this terrible sentence,
neither does any court of law on Earth or in Heaven.

Yet, death pursues the idolater,
for he who worships himself
is worshiping death.
Every day, the selfish call out for death to embrace them.
This is, after all, what selfishness is.

The day will come and death will hear their call.
Death will come to the idolater,
not by the Hand of God
and not by the hand of any fellow,
rather death will embrace the idolater
by his own hand,
by his own decisions,
and by his own choices.

How many have already died
because of the foolish choices
they have made in life?
The number is high,
and my point is proven.

Continue to complain
how you do not like what I say,
but my job is to speak about
life and living,
I even seek to resurrect the dead!

We can all become alive,
if and when we turn to life,
and there is no life
that is not God.
Turn to God and live!

67

In order to understand (Binah) me,
you must slow down.
We are not in a race,
and I have no intentions
of trying to keep up with you.

In order for you to hear (Ta Sh'ma) me,
you must first silence
all the noise that drowns me out (Sh'tika).
You cannot hear me
because you are too busy
listening to everything else.

I will not run.
I will not scream.
If you wish to walk with me,
you are welcome.
Come with me side by side.
If you wish to hear me,
then silence your mind
from questions,
and silence your tongue
from speech.

We will walk together,
and we will walk the pace
that nature itself sets for us.

At times, we will move fast,
at times, we will move slow.
We will move as nature so dictates,
for in this will we see the Way of God (Elohim).

We will be silent,
and we will talk,
at times we will even shout.
At times we will debate,
and at times, we will communicate wisdom.
We will know what to do
and when to do it
because in the silence that nature provides,
we will hear within
the still soft voice of Divine Guidance (YHWH).

In movement and in stillness,
in speech and in silence,
we will live,
for true life is the flow
of the Divine Spirit (Shekhina).

In between the silence and the noise,
in between stillness and movement,
we will meet and reside,
there, we will wait,
and there we will commune.

THEY will come to us,
but THEY come in their own way,
not ours.
We must reach out to THEM.
As we reach out in the right way,
THEY too will reach us in the right way,
in the right time and in the right place.
We must first trust
to walk in the darkness
and sit in the silence,
and wait for the light to shine.

You still cannot understand me.
You still cannot hear my voice.
You are listening to my words,
when you should be hearing my spirit.
You can understand me, you have what it takes,
but your understanding is buried deep within you,
it is sleeping and in need of awakening.

I will not awaken you, it is not my job.
God will awaken you for this is the Divine Way.
He has already sent THEM
to awaken us all,
and THEY are already busy at work.
If THEY do not succeed in awakening us
with ease, then they will resort
to awakening us with force,
and do not underestimate the power of this FORCE.

The awakening is coming.
You will not avoid it.
Understand! Listen!
THEY are talking to you.
Are you listening?

68 (Hayim)

One day a group
of three of my students,
whose names were
Left, Right, and Center,
approached me and asked,
"teach us something new.
We have learned from you
for a long time,
and we have already learned
what you have taught us."

I gazed upon them
with surprise and disappointment.
In turn I responded and said,
"tell me what have you learned,

and I will show you
what you have not learned.
Tell me what you know,
and from within it
we will discover that
which you do not know."

In surprise the students stood there,
in silence,
not knowing how to answer.
Again, I said to them,
"what I teach you is concentrated.
What I show you contains
many details, which are hard to see.
What I have shared with you
over many years,
you glean the surface
but fail to dive to the depths.
How can I give you
something new,
when you have not yet
mastered the old?
Do not seek to
broaden your horizons.
Instead, seek to delve deep
into where you are,
and into who you are.
You will there discover
that the new that you seek,
is contained in the old
that you already have.
You need to study
with greater depth
that which you have
before you move on
to that which you
do not have yet.
When you reach the depths

you will know it,
for therein will you find
that which you seek.
My job is not to give to you.
My job is to guide you
so that you may learn
to take for yourself.
Ask not of me.
Ask of yourself!"

The students pondered my words
and one by one
each walked away,
each into their individual interpretations
of what each thought that I said.

Left heard in my words
a rejection.
He chose to abandon wisdom
and to seek his fortunes
elsewhere in folly.
He has not yet reached his end,
and may never do so.
It is a shame to be lost,
and to not know it.

Right heard my words
but chose not to believe them.
He chose to broaden his path
just as he decided to do
before he came to speak with me.
He spread himself so thin
that he was everywhere,
and into everything.
But alas, the one thing
that he missed
was to be in himself.
I could ask him any question,
and he could answer
from the knowledge he learned in books.

When I asked him to explain
and apply what he had just said,
he began to talk,
but had nothing to say.
It is sad to see
the one who knows not
but thinks he knows so.
His words deceive him,
whereas his own heart
bears testimony to its emptiness.

Center heard in my words
that I which I said,
and that which I meant.
In silence he withdrew
to contemplate and to meditate.
He gazed within himself
to discover the unrevealed depths.
His path was long and arduous.
But he never gave up.
He explored his every feeling.
He asked of himself, why.
Why does he feel this way.
Why does he think this way.
Why does he do one thing,
and not the other.
In time, he received all his answers.
Light then shined
and filled his heart, his mind, and his soul.
He returned to me,
with a strange grin,
and said,
"I understand now,
thank you for guiding me."
I in turn responded and said,
"Thanks to you,
for accepting guidance,
and for walking the never-ending path."

My student took his place
by my side
and we continued walking down the path,
exploring together the depths of that
which we saw,
and which we contemplated.

In everything old
there is something new.
In everything new,
there is something old.
One who looks out there
will forever not see
that which is in here.
Know where to start
and you will know where to end.
This is the Way of
the Never-Ending Story.
Contemplate this well.

SECTION SEVEN

THE HOLY GORAL OF AHITOPHEL

"These are the names and words which dwell in the hearts of all.
117 in total, representing the 117 Angels who are over all spirits.
They reveal what is hidden in the heart, all things, be they good or bad;
all advise, all give counsel, with the help of Him who rides upon Aravot"

Originally published in Sefer Segulot (1993)
& in Walking In The Fire (2007).

The Holy Goral of Ahitophel

"These are the names and words which dwell in the hearts of all.
117 in total, representing the 117 Angels who are over all spirits.

They reveal what is hidden in the heart, all things, be they good or bad;
all advise, all give counsel, with the help of Him who rides upon Aravot"

Originally published in Sefer Segulot (1993) and in Walking In The Fire (2007).

Introduction

It is written in a number of places in the Bible (ref. Lev. 16:8-10, Numbers 25:56; Joshua 7:16-18, 18:6,8,10), how in times of need, the Elders of Israel would cast a Goral (a Biblical style lottery), in order to ascertain the will of God and receive an answer from Heaven to that which they sought to know.

The Goral (lottery) of the Bible was not, as some might wrongly assume, an arbitrary game of chance as a lottery is today. Rather, the Biblical Goral was an oracle, a tool used for psychic communion, to direct questions to God, the King of the universe, regarding important matters and to receive answers directly from Him.

The most famous of these psychic communion tools were the Urim and Tumim, which along with the Hoshen Mishpat (Breastplate of Judgment), was worn by the High Priest (ref. Exodus 28:30).

When the Elders of Yisrael wished to address a question to Heaven, they would approach the High Priest, who would then don the Hoshen Mishpat along with the Urim and Tumim. He would then perform the necessary supplicatory prayer that consisted of the recitations of many of the holy Names of God. This was coupled with a non-verbal telepathic communication of the question whose answer was sought.

After all this, the Urim and Tumim would, as if, "come to life" by starting to make sounds, similar to the Ta'amim (cantellations) sung while reading the Torah. The jewels of the Hoshen would also begin to glow in a sequence which was code known to the Kohen Priests of those days.

God would thus answer the High Priest by sounds and lights emanating from the Urim and Tumim and Hoshen Mishpat. The Kohen who was trained in the meditative usages of these psychic communion tools would be able to interpret the lights and sounds and provide a clear answer, which had come direct from God, Himself.

With the destruction of the First Temple in Jerusalem in 586 B.C. E., the Hoshen, Urim and Tumim, along with the Ark of the Covenant were hidden, only to be returned to humanity when the time comes for the true King Mashiah (the Messiah) to be revealed on that day known only to God.

Since the absence of the Hoshen, Urim, Tumim and Ark, many other types of Gorals have been devised. Each one was formulated according to the ancient prophetic pattern as revealed in the Oral Torah that has been passed down to us by word of mouth in direct succession from the days of Moses, himself. So today in absence of a prophet, seer, or properly consecrated Aaronic priest; the Sages of Israel still have access to Heaven and can ascertain the council of the Divine by using one of these ancient Gorals.

The Gorals that are in use today have each been formatted in a similar manner. Following the pattern described in both, the Written and the Oral Torah, the Goral is a layout of boxes, or squares, each having within them a certain name or group of letters. This was the format of the Urim and Tumim, which had the names of the Twelve Tribes of Israel engraved upon the twelve jewels. These were then sewn onto Hoshen which was worn by the High Priest.

This format of boxes was then meditated upon with complete mental focus and devotion until they would "light up" in the mind's eye of the questioner. This display would then reveal the sought after answer to the question. Along with the format of the squares came an answer book of sorts that explained what each of the boxes meant. The Gorals that we have today do not emanate "noises" or "light up," as did its Biblical counterpart, the Urim and Tumim.

Today, there are several known Gorals attributed to some of the great Sages throughout Jewish history. Among these include the Exilarch of Babylon, Rav Sa'adia Gaon and the famous astrologer and Torah commentator of medieval Spain, Rabbi Avraham ibn Ezra.

Another format of Goral is derived from the use of the text of the Bible (Hebrew Bible). Instead of the "lights" shining forth from a format of squares, one finds one's answer "shining" from a verse in the Hebrew text. This system was used by the famous 16th century Kabbalist, Rabbi Haim Vital, as well as by Rabbi Eliyahu, the Gaon of Vilna.

The Goral Ahitophel that is here before us is said to have been devised by the "Men of the Great Assembly." This was the body of Elders who were responsible for resettling the Jewish refugees returning from the Babylonian exile. It included amongst them Ezra and three of the last Prophets, Zechariah, Hagai and Malachi.

The Goral is named for Ahitophel, yet just who he is, is never stated. The only Ahitophel that is known in Jewish tradition was one of the teachers of King David, (referred to in 2 Samuel 15). Yet, nowhere does the Goral claim to be attributed specifically to him. Therefore, we cannot accurately say who the Goral of Ahitophel is really named after. He may have been a member of the Great Assembly, or the name might be a code name for someone else (which was a traditional Jewish practice at that period in history due to the persecutions of the time that forbade the writing of

Jewish books). Without further information from as yet unknown sources, we will never be certain as to who Ahitophel was or who truly arranged this Goral, attributed to his name.

According to tradition, during the time of the Greek occupation of the Holy Land, the Goral Ahitophel was concealed, and for its protection taken out of the Land of Israel. For a number of years its location was said to be unknown. However, during the time of the Roman occupation, it was again revealed, used and re-hidden. It was not to be seen again for hundreds of years until the Muslims were in control of the land of Israel. At this time, it was decided by the Elders of the land that the Goral not disappear again, so from that time forward the Sages passed down the Goral from generation to generation to the present day.

The Goral as we have it at present was rediscovered in manuscript, amongst the writings of Jewish Kabbalistic community of Yemen. From there it made its way to modern-day Jerusalem, Israel, where it was published for the first time in its original Hebrew. This English edition (published by me originally in 1993) is the first time the Goral has been published in translation.

Gorals, in general have been used by Jewish Sages for thousands of years. Now, they are readily available for usage by the everyday laymen. Yet just because it is available, does not mean that just anyone should pick it up and try to use it. There is an old saying, that says, "the right means in the wrong hands will cause the right means to work in the wrong way."

Unfortunately, the everyday person is often not careful in following the instructions regarding honoring the holiness of the Goral and have abused it by using it as a fortune-telling device, to see if they will prosper in this or that endeavor.

We must remember that the Goral of Ahitophel is a holy work. It should never be demeaned and used as a gross method for fortune telling. Rabbi Joseph Karo, (master Kabbalist and author of the Shulkhan Arukh, Yoreh Deah, 179:1) quoting earlier authorities goes so far as to recommend that Gorals not be used at all. He gives the sound Jewish advice that people should better put their faith directly in God and walk before Him in innocence and not succumb to temptation of "fortune telling."

Regardless of R. Karo's clear prohibition against using any Goral, as recorded in his Shulkhan Arukh, many Sages over the centuries have properly respected the Goral, and use it correctly with proper devotion and holiness. To them Heaven reveals its will, that they who fear YHWH, may know His Will, and walk in His Way. From them YHWH does not hold back any good.

Therefore, today, this English version of the Holy Goral of Ahitophel has been made available for all who sincerely seek direction from YHWH, God of Israel, and request insight from Him regarding an aspect of one's personal life.

I must however insist that all who wish to make use of the Goral do so with sincerity and awe. God is Alive and knows the hearts of each and every one of us. Heaven will respond to each inquiry based upon the sincerity within each one's heart.

If you are seeking Heavenly guidance, then you must be open to receive that which you are requesting be given to you. The Goral may indeed give you an answer that you may not want to receive. Nevertheless, once the Goral has spoken, its answer should be respected.

One cannot ask a question a second time because the first answer was not acceptable or understood. Another attempt at the question or another question is of no avail here. One can ask only once. Any second try is considered a lack of faith in God and Heaven will not be moved to guide the Goral to answer you a second time. Though you might try the Goral again, any answer coming at this point would be arbitrary and cannot be said to be given to you from Heaven.

It is taught that only when one completely does not understand the answer given, can one then he repeat his question, but only after waiting until the next day. So, please take this work seriously and do not intentionally aggravate Heavenly powers. Be in awe of God and request your needs in sincerity and truth. Pray the opening prayer with full intention and God, knowing the sincerity in your heart will answer you for good.

Instructions For Using The Holy Goral of Ahitophel

- It is imperative that one use the Goral with a sense of complete awe.
- Lay out the table of the Goral, placing it directly in front of you.
- Meditate specifically; with complete devotion upon what it is you want to ask of God through the Goral.
- Recite the opening Goral prayer. In the appropriate place, recite out loud your specific request. Be as precise as possible, this way your answer will be more clearly understood.
- After reciting the prayer, close your eyes and place your left hand over them.
- Take your right index finger and cast it out over the Goral and let it descend downwards onto one of the boxes of the Goral. Feel your finger as if it is guided by the Hand of God.
- When your finger has landed firmly upon the table of the Goral in front of you, open your eyes and see in which box your finger has been guided to land in.
- Open the Answers section and see what it is that God has given you for an answer.
- Remember the answer you receive might require contemplation, in order to understand the true depths of its meanings. For it is the way of God to speak cryptically, requiring one to be spiritually minded in order to be able to discern the wisdom of Heaven.
- Be patient and contemplative, if after a few minutes you are still unable to fathom the meaning of what has been revealed to you, lay aside the Goral until the following day. Pray to God, that He might have mercy upon you and grant you the wisdom to understand His truth
- The Goral can only be used at specific times. It must never be used at night, and best not to be used on a cloudy day. Under normal conditions, it should only be used on a Sunday, Monday, Thursday, or Friday. This is because of the proper astrological

windows are then open. Even on these days, the Goral should not be consulted during the hours when the planets Saturn, Mars or Mercury are in ascendant (in accordance to Jewish astrology). Some say the Goral should not be used on the day prior to the New Moon.

The Hours of the Day And the Planets that Rule Them

There are 24 hours to a day, 12 for night, 12 for day. The length of all hours are seasonal. Each hour is 1/12 of a day or night measuring from sunrise and sunset. Therefore a summers day hour might be equivalent to approx. 72 minutes on the clock, whereas a winters day hour may be only approx. 50 minutes on the clock. The same, of course applies to night time hours as well.

E = evening, D = day
ME = mercury; MO = Moon; SA = Saturn; JU = Jupiter; MA = Mars;
SU = Sun; VE = Venus

Hr.	Sat E	Sun D	Sun E	Mon D	Mon E	Tue D	Tue E	Wed D	Wed E	Th D	Th E	Fr D	Fr E	Sat D
1	ME	SU	JU	MO	VE	MA	SA	ME	SU	JU	MO	VE	MA	SA
2	MO	VE	MA	SA	ME	SU	JU	MO	VE	MA	SA	ME	SU	JU
3	SA	ME	SU	JU	MO	VE	MA	SA	ME	SU	SU	MO	VE	MA
4	JU	MO	VE	MA	SA	ME	SU	JU	MO	VE	MA	SA	ME	SU
5	MA	SA	ME	SU	JU	MO	VE	MA	SA	ME	SU	JU	MO	VE
6	SU	JU	MO	VE	MA	SA	ME	SU	JU	MO	VE	MA	SA	ME
7	VE	MA	SA	ME	SU	JU	MO	VE	MA	SA	ME	SU	JU	MO
8	ME	SU	JU	MO	VE	MA	SA	ME	SU	JU	MO	VE	MA	SA
9	MO	VE	MA	SA	ME	SU	JU	MO	VE	MA	SA	ME	SU	JU
10	SA	ME	SU	JU	MO	VE	MA	SA	ME	SU	JU	MO	VE	MA
11	JU	MO	VE	MA	SA	ME	SU	JU	MO	VE	MA	SA	ME	SU
12	MA	SA	ME	SU	JU	MO	VE	MA	SA	ME	SU	JU	MO	VE

<u>Prayer Recited Prior to the Use of the Goral</u>

Elohim, God of Gods and Lord of Lords, the King who is the King of Kings, the great powerful and awesome God who dwells amongst the Cherubim. I have come with shuddering, fear, and awe, in panic, trembling, and quaking to request grace by prayer and supplications from before the Throne of Your Glory, kneeling, bowing, falling on my face I have come before the essence of Your kingdom that unfolds by the grace of Your attributes.

At this time reveal to me and enlighten me as to the secret of my question, the truth of my request and my desire. According to this Goral (lottery) that was arranged by your prophets and seers who have shown your way, revealing your visions and your covenant as it is written, "The secret of God is with those that fear Him, and He will reveal to them His covenant" (Psalm 25:14).

However, it is revealed and known before you Adonai my Lord, my God and God of my fathers that all the while that the Holy Temple stood in Jerusalem, there were your prophets and seers who prophesied, as well as Your priests who used the Urim and Tumim. They revealed to us what the future would hold whether good or bad.

But now, because of our many sins and transgressions, our Temple is destroyed, prophesy has ceased and we have no prophet, no seer, no priest to reveal to us this needed thing. Therefore, I come before you, Adonai my Lord my God, with a complete heart and needy spirit, for I have no better way to distinguish right from left. Enlighten me by your great mercy according to this Goral that which I ask to know.

At this time verbally express your question in precise and specific terminology.

For you, Adonai my Lord, have desired the use of Gorals, for by it was the Holy Land divided (amongst the tribes.) Therefore now reveal to me Your way for You are my portion and my lot (Goral) even as it is written: "Adonai is the portion of my inheritance and of my cup, You maintain my lot (Goral) "The lines are fallen to me in pleasant places, yes I have a good heritage. Bless Adonai my Lord who gives me counsel, my reins also admonish me in the night. I have set Adonai my Lord always before me, surely He is at my right hand, I shall not be moved." (Psalm 16:5-8).

"Therefore Shaul said to Adonai, God of Israel, "Give us a perfect lot (portion)." And Shaul and Yonatan were picked, and the people escaped." (I Samuel 24:41.)

Blessed be Adonai my Lord who has made Holy His Name and revealed His secret to His merciful ones, to show His power and strength, by His Name, and the word of His mouth, orally and written. The blessed and holy King is to be honored forever.

Daniel spoke and said, 'Blessed be Adonai my Lord forever and ever: for wisdom and might are His: and He changes the times and the seasons: He removes kings and sets up kings: He gives wisdom to the wise and knowledge to those who have understanding: He reveals the deep and secret things: He knows what is in the darkness and light dwells with Him." (Dan. 2:20-23).

8	7	6	5	4	3	2	1
16	15	14	13	12	11	10	9
24	23	22	21	20	19	18	17
32	31	30	29	28	27	26	25
40	39	38	37	36	35	34	33
48	47	46	45	44	43	42	41
56	55	54	53	52	51	50	49
64	63	62	61	60	59	58	57
72	71	70	69	68	67	66	65
80	79	78	77	76	75	74	73
88	87	86	85	84	83	82	81
96	95	94	93	92	91	90	89
104	103	102	101	100	99	98	97
112	111	110	109	108	107	106	105
===	===	===	117	116	115	114	113

אמת א	כוהן ב	גואל ג	דגול ד	הדור ה	ועד ו	זכי ז	חנון ח
טוב ט	יה"ד י	כפי' יא	לובי' יב	מושי' יג	נורא יד	סומי' טו	עוזר טז
פ"דה יז	צדיק יח	קדו' יט	רהום כ	שדי כא	תמי' כב	ארי' כג	בונה כד
גוזר כה	דובר כו	האיד כז	ותיק כח	זכאי כט	הושי' ל	טהור לא	יודע לב
כביר לג	לוקי' לד	מישי' לה	גאמן לו	עני' לז	סיכי' לח	פות' לט	צופה מ
קרוב מא	רוא' מב	שומר מג	תקי' מד	אהוב מה	בורי' מו	גימל מז	דעה מח
האל מט	והשר נ	זוכה נא	הזק נב	יועץ נג	טיב נד	כותבי' נה	לובש נו
מהי' נז	נוצר נח	סוטי' נט	עושי' ס	פודי' סא	צבאו' סב	קורא' סג	רב סד
שמו סה	תמי' סו	אלהי' סז	ברי' סח	גבור סט	דיין ע	הבהיר עא	והוא עב
זיין עג	חי עד	טוב עה	ישר עו	כיבי' עז	לוחם עח	מפרנ' עט	נכון פ
סלה פא	עוזז פב	פוקד פג	צוד פד	קיים פה	רם פו	שוכר פז	תמיד פח
אלי' פט	ברי' צ	גלוי צא	דורי' צב	העוון צג	והיש' צד	זך צה	הסין צו
טופח צז	יהיד צח	כופל צט	לובש ק	מוחל קא	נותן קב	ס'תר קג	עושה קד
פועל קה	צדק קו	קיים קז	רופא קח	שופט קט	תדיר קי	האדיר קיא	האבר קיב
הגיזר קיג	הרן קיד	האדון קטו	ורוב קטז	החזקה קיז			

The Holy Goral of Ahitophel - Answer Guide

1.   This thing which you fear, do not be afraid of it, for all your desires shall come to you with joy and gladness. All good shall come to you by this which you seek.

2.   The end and thus good times will come to you with joy. However, you must pray and fast before God. You must submit your will to Him, though you find this difficult, because you are unable to listen to admonition. If you repent, great good will be awaiting you from Heaven.

3.   God watches over you with mercy, He sends to you His angels of mercy, they will come and guide you. Give thanks to God, for salvation and goodness are given to you from Heaven.

4.   Distance yourself from this thing. It is not good for you. It shall not come into your hands. Pray to God. What's right in His Eyes shall He do and He shall rectify your end.

5.   Rise up fast and do your desire, rejoice in this which you seek. God shall prosper your way. Do not delay.

6.   Joy, gladness and richness are prepared for you, what you seek shall be granted you from Heaven, soon with love.

7.   Don't worry about this which you seek, for it shall come to you. Don't be distraught with worry in your heart, don't try yourself. Wait a little until God covers you with His grace.

8.   You boast and say you shall do such a thing. Know that you are unable to do it. Be careful with your soul. Pray, and ask for God's Mercy.

9.   What you seek speaks of good tidings coming soon. Your destiny brightens up by Heaven's hand. A good hour is upon you. Trust in God. What you seek is very close.

10.   Why do you worry your soul about nothing, repent and be careful regarding this which you seek, for herein is much trouble, sickness and financial loss. Now wait a few days and good reward shall come to you from Heaven and you will then rejoice in goodness.

11.   My brother, know that all is from God. Turn back, trust in God. Place Him as King. Then He shall prosper your ways and shall grant you your desire. Then shall He give you that which you seek with joy. All your enemies, those that hate you shall be disgraced

and shall submit to you. Your desire shall come to you. God shall topple your enemies, both in public and private.

12.   My love, in regards to this request you must ask for mercy from the Blessed God. He will comfort and help you.

13.   God sees trouble in regards to this which you desire in your heart. If you are sick, it is due to the Evil Eye. You will need a good amulet from an expert.

14.   Do not worry or fear from evil men, for they are not able to move you. God is your help. They cannot cause you to fall.

15.   You dwell upon a thing wondering to do it, but God does not wish it for today. Turn from it and it shall be good for you.

16.   This worry that has been in your heart for a while is not from God, but from evil men whom you have befriended and associate with. You can choose to be free of them and their advice, for God is with you.

17.   My brother, separate yourself from men who lead you astray by what they say, who flatter you, yet are evil in their hearts.

18.   My beloved, because you are in awe of God, you will receive good tidings and God shall grant you your request in joy and abundance. With this you shall find all your desires in peace.

19.   My brother, you have already received abundance from God in Heaven and also honor from men. Give thanks to God, for in regards to this question, there will be goodness and joy in your home.

20.   Persist in this request, for it is for your good. There shall be no pain or anger. Only joy and prosperity will be ready for you. All will rejoice in your gladness.

21.   What you seek shall be given to you, because you trust in God with all your heart, thus God will prosper your way and give you mercy, grace, life and prosperity, for God brings down and raises them up. Trust in God and do good deeds.

22.   This question which you ask is good, but wait a bit, then you will be comforted. You shall rejoice in your heart over this thing, in the times to come.

23.   Why do you curse yourself with this that you seek. Today you cannot achieve this. Wait a while, until it comes to you with goodness and love.

24.   The one who is patient will find much good. If you only wanted to, you wouldn't curse yourself. Guard your soul, ask for mercy before our blessed God and He will save you from all your enemies and from those who bewitch you. Also God will enlighten your eyes with this that you seek.

25.   God encompasses you with His great mercy and shall prosper your path. He shall send His angels of peace before you and save you from every evil thing. Now, quickly do this thing, for it is good. Rise up, do it and prosper.

26.   Rise up fast, for this is the right and good time. God's grace shall come to you, both your destiny and fortune presently shine.

27.   Be strong of heart, do not fear, but be aware of evil, and bad men who are able to curse you. Separate from them and do what is right. They only give you bad advice. You kill yourself in order to make a living, but your time has not yet come. Fast and pray before God, He will quickly bring you joy and that which you seek.

28.   Rejoice and be glad, for there is nothing wrong in this which you seek. Settle your heart, relax, for you shall find all that you desire. Do not worry, request grace from God and He will give you mercy, favor and grace. He will straighten your path and your heart will rejoice.

29.   A good period of time is coming your way. From now on you have no cause for worry or concern. Don't worry, for your joy shall be great. God will give you grace, you shall receive mercy and favor. Your star shall shine brightly soon; shortly will you rejoice.

30.   My brother, know that your loved ones in reality hate you. Without reason they speak about you hypocritically. They lie to you as they eat and drink with you; they think always to do you harm. Separate from them wisely, for they wish only to bewitch you. Pray to God, request from Him that you don't fall under their control. He will save and redeem you.

31.   You are very tired, yet God has mercy upon you. There is nothing wrong in what you seek No one can touch you, to do you harm. God shall give you what you seek; He shall make your star shine. He will extend to you mercy and honor.

32.   My love, don't curse yourself for no reason, for this is how you weaken yourself; the end has not yet come. Allow God to rule, let Him do what is needed. Wait until these days have passed. God

will give you joy, He shall straighten your path and give you that which you seek.

33.   A good time, great fortune and a shining star arises for you now. Give thanks to Heaven, for all is ready for you, from the hands of God, Himself. What you seek shall be given to you.

34.   Why are you hypocritical, testing God? You say you shall do such and such. Now, do not pursue this, for it is not good. Guard your soul.

35.   What you seek, you shall richly receive with joy and gladness. Give thanks to God and prosper.

36.   God is with you. What you seek shall come to you. Praise God for He has heard your voice and answered you.

37.   My brother, pray to God and be patient. He will deliver you from all evil and grant you that which you seek.

38.   What you seek shall be given you, even as you desire it. As you wish, you shall have a good name.

39.   Son of man, know that the desire for what you seek was given to you from Heaven. Do not fear, what you seek shall come soon.

40.   You shall be victorious over all who rise up against you. Your fortune is great. What you seek shall come to you shortly.

41.   God shall deliver you from all evil. What you seek shall come to you. Be patient with God and your future will be good.

42.   People are lying to you and speaking bad things about you. Beware of them and you shall be spared.

43.   You have worried about this for a long time. You can be free at any time you wish. Pray to God and guard yourself; He will topple your enemies before you.

44.   Joy and gladness shall come to you. God shall correct your path. What you seek shall come to you and you shall rejoice in it.

45.   God will raise you up over all your enemies. Rejoice in what is right and do what is right in the eyes of God.

46.   People are speaking badly about you, and advising ill against you. Repent before God and be aware of them and God will topple them before you.

47.   You have nothing to gain in this which you seek. You are full of pride. Listen to me and listen to truth, then you shall become

very rich and never again be in need. God will answer you, because you fear Him; He will of great assistance to you.

48.   Your thoughts are confusing. Strengthen your heart before God. Pray, for God will support you. He will give you great fortune. Rest and joy are coming.

49.   You are a lover of the truth. There will be no success in this which you seek. Don't worry about it, for its time will come and then shall you prosper.

50.   Refrain from this which you seek, for it is not good. You are viewed as being wicked before God. Repent of your actions, for you do not know God's decrees and His judgments, and just how patient He is with you.

51.   My brother, rectify your heart so you will not be confused. Abandon this which you seek, for it is bad. If you do so, then all will be well.

52.   You believe that you shall proceed and prosper. Know that you shall not prosper in this which you seek. For you, it is not good. Heed my advice and leave it alone.

53.   I see you desire this that you seek; now run after it, for you will prosper. You will find honor in all your endeavors.

54.   God shall prosper your path and give you what you seek. If your heart is right with God, then shall you rejoice.

55.   My brother why do you tire yourself, wasting your money and strength over nothing. Wait, for the end has not yet come and it is still far away. But what you seek will eventually come to you joyfully.

56.   My love there is no harm in this which you seek. It is waiting for you. Rejoice.

57.   You ask of a great thing and are in awe of it. Now do not fear the future, for you will suffer no pain. You shall receive that which you seek.

58.   You believe that you are able to receive what you seek with ease. This is not so. You are lying to yourself. It shall not come into your hands.

59.   Leave this alone for today is not a good day to ask. Be a little patient and then you will succeed.

60.   Abandon this search. Throw it out of your heart. Guard yourself from your evil enemies. Rejoice that God will turn your quest into something good.

61.   My brother, I see goodness and peace prepared for you from Heaven, coming in a little while. There is good fortune in this which you seek. Give thanks to Heaven.

62.   Fear God and all will go well with you. For He lives and sees all, though He is not seen. Humble your heart through prayer and fasting. Cry out to your Creator, turn away from this which you seek.

63.   Don't push too hard to receive this which you seek, for you do not yet have the keys to open all the necessary doors. Pray to God and what you seek shall come to you with joy.

64.   Son of man, repent of this bad course of action that you pursue with a bad heart. Do not condemn you soul to judgment by proceeding further. Be careful to give charity and your reward will come.

65.   Richness and joy shall be given you from Heaven. That which you seek shall also be given to you, for a good time has come upon you.

66.   God sees that your heart is at times strong and at times weak. Dedicate your heart to God and He will have mercy on you and help you with everything.

67.   My brother, how peasant you are in the eyes of God. What you seek is good and your fortune is bright. you shall prosper with this that you seek Don't wait for it to come to you, for it already is in your hands. Quickly, don't wait, for you might lose it.

68.   Submit your heart to Heaven, don't be split inside yourself. What you seek you shall have and it will be good; but not now, it will take some time.

69.   Know that what you seek is of interest to you because you are depressed. I have warned you of this in the past. Now, rise up and give praise to God.

70.   Rise up quickly, for this is a good time with good fortune. You shall receive what it is that you seek.

71.   Rejoice, for what you seek has already been granted you. It is right for you and it is in your hands, even as you had wished.

Would you go to the ends of the Earth, God will strengthen you and be with you.

72.   Don't tire yourself with this which you seek, for it shall not come into your hands. There is no reason for it, nor is there any wisdom in it. Now, turn away from this which you seek.

73.   Why are you making yourself crazy? Leave this thing alone. Do not be proud and all will go well for you.

74.   Know, that no one can do anything to you that is not the will of Heaven. Don't curse yourself today. Have faith in God and He will prosper you.

75.   Know that what you seek is not good for you. Seek something else and I will answer you about that whether it is good or bad.

76.   At this time there is goodness, joy and good fortune for you. Give thanks to God, for you have a good reward in this which you seek.

77.   A good sign and a good word shall come to by this which you seek. Heaven shall do it for you, they are close at hand.

78.   There is great pain, suffering and worry in this which you seek. Now, be patient and good news shall come to you. You will find what you seek.

79.   My brother, keep away from the bad thoughts that guide you, for there is no good in them. Be careful of them so you don't stumble and be embarrassed. Another pursuit would be better for you.

80.   Joy and gladness shall you find in this which you seek, it is awaiting you now. Stand up and be strong.

81.   My love, I see for you much good and many fruits with this which you seek.

82.   What you seek brings with it testing and financial loss. Wait until these days shall pass, then shall you prosper.

83.   Request what you seek from Heaven and then it will be good for you. Do not request this of men, but only of God. He will give you that which you seek.

84.   If you seek to take a wife so as to have children or any other similarly good thing, do so for you shall prosper.

85.   My brother, rise up. Stop your joking. Guard your secret. Do this thing that is in your heart and you shall rejoice and be glad in it.

86.   Rise up like a strong man and do that which you request. Fear not, for your prayer has already been heard by your Creator.

87.   You have three different feelings in your heart, and you say that you don't have any luck. You really have great fortune, but because your actions are bad you have not yet prospered.

88.   My brother, don't be afraid of those who chase you, without you even knowing about it. Though they do evil, your fortune is still strong.

89.   My love, do not be afraid of the thoughts in your heart, for you have good fortune with this that you seek.

90.   My love, concern yourself with matters of the home. Do not associate with the wicked, for prosperity comes from Heaven. If your wife is pregnant, she is carrying a son. There is good fortune.

91.   Son of man, do not multiply troubles. If you have made a vow, fulfill it. I see for you joy, you will find good living, prosperity and long life.

92.   My brother, that which you seek you already have in joy and peace. Trust in God.

93.   You ask yourself when you will be healed of this affliction and when will you have good fortune with the work of your hands. The end has not yet come, wait a while and do not curse this which you seek. You will be healed and you will prosper.

94.   Abandon this which you seek. For if you don't abandon it and repent, great sufferings will befall you. If you repent, all things will be well.

95.   You ask of me regarding something evil that you have done, about which you have no remorse. You have no mercy, you have acted cruelly. Repent and you will be accepted back.

96.   My brother, God has already had grace upon you and helped you. In the future He will give you great joy and you'll be happy you sought this.

97.   Request this thing from God, for there is nothing wrong in what you seek. Rejoice for your star now shines and your fortune is very bright.

98.   That which you think about is good, there is no bad in it. Now do that which you want do to and don't be afraid, for God is with you.

99.   Leave this thing, for it is not good. These are not good times for you. Now be patient, these days will pass and then you shall rejoice.

100.   Leave this thing, for it is not good for you, by this will you rejoice before God. If you have made a vow, fulfill it, then shall you rejoice in this which you seek.

101.   My brother, be patient for a while, until the good times come, then shall you rejoice in this which you seek.

102.   Do not walk this path and do not do this thing that is in your heart, for it is not good for you. Therein you will find nothing, for your actions are evil. Repent, seek grace and then shall it be good for you.

103.   My brother, take a rest, humble yourself with fasting and supplications before God. Now wisely separate from them, for God is with you.

104.   My brother, the one who will be speaking to you is desirous to do you harm. He thinks only evil about you. Beware of Him, for God is with you.

105.   What you seek is good for you, it is from Heaven. God will send to you good tidings, therefore do what is right before Him. You are a wise and God fearing person and God will give you joy in the desire of your soul; you will be very glad.

106.   Rejoice and be glad, for your future speaks of peace. You shall receive your desire, even as you request it.

107.   How pleasant and nice is it that you seek this, for this is a good time. What you seek is correct. If you wish to go to a place, then go, you will be healed soon.

108.   My brother, know that what you seek cannot come into your hands. You cannot succeed. Now stop desiring this, serve God with all your heart and soul, that God will make your path prosperous.

109.   Rise up, my brother and do that which you wish with all your truthful desire. You will rejoice in goodness and peace.

110.   My love, hear my words, be strong and do not stretch this thing out, for it is not good, it's not for you. You cannot handle this for it is dangerous. Don't pursue this and all will be OK.

111.   Joy, richness and gladness are waiting for you, with plenty. It is known that you suffered from great sorrow, but now it's time to rejoice.

112.   My brother, know that I will tell you what is to be. This secret is for you, your fortune is great, with much joy awaiting you. Give thanks to God.

113.   Rise up and quickly pursue this which you seek, for it is good. God will rejoice with you and bless you. He will topple all your enemies and those who seek to do you harm. You will become very great and wise.

114.   My brother, you are a good person, what you seek shall be given to you. Your enemies are removed far away from you, yet be aware of them. I have warned you.

115.   Abandon this which you seek for it is not good and you cannot attain it. Heed my word and you shall prosper.

116.   There is nothing wrong with what you seek, rather joy and gladness are headed your way. Many will rejoice with you. Give thanks to Heaven.

117.   What you seek is right for you, it is from Heaven. It will arrive shortly. Put your heart right with God and all shall come to you with joy and gladness, even as your heart desires. Give thanks to Heaven.

Blessed be God, who has given to His servants wisdom and prophecy.
He has revealed to them His secrets to do all the works of His word.
As it is written: "God will do nothing
before He has revealed His secret to His servants, the prophets".
Therefore will we give thanks to Him who has done this.
Blessed be He, who gives wisdom to those that fear Him
and reveals His secret to His servants the prophets.
Amen

About Ariel Bar Tzadok
& the KosherTorah School

Rabbi Ariel proudly welcomes to the KosherTorah School all peoples, of all backgrounds, who wish to learn about the authentic and original Biblical world outlook.

KosherTorah is not just about the Bible.

KosherTorah is not just about Judaism.

KosherTorah is not just about religion.

KosherTorah is not just about God.

KosherTorah is about us!

KosherTorah is about building bridges!

KosherTorah is about becoming a more decent human being!

KosherTorah is about common sense, simple living, righteous behavior, and liberty and respect for all.

For over thirty years, Rabbi Ariel has been a world renowned expert of the authentic, Biblical "Secrets of the Torah" teachings, that many today simply call "Kabbalah."

Rabbi Ariel teaches the sulam aliyah (ladder of ascent) school of Kabbalah, which consists of the Biblical teachings of the works of Ezekiel's chariot (Ma'aseh Merkava), and the prophetic meditative techniques passed down through the centuries.

The purpose of these teachings is to cultivate actual, authentic, and personal spiritual experiences, the likes of which are psychological, and transformational. The purpose of spirituality is to explore one's inner self, and to discover, and unleash one's inner, latent potentials. To this task is the KosherTorah School dedicated.

While knowledgeable of the theoretical/philosophical schools taught by others, Rabbi Ariel places special emphasis on teaching the "other schools" which most today are unaware of, or not qualified to teach. These specifically are the prophetic/meditative and so-called "magical" schools. Rabbi Ariel teaches others HOW-TO practice these ancient methods for each individual to acquire their own unique spiritual experiences.

The KosherTorah School focuses on teaching Biblical, and later mystical literature in a rational way to enable the student to extract their universal teachings from their numerous layers of myth and metaphor. The school proudly serves the educational needs of a global audience, and welcomes students from all walks of life.

Born and raised on Long Island, New York, Ariel Bar Tzadok studied abroad in Israel for a number of years. He studied in Jerusalem at the premier Sephardic institute, Yeshivat Porat Yosef (Old City), and later in Kollel Hekhal Pinhas. While studying for his rabbinic ordination, he was blessed to become the private student of the renowned Kabbalist, Rabbi Meir Levi, *obm*, the foremost student of the leading Kabbalist of Jerusalem, Rabbi Mordechai Sharabi *obm*.

In June 1983, Rabbi Ariel received his rabbinic ordination (Haredi/Orthodox) from Rabbi Ya'akov Peretz, Rosh Yeshiva (Dean) of Kollel Hekhal Pinhas, and Beit Midrash Sephardi in the Old City of Jerusalem.

Rabbi Ariel augmented his religious education with studies in the other religions of the world, esoteric studies and practices, philosophies and psychological systems, particularly studying Jungian psychology at the Jungian Center in New York.

In 1992, after teaching privately for many years, Rabbi Ariel officially established his school (with the original Hebrew name Yeshivat Benei N'vi'im) to address the growing concerns of spiritual misguidance, and misinformation that is pervasive in the Jewish community at large. Since then, while staying faithful to his Orthodox Torah origins, Rabbi Ariel has expanded the KosherTorah School to meet the needs of an ever widening audience.

Rabbi Ariel is a regular featured guest on the popular TV program Ancient Aliens. He also appears in other TV programs, speaks on radio talk shows, and is published in scholarly journals and newspaper articles. His YouTube page hosts hundreds of his videos and he regularly teaches live public classes on Facebook. He has spoken before religious congregations, university groups and lectures around the country.

Made in the USA
Las Vegas, NV
26 August 2024

94451102R00223